RUN, HIDE, REPEAT

RUN
HIDE
REPEAT

A Memoir of a Fugitive Childhood

Pauline Dakin

VIKING

VIKING

an imprint of Penguin Canada,
a division of Penguin Random House Canada Limited

Canada • USA • UK • Ireland • Australia • New Zealand •
India • South Africa • China

First published 2017

www.penguinrandomhouse.ca

LIBRARY AND ARCHIVES CANADA CATALOGUING IN PUBLICATION

Dakin, Pauline, author
Run, hide, repeat : a memoir of a fugitive childhood / Pauline Dakin.
Issued in print and electronic formats.
ISBN 978-0-7352-3322-5 (softcover)—ISBN 978-0-7352-3323-2 (EPUB)

1. Dakin, Pauline—Childhood and youth. 2. Journalists—Canada—Biography.
I. Title.

PN4913.D327A3 2017   070.92   C2017-900162-0
                                            C2017-900445-X

Cover and interior design by Five Seventeen
Cover photographs: (front) courtesy of the author;
(back) Blue Bird Motel, Schermer Photo Ltd.

Printed and bound in the United States of America

10 9 8 7 6 5 4 3

Penguin
Random House
Canada

For my mother, Ruth, who taught me about love;
my brother, Ted, who was my fellow student;
and my daughters, Avery and Laura,
who continue the lessons.

PROLOGUE

I WAS RUNNING ALONG the Upper Blandford Road this morning, watching the little islands emerge from the morning mist, when I came upon a fisherman stacking lobster traps by his shed.

"Running like the dogs of hell are behind ya!" he remarked with a smile and a salute. I laughed, waved back, thinking, *You have no idea.*

I spent much of my early life on the run, in one way or another. I escape to this place on Nova Scotia's Mahone Bay when I can, and hunker down in my old trailer. I take reassurance from the enduring beauty of sea and sky, the sunsets across the bay that soothe me. And I sift through memories I had so firmly put away for so long.

The cast of my story revisits me in this quiet place: my mother, my father, and Stan. All gone now. I have learned to remember them without the heat of anger or the searing sting of betrayal.

In this retreat I am surrounded by the physical evidence of my mother's life. The wooden table and chairs from her kitchen. Her spice rack, the earth-toned spices painstakingly chosen. I can sense the pleasure she took in the careful printing of the hand-written labels, the alphabetical ordering of the round glass bottles. I think that organizing and ordering, the imposing of a predictable architecture, was a response to how little control she felt over so much else. Her dishes are in the cupboard over the sink; we bought them in Winnipeg after renovating the kitchen. Her cookbook is on the shelf above the fridge. Her belongings, what I chose to keep of them, have furnished this place where I so often find myself reflecting on the life we lived and, now, wrestling its strange narrative into submission and meaning. I bring them all back in my mind and on the screen before me.

My mother often said I should be a writer. And then she gave me a story—our story—the story I was warned never to tell.

ONE

I T W A S D U S K, late February of 1988. The air was cold and
clear as I stepped out of my car in the parking lot of the highway gas station. A crescent moon to the southwest was perfectly outlined in the darkening sky. At its tip winked a bright,
large star, perhaps a planet. The horizon still glowed a deep
magenta. My mother's aging blue Toyota Tercel was parked
nearby, under a light. We'd agreed to meet here, in the small
farming community of Sussex, New Brunswick. She would
drive from Halifax, Nova Scotia, where she was doing her
theology degree, and I would drive from Saint John, New
Brunswick, where I was working as a reporter at the local newspaper, *The Telegraph-Journal*.

As I approached our rendezvous, I saw the lights of a motel
just off the highway, a few hundred metres from the gas station.
I'd driven by the large, lit-up block letters of the Blue Bird Motel
many times.

I walked over to Mom's car and got in, said hello, leaning across for a hug. She held me just a beat longer, tighter than normal. As she pulled back, her smile was sad, almost apologetic. She handed me a note and an empty envelope. She put one finger over her lips, hushing me, although I wasn't speaking. She pointed at the note. Puzzled, I unfolded it and read, in her distinctive handwriting: "Don't say anything. Take all your jewellery off and put it in the envelope. Don't talk until we get out of the car again. I will explain."

I sat staring at the note. I could hear my pulse as silence descended between us like a wall. My mother suddenly felt like a stranger whose intentions were unclear. Why this bizarre drama? I looked at her for a long moment, then slowly took off my rings. The small diamond cluster my father had given me for my sixteenth birthday. A square-cut peridot, my birthstone, that was a Christmas present from his third wife, Thora. I pulled the long, heavy chain that held an antique-style watch out of my shirt front and over my head. A gift from Mom the Christmas I was fifteen. It all went into the envelope. I passed it to her. She licked the flap, sealed the envelope, and set it on the console between our seats. As she put the car into gear and eased onto the now-darkening winter road, I braced myself for what was to come. We drove the short distance in silence.

EARLIER THAT WEEK, Mom had called me at work. We usually talked in the evening, but I was glad to hear from her. She'd moved to Halifax the previous year to go back to school and I missed her and our day-over debriefs.

"Can you talk for a minute?" she'd asked.

"Sure," I answered. "I have an interview, but I don't have to leave for twenty minutes."

Around me the newsroom of *The Telegraph-Journal* and its sister paper, *The Evening Times-Globe*, buzzed with the usual background chatter of the police scanner and clatter of the old teletype printers spewing wire copy and photographs. It was a relatively quiet news day, but I was aware that could change at any moment. Two years earlier I'd witnessed a newsroom responding to the first word of the explosion of the space shuttle *Challenger*. It was the only time in my years at the paper I ever heard the order to "stop the presses" and it left a strong impression of how quickly life can go off the rails, without any warning or any chance to prepare. Normal one moment, irreversibly changed the next.

I was sitting at my desk now, one in a row set sideways to a bank of windows that looked across mud flats near an inlet.

"What's up?" I asked.

I could hear Mom inhale deeply. She was bracing herself to begin. My interest increased.

"You know so many times in your life I've told you that someday I'd be able to explain things," she began. Yes, it was a refrain I'd grown sick of through my childhood. Why are you crying? *I'll explain when you're older.* Why are we missing school to go bowling in Portage la Prairie today? *I'll tell you someday when you're old enough.* Why do we have to move without telling anyone we're going? *When you're bigger, I'll explain.* Why can't we ever tell anyone we're going on vacation, or even if we're going out for dinner? Why is everything such a big secret all the time?

"Well," Mom continued, "it's time. I have to tell you some things that will make a lot of the strange events in our lives make sense to you."

I could hardly believe my ears. At some point I'd decided "I'll tell you when you're older" was a placating reaction, designed to deflect more questions. Now, at the age of twenty-three, it seemed I would finally learn the mystery, the cause of the behaviour that had so often confused and frustrated my brother and me.

"What do you mean?"

"We can't talk about this on the phone," she said, an echo of another warning I'd heard many times before. She gave me instructions to meet her that Friday night at the highway gas station in Sussex.

"Don't tell anyone you're meeting me."

"Yeah, I know, I know."

The rest of the week dragged on. I knew I was acting strangely. I wanted to tell Terry, my live-in boyfriend, and my friends, Robin and Margaret. Several times it was on the tip of my tongue, but in the end I said nothing. At various times through the years we'd all talked about the strangeness of my family, the oppressive secretiveness, the unpredictable comings and goings, and speculated what might be behind it.

"It has to be something to do with my dad," I always said.

My parents separated when I was five, the summer before I started school. They spent the next decade engaged in legal warfare over late support payments, unpaid dental bills, and my father's access to me and my younger brother, Ted.

My dad was an alcoholic and I knew there'd been some violence at home when I was small, but my mother wouldn't talk about that. I remembered being whisked to the basement playroom on weekend mornings to eat breakfast there, so as not to wake Dad up. He was sleeping it off upstairs and was volatile when he was hungover. My mother was afraid rambunctious children might provoke his anger, an incident.

According to the court documents, their separation agreement awarded Mom eight hundred dollars a month in spousal and child support "on the condition that, and so long as, the wife shall continue to live a chaste life." She got the house and the furniture. He got his family heirlooms: the crystal, china, silver, some paintings, and the swords his father had brought home from his commission as an officer in the First World War.

The court also gave Dad "reasonable access" to my brother and me, including alternate Christmas and Easter holidays and the month of July each year. But, despite the order, we never did spend much time with Dad when we were young. I remember a few weekends watching golf at the West Vancouver apartment where he lived after he moved out of our home. It had a pool, which we loved. One afternoon when I was five and Ted was three, we spent the afternoon in that pool. I wore my white bathing cap with the bright blue plastic flowers Mom had attached. They made it easier for her to keep an eye on me in a crowded pool or at the beach. Ted wore his red swimming trunks with the navy stripes up the side. It was a golden day, sunlight reflecting off the waves Ted was creating by jumping in off the side, scrambling out, jumping in again.

I looked up to see Mom's red station wagon roaring up the driveway and into the parking lot. She jumped from the seat and came running over, startling us in her frantic haste.

She almost ran through the pool gate, yanked Ted unceremoniously out of the water by his arm, and told me tersely to get out too. I didn't understand why she was angry.

She hustled us across the lawn to the nearby door of Dad's apartment, which was ajar. We must have forgotten to close it behind us on the way to the pool.

"Warren!" Mom called, in her I-mean-business voice. There was no reply. She barked his name more loudly. Nothing. We walked in. Dad was passed out on the couch, a golf game on the television set, empty bottles and a tumbler with a thick glass bottom on the coffee table, beside an overflowing ashtray.

"I've been trying to call," she said to Dad's prone figure as she nudged his shoulder. She couldn't wake him. She gathered up our clothes and toys and marched us out to the station wagon, still in our dripping bathing suits. We were silent, eyes wide. Once we were belted into the back seat, she looked at us in the rear-view mirror.

"You could have drowned," she said, and began to cry.

As we drove down the winding driveway away from the apartment building, I felt sad for Dad, left alone with only the murmuring TV for company.

MORE OFTEN I remember waiting by the window for Dad's blue Oldsmobile 98 to come around the corner and pull up in front of our house. The appointed hour would roll by, and the longer we waited, the more my stomach would ache. Ted would become increasingly agitated, his misbehaviour escalating as the minutes passed. One Saturday afternoon, the house thick with the smell of anxious waiting, Ted broke every section of track in the expensive electric train set Dad had given him for Christmas that year.

A few days later, Dad called and explained he'd had the flu. Again.

We were Dad's second family. He had two older children, our half-siblings Linda and Tom. My impression was that their mother was wealthy; I often heard how she'd owned the first ski resort in Whistler, British Columbia.

When I was a baby, Linda was a teenager. Sixteen and rebelling. She'd visit Dad and my mother and smile stiffly for the pictures I still have of her holding me, a chubby grinning baby, unaware of the family fault lines. Usually in the photos it's Christmas, or some other occasion for which she's wearing a formal dress, full-skirted, her blond hair bouffant and curled up at the ends, and she looks beautiful and glamorous.

After Mom and Dad split up, the only time I saw Linda for many years was the Christmas I was eight. She stood at our door yelling at my mother to take the presents Dad had sent. "It's Christmas, for Chrissakes. He's their father."

My mother sent them back. "If he wants to give them presents, he should sober up and bring them himself." I've heard this story from both Mom and Linda. Both retellings were venomous.

We didn't see much of Tom, who was younger than Linda. He made an occasional appearance in a Christmas photo, but by the time I came along he was mostly away at boarding school. He was a tall, amiable kid with a big infectious laugh who finally dropped out of school in grade eight and focused his self-education on learning new ways to get to Mexico.

Not long after the pool episode, Dad introduced us to Thora. She was petite, older than Mom, with a bleached blond ponytail that reminded me of the genie's in *I Dream of Jeannie.*

Thora wore high heels, drank Scotch straight-up, and made frequent trips to Hawaii. She seemed very glamorous too, and she would let me take out her ponytail and brush her long hair, with me sitting behind her on the bed in the new apartment she and Dad were sharing. She didn't even mind when I hit a tangle. She won me over completely when she gave me one of her many scarves, a deep purple one, diaphanous, and etched with a sparkly silver design.

When I got home and showed it to Mom, something about her cool response made me hide it in the back of the drawer.

Sometimes I'd take it out and fashion elegant dresses for my Barbie with it, wrapping it around her large plastic breasts and down around her impossibly tiny waist to trail behind her in its purple and silver glory. But I never left it out for Mom to see.

THE LIGHTS OF the Blue Bird Motel, a Sussex landmark, illuminated Mom's face as she shifted down into second gear and turned onto an otherwise dark country road on the edge of the town. Her face was set, her brown eyes trained with determination on the road ahead, her body tense. She looked distant, unfamiliar. It was all I could do not to speak, not to ask what was going on.

Our destination was the courtyard of the horseshoe-shaped motel. It was an aging but well-kept place with a brightly lit diner-style restaurant at the front. The garish blue fluorescence loomed out of the darkness of the countryside.

We parked outside one of the motel rooms and got out of the car. My mother's evident anxiety fed my growing misgivings, and I was aware of feeling warm despite the chill air.

She took out a key attached to a large plastic tag with the room number on it and walked to the door. I was right behind her, anxiously looking over her shoulder into the room as the door swung open.

It was an unremarkable room, lit by a bedside lamp. A sink, small fridge, stove, and stretch of cupboards and counter lined the back wall. A housekeeping unit. The bed was on the left, covered by a dated but clean patterned bedspread stretched taut, undisturbed. To the right, a TV set, and beside it, a small table and chairs. Beyond that was a door with a sliding bolt, presumably to an adjoining room.

I let my breath out. Nothing threatening here. I looked at Mom. Was it okay to talk now?

She walked over to the connecting door and tapped, acknowledging my surprise with a nod, and stepped back.

The door opened. Stan came through the doorway into our room, smiling uncertainly.

I stared, shocked, and then burst into tears.

TWO

THE FIRST TIME I met Stan—Reverend Sears to me back
then—was on the street outside the large old clapboard
church where he was the minister. He was in his late forties,
medium height, with a wiry build and dark hair, generously
streaked with iron grey, parted to one side. He had brilliant blue
eyes, a nose that pulled slightly to one side, and a deep scar that
travelled down one cheek and across his neck. I later learned it
was the result of tobogganing into a barbed-wire fence as a
child. He had almost bled to death. Later still, I would think
about that accident, how his rescuers not only saved his life but,
in the way every action reverberates through time and circumstances, changed ours too.

Stan had a compelling face, possibly because of the intelligence and humour that illuminated it. He was always quick to
smile, and liked to laugh.

He knelt down in front of me when Mom introduced us. "I'm

glad to meet you," he said in a way that made me believe it. "You're in grade two?" he asked. I nodded.

Ted, who was then five, had been running around the church lawn. He came over now and sidled up beside me, uncharacteristically shy for a moment beside this new man.

"Well, hey, you must be Ted." Stan held out his hand. Ted took it and shook vigorously, a smile spreading across his face. Stan took his hand back and wiggled his fingers in a pantomime of getting the blood flow going again. "Strong shake you've got!" Ted's grin widened proudly.

That morning Mom, Ted, and I had sat in a pew midway down the left side of the church. I looked at the soaring ceiling of the dim sanctuary, the stepped tubes of the pipe organ whose bass notes rumbled deep in your chest, and the stained-glass windows spilling multi-hued light across the pews. We'd been baptized in the Anglican Church but I could remember going there only once, maybe for Ted's christening. This was the United Church, Mom had explained; we'd be coming here on Sundays from now on. This was the beginning of Mom's return to the church of her childhood and a faith that had always been part of her life. After her mother's death, she had pushed it away, angry with a God that would inflict such pain. But with a faltering marriage and two small children depending on her, she knew she needed the comfort of a sacred space and a faith community. And the support and wisdom of Rev. Stanley Sears.

We got into the habit of dressing up for church on Sunday mornings, Ted in his dark blue corduroy suit, Mom in skirt and heels. Ted fidgeted, unable to sit still. We'd giggle at a large woman several rows ahead who sang with more gusto than tunefulness. Without even turning her head, Mom quietly reached across, rested one finger on Ted's thigh, and tapped lightly, a silent and surprisingly effective warning to behave.

What often kept us quiet in church was our concern and embarrassment, our wish to sink down into the old wooden pew and disappear, as each Sunday, usually during the pastoral prayer, Mom would cry. She wiped the steady, silent tears with tissues pulled from a generous supply at the ready in her purse. I looked at her, trying to catch her eye, my eyebrows raised in question. She only glanced at me, an almost imperceptible shake of her head her only response.

I looked up at Reverend Sears, in his black robe and white collar, as he leaned over the ornate wooden pulpit with his glasses on but slipping down his nose, his face serious and yet alive with some inner emotion. I tried to understand what it was he was saying that made my mother cry. He was praying for people who didn't have enough to eat, or didn't have anyone to eat with; for people living in fear of war and violence; for those struggling with addiction, illness, loss.

Once as I was watching him during the prayer, he caught my eye and smiled with an almost imperceptible wink, a connection that somehow reassured me, making us the unpious co-conspirators among the bowed heads and closed eyes of the faithful.

That first day, on the sidewalk by the church after the service, he was full of mischief. "Next time you come you might want to visit the kids in the Sunday school. They have a lot of fun." His voice dropped to a whisper, and he held his hand to the side of his mouth, as if to prevent Mom from hearing. "Once they snuck into the balcony and dropped spitballs on the old ladies' hair!"

"Really?" I breathed, shocked. Ted laughed.

"Really," he confirmed. "They don't realize I can see them from the pulpit." He chuckled, smiled at me, and then straightened his legs. He chatted with Mom for another minute, then walked across the street to a sporty orange car and drove away with a wave.

I would find out only on that February night at the motel room when I was twenty-three that Mom had first met Stan many months earlier than my first encounter with him—when she was struggling with the decision to leave her marriage.

She'd been going to Al-Anon meetings, a support group for families of alcoholics, in the months before Dad moved out. A friend there, recognizing she was in shaky emotional shape, recommended a counsellor, Rev. Stan Sears. He was also a psychologist, she said, and did a lot of counselling work, as well as ministering to his own congregation. By the time I met Stan, he'd heard Mom's story over months of weekly appointments. He'd slowly won her trust and become her source of strength and hope in the midst of a deep depression.

Sixteen years later during the weekend of revelations in Sussex, while Mom was in the shower, Stan told me how fragile she had been when she started coming to see him. His case notes confirmed this, I discovered many years later. "Mrs. Dakin is in an extremely depressed state," he wrote after their first session. "Very withdrawn, guard up, has built a wall around self. If she trusts anyone I don't know who it is."

Sometimes, he said, she would cry. Often she would shake uncontrollably as she talked about her marriage, her children, her own childhood, growing up in the poverty of the Depression-era Canadian prairies. I had only a vague sense of this from some family stories she told, and old dog-eared photographs.

During her continued counselling with Stan in the months after my father moved out, Stan's notes chronicle her weight loss, her continuing spiral. "Nervous and depressed state has increased alarmingly despite medication." He compared her to an injured fawn he'd once come across in the woods that wanted help but refused it because of fear.

"I didn't dare come out from behind my desk," Stan told me. He said if he got up, even to go to a nearby bookcase, she tensed, flinched. He said years of being brutalized by my father—physically, sometimes, but more often emotionally and psychologically—meant she always needed to locate the exit from any room, and would choose the closest seat to it, preferably with her back to a wall.

There were stories she eventually told me, years later, that explained this.

MY DAD HAD come home drinking again, the slam of the taxi door on the street outside a warning that he'd had to leave his car at his club downtown. Mom always took that as a sign he must be in pretty rough shape.

She was at the kitchen table with her father, who was visiting from Vancouver Island. Ted and I, then preschoolers, were in bed. I now imagine Mom bracing herself as the door to the carport opened and my dad bumbled in.

He would have greeted Grandpa Cliff heartily and asked after Stella, my grandfather's new wife. Grandpa Cliff liked to drink too; it made him more social and outgoing. But he was cold sober that night, and my dad's loud joviality likely made him uncomfortable.

Dad retreated down the hall to the den, where he poured himself a Scotch and loudly offered one to my grandfather, who accepted. Mom recalled her worry that they'd get out of hand

and wake Ted and me. She followed my dad into the den, saying something like "Don't you think you've had enough tonight?" She tried to sound conciliatory, struggled to keep both the judgment and the fear out of her voice. But as he turned to look at her, she saw his eyes narrowing and felt afraid. She stayed in the den when he returned to the kitchen.

I picture Dad walking back with two generously poured tumblers of Scotch, ice cubes tinkling against the glass with his unsteady gait, Dad offering a tumbler to Cliff, regaining his joviality.

I imagine my mother, sitting in one of the big leather chairs in the den, trying to calm herself. It was a male room, in a house that was probably much grander than any she'd expected to live in. A large neo-Tudor style two-storey with cedar and stucco siding, it stood on a generous, landscaped lot in a newer subdivision in North Vancouver, on the approach to Grouse Mountain. It was a neighbourhood of upwardly mobile families. Yards had pools, or patios with built-in barbecues where cocktails were served on Saturday nights.

Our yard was tiered, and seemed like a magical place full of hiding spots. The covered patio off the den opened to a cement terrace surrounded by manicured gardens. From there, steps led down to a large horseshoe-shaped lawn, guarded by soaring old Douglas fir trees, rhododendrons, and azaleas. Another set of steps marched down again, to the inner curve of the horseshoe, a shaded stone garden surrounded by ferns, with a miniature Japanese pagoda and a small stream that ran by after it rained.

There was a gardener who came to mow and help keep the aggressive greenery of the rainy West Coast in check, and a lady who cleaned the large four-bedroomed house and its four bathrooms, and a living room that was used only when there was company or on Christmas mornings. It was a house full of expensive reproduction furniture, complemented by two late-model cars in the driveway. There'd been a recent trip to Hawaii, and Dad had come home a few months earlier announcing he'd bought a summer cottage at the beach in Point Roberts, Washington, on the tip of a peninsula that jutted into the waters of the Juan de Fuca Strait.

It was everything anyone could want, materially. Her family clearly felt she'd hit the jackpot and was happy to be charmed by Dad, eager to overlook any cracks in an attractive facade. And yet none of this pretty life had brought my mother happiness or any sense of security.

As she sat in the den she may have looked up to see the weapons mounted on the wall: Dad's hunting rifle, a couple of guns he'd brought back from the Second World War, and his father's decorative military swords from the Great War. She always shuddered when she talked about them. She couldn't stop herself from imagining the destruction and suffering they had wrought, the threat they implied. This was not the life she had imagined.

My parents met on a Vancouver–Toronto flight. She was a stewardess with Trans-Canada Air Lines, based in Vancouver. Dad was an investment dealer and director with a securities company that had regular meetings in Toronto. A guy on the rise, Warren was tall, charming, and had a ready smile.

Mom recalled taking his coat as he ducked through the doorway of the DC-8. During the flight she served him his meal, drinks. He flirted with her. She was reserved, proper. The airline had strict rules regulating everything from the height of shoe heels and the colour of her nail polish to the angle of the jaunty little caps she and the other female flight attendants wore.

Certainly there were rules about mingling with paying passengers, and the airline, which was soon to become Air Canada, had a no-marriage rule for its stewardesses. But eventually, during one of his monthly trips, Warren asked her out for dinner and she said yes.

She described Dad as self-assured, well-known in the best restaurants in Vancouver. He was a member of The Vancouver Club, a haven for well-heeled businessmen, and the Capilano Golf Club. He spent freely, entertained frequently, and many have described him to me as a generous host. His first marriage had ended and he was a single man with good prospects. To Ruth, my mother, fifteen years his junior and having escaped a hardscrabble life on the prairies, he must have seemed impossibly suave, a man of the world.

But a wedding and two children later, the shiny facade had worn thin and she had become intimately acquainted with shortcomings that materialized and were magnified when he was drinking. My half-brother, Tom, always described our dad as a friendly drunk. That might have been true in Dad's first marriage, but it wasn't the dynamic in our house. I wonder now if something about my mother's sensitivity, her vulnerability, her disapproval, maybe her fear, brought out a nasty impulse in my father.

According to Mom, that impulse flashed to life the night Dad and Grandpa were sharing drinks in the kitchen. Dad had come weaving back into the den for refills, empty glasses in his hand, headed for the collection of liquor bottles on the cabinet. He stumbled, righted himself against the doorway, but dropped one of the heavy tumblers. Mom jumped at the explosion of sound and hissed at him that the children were trying to sleep.

She described how the change in Warren was immediate. The affable drunk was gone. As his face turned hard and dark, she said something about how she and the children could not live like this anymore.

"*My* children," she remembered him yelling. "You won't take *my* children anywhere." He told her if she tried to leave and take us, it would take only two doctors' signatures to have her committed to a mental institution where she would never see us again, and she knew he had the contacts.

My father was six-foot-four to my mother's five-foot-six and she was frightened. She said that as she stepped back from his anger, this seemed to further enrage him. He reached up, grasped his father's decorative war sword, lifting it off its brackets, and unsheathed the blade.

Mom decided to run, intending to flee up the stairs, perhaps lock herself in the bathroom. But before she could move, he raised the sword over his head, back behind his shoulder. She closed her eyes as it sliced through the air toward her. Mom's voice wobbled years later as she remembered it.

When she opened her eyes again, the heavy decorative handle of the sword was swaying beside her, the point of the blade embedded in the wooden floor a short distance away. When she turned she saw her father, Cliff, standing in the kitchen doorway, also watching the sword, a stunned expression on his face. She said he didn't meet her gaze, but without a word went up the stairs to the spare room.

The next morning, as Dad was sleeping it off and we were having breakfast, Grandpa came down to the kitchen, suitcase in hand, headed for the door. Mom asked him where he was going; he was supposed to stay the week. But a taxi was waiting outside.

Mom cried as she related his answer. He opened the kitchen

door, saying, "Last night . . . that was the worst thing that ever happened to me." And then he was gone.

I REMEMBER MY grandfather as a man who always had a toothpick and a lopsided grin. His laugh was a wheezy series of exhalations that reminded me of Sylvester the cartoon cat who was always trying to eat Tweety Bird. To me, too young to make the distinction between funny and cutting, he seemed jovial and likeable. He fished and canned his own salmon, samples of which would arrive in the mail in a box at Christmastime. He did some woodwork, had a lathe on which he turned wooden lamps. His second wife, Stella, a schoolteacher, seemed to propel their lives, keeping it on track, but she always made a point of deferring to Grandpa. "Isn't that right, Cliff?" she'd ask. Or "Let's just see what Grandpa thinks."

My grandfather had had a hard life, my mother told me. He grew up poor. Rode the rails during the Depression. It's not hard to picture him as a hobo, hunkered down in boxcars of speeding trains, begging for meals at houses along the tracks, asking for work wherever the trains stopped. When he met Jessie, my grandmother, she'd just finished normal school and was a young teacher. He joined the air force. They married. He worked as a mechanic during the war, mostly on planes. When the war ended, he used his military discharge benefits to buy a small garage and coffee counter on the highway near Summerberry, Saskatchewan.

He worked long, hard days, Mom would recall, bent over engines, or splayed beneath them on a crawler, the lines of his hands permanently etched with oil grime. Or out pumping gas, washing windshields. All for little pay. He was honest, Mom said. He wouldn't stoop to the tricks of the guy who ran the gas station down the highway. "Fanbelt Frank," as she and Grandpa called him, would smile at the tourists as they drove up and then slice their fanbelt while he was under the hood checking the oil. "Oh look, you're gonna need a new one a' these," he'd say, emerging from behind the hood with the length of sliced rubber. I guess no one ever thought to ask to see the old belt. Never saw the cleanly cut ends. Fanbelt Frank made a lot more money than Grandpa, Mom said. But Grandpa made an honest living.

When we were kids and she talked about Grandpa, these were the stories she told. But when I became an adult, asking more probing questions about her life, another story emerged that now makes me look at an old photograph from her childhood with a feeling of profound sadness for that little girl, a small Ruth, posing with her dolly and her toboggan, its metal runners pressed tightly to her chest, standing on the edge of the prairie on a winter day. Her smile in that old photo now seems brave.

In the black-and-white background behind her, the street runs into town. A church, a few houses, a grain silo are in the far background. Ruth looks excited under the hood of a heavy wool coat. There is no one else around, except of course the photographer. Her mother? Likely.

In another shot, this one a professional photograph with "The New Hollywood Studios—rough proof only" stamped in red on the back, Ruth sits next to her older brother, Murray. She might be three, Murray a few years older. Their little sister, Penny, hasn't been born yet. Ruth and Murray are dressed to the nines. Having a studio photo taken would have been a special occasion, a rare splurge in hard times. Murray is wearing a suit, maybe borrowed. It's too big and wrinkles around his chest and shoulders. His polka-dot tie is just off-kilter. He's seated on a piano bench, one hand gripping its edge, and his feet almost touch the ground.

His unseen hand has disappeared behind the back of young Ruth, who's wearing a white dress. It has short puffy sleeves, gathered with lace at the cuff and collar. In her short, blunt-cut hair is a ribbon that drapes down one side. Her legs are bare, her little feet in ankle socks and black patent leather shoes. One of her feet appears to be caught in mid-swing. But what stands out in the formality of this picture is Ruth's grin, somehow out of place. It's broad, although it seems she's just finished licking her lower lip. Her upper teeth are showing and her cheeks are rounded, pushed up by the smile, which extends to her eyes. There's something mischievous about it, in contrast to the more serious half-smile on Murray's face and the wariness in his eyes.

This proof would not have been chosen for printing because of Ruth's funny, lip-licked smile, her laughing eyes, her swinging foot. The very brightness and energy that emanate from her would condemn the photo as not solemn enough for a family portrait. She was likely reprimanded and told to sit still.

It wouldn't have been the first time. Mom described herself as the kid who couldn't sit still. She recalled a day when she was six and she and Murray were in their father's truck as he drove to the next town on some errand. Their father repeatedly barked at her to settle down, stop wiggling. But there was so much to see . . . The way the power lines dipped and climbed. The stooks of harvested hay lined up in fields that stretched to the horizon. A flock of birds swooping and then coming to rest in a slough.

But Cliff had had enough. The wiggling irritated him, Mom said. He jammed the brakes until the old truck skidded to a stop on the dirt road, kicking up a cloud of dust. He ordered Mom out. "If you can't sit still, you can walk," he said, nudging her out the door and then reaching past a surprised Murray to pull the door shut behind her. He pulled away in a spray of gravel.

Mom described watching the truck disappear into the distance, seeing the billow of dust trailing behind it, and feeling alone and afraid. She was miles from home and there weren't even any farmhouses within sight. She started to cry. She couldn't ever remember being all alone before.

She recalled walking for a while, deciding to head back in the direction of home. Every few minutes she'd turn her head, hoping to see the rusty old truck coming back for her. The sun was getting higher in the sky. She was hot, sticky, and getting hungry. It seemed hours since her banishment. She thought of going into the field beside her, to sit in the shade of a swathe of cut grain stalks and rest. And then in the distance she heard something coming down the road.

She turned and tried to see through the approaching dust cloud. Slowly the rusty curved hood and round headlights of Cliff's old truck came into focus. As it came closer she could see her father's glasses glint in the hard sunlight, and make out the shape of his hat.

The truck pulled alongside. She remembers approaching it tentatively. Murray swung the door open. He didn't look at her. Cliff was laughing, his wheezy huff-huff. "Think you can sit still now till we get home?"

She sat very still. She didn't look at Cliff or Murray but kept her eyes trained on the passing fields.

THREE

STAN STOOD UP and crossed to the motel-room kitchen-ette, where the kettle was whistling. He returned to the table with a brown teapot and three mugs. I felt disoriented. This was like playing house with a differently constituted family, as though I'd stumbled into some alternative universe in that motel room. Nothing was as it had always seemed.

When Stan had first walked in from the adjoining room, my shock had quickly been overtaken by an overwhelming relief, as if a sustained tension I'd been unaware of had suddenly eased. I hadn't seen him in a couple of years, during which I'd tried not to feel abandoned by him. I was hurt that after years of a close, father-daughter-like relationship he had moved away and writ-ten me only one letter since.

He hugged me as I cried, and told me he'd missed me too. When I pulled back to look at him, his startlingly blue eyes were wet. He smiled. It felt as though something missing had slipped back into place. The three of us sat down at the little round table. Stan asked about my life, my job, my boyfriend, the fixer-upper house we had recently bought.

As he poured the tea, I saw him look meaningfully at my mother. She nodded. *Here we go*, I thought. I couldn't imagine what was to come. No one could have.

They began, and took turns telling me the story that would explain the upheavals that had divided us from friends and family, twice. My life's direction was about to change.

"YOU REMEMBER WHEN you started coming to my church in North Vancouver?" Stan asked. I nodded.

"Your mother was also coming to me for counselling." This was not a surprise. In recent years Mom had told me that by the time she actually left my dad, she was suicidal. His threats, his lawyers, and the abandonment by most of their friends left her feeling isolated and afraid.

"I actually had a moment of believing an overdose for you, me, and Ted might be the only way out," she told me. "I couldn't see a way to go on, but I couldn't imagine leaving you kids in such a situation with no one to protect you."

She described how, in the months after her separation, she had barely been able to haul herself from her bed in the mornings, and had forced herself to grocery shop and to make meals for us that she could only pick at.

This was the time Stan had written about in his counselling session notes. In them he talked about how long it had taken him to earn her trust—speaking softly, gently, never making any sudden or unexpected moves, always listening calmly.

After six months of regular sessions, Mom had begun to

relax, and there were signs the depression was lifting. "It's like watching the first bright rays of sun hit mountain peaks," Stan wrote after one appointment.

"Thank God my Al-Anon friend put me in touch with Stan," Mom said as we all sat around the little table in the Sussex motel room, sixteen years later. She smiled across at Stan, a smile he returned with such intimate warmth that I had to look away.

That was the first revelation of the weekend. They told me they had fallen in love. For many years they had not acted on those feelings, but they had eventually agreed they wanted a life together. Stan joked that he fell for Mom the first time he met her, when she came to his office for their first appointment.

"I watched her getting out of her car from my office window. She was wearing a skirt. I thought, I've never seen more beautiful legs." He laughed at the memory and the silliness of his own admission, and then grew more serious. "But I really fell in love with her watching her fight her way out of such pain, and realizing what a beautiful person she was."

Mom had fallen more slowly, she said, unaware of Stan's feelings for months. After she had stopped seeing him as a counsellor, she became his secretary when the previous one retired. I remembered how church had become important in our lives. At a dark time, it must have felt like a homecoming to Mom, whose own mother had always taken her to church when she was growing up. She told me Stan was the first man who had respected her, admired her intellect and her sensitivity. Slowly she had opened her heart to him, despite his marriage.

As they told me this, I was mentally calculating. I remembered the infrequent weekends, maybe two or three times a year, when I was a teenager and Mom would have a friend stay with Ted and me, vaguely saying she needed a little break. I now realized that they had been spending time together alone. So many nights as a child and teenager I'd arrive home from my activities to find Stan's car in the driveway, Stan and Mom drinking tea in the living room, each seated in one of the tall blue armchairs. Often Mom was crying, and she'd laugh self-consciously as I came in, wiping her eyes.

It was strange, watching them that weekend, as an adult, trying to reframe my family history and square it with this new information. I'd always thought of my mother as strong and independent, having no need of a man. Did this diminish her in some way, or just make her more human?

That weekend was the first time I'd seen her being affectionate with a man. In my memory, my parents had mostly interacted in controlled exchanges, or studied public politeness. It was odd to watch her relax into Stan, her evident pleasure at his attention, her enjoyment of being the butt of his gentle humour. It was funny how she became shy in front of me when he'd reach for her hand. She wasn't sure how I was reacting to this. Neither was I.

In some ways it was a childhood fantasy come true. Stan had been like a father to me from the time I was seven. He was the guy who showed up for the father-daughter tea at school, who taught me how to start a campfire, and always had a goofy joke to make Ted and me laugh.

After the first time we met, he would often stop me outside the church service to ask how school was, how things were going. One early summer weekend he invited us to a church camp, a retreat off the highway between Vancouver and Whistler. It was called Paradise Valley, a circle of cabins in the woods across from a large pond. A fast river ran behind that, and beyond were the large, craggy mountains in the distance.

On the first afternoon there I wandered over to a small group of kids my own age who were hanging around a swing set. It was hot for June. We were all in sandals and shorts.

"There's a nest of baby robins in that tower," said one boy, pointing across the field to an old wooden building, I think it was an old church. I'm not sure what our purpose was as we all began to walk toward the building. The door was unlocked and we went in cautiously. No one was around.

On the spiralling stairway leading to a belfry, dust motes danced in the light pouring through a window at a landing about halfway up. As we climbed, our passing sent them spinning. There was a dangerous sense of excitement that deepened the closer we got to the top. I wanted to see, maybe touch. I was drawn to the hatchlings' vulnerability. I'm not sure whether the boys had some more nefarious plans. There was no chance to find out.

"Hey!" Heavy feet were thumping up the stairs behind us, coming fast. My heart pounded.

"You kids leave those birds alone!" said the stern voice, followed by a serious face emerging from around the corner of the stairs.

It was Stan. "Reverend Sears" to us kids. He was taking the stairs two at a time to catch up to us. I don't know how he knew what we were up to, or even that there was a nest above. I had the sense he knew everything, was omniscient, maybe because he was God's man.

"Back down you go. They're fragile. You can't touch them." His voice was commanding.

I'd never seen Stan angry. But now he looked fierce in his defence of the baby birds, and I felt my eyes well up in some combination of fear, unexplained shame, and relief that he'd come to the birds' rescue.

The other kids ran away. I stood frozen, sniffling. Stan knelt down in front of me. "Were they going to hurt the baby birds?"

he asked, his voice gentle now. I shrugged, wiping hot tears from my cheeks.

"I was afraid those boys were going to throw them out of the nest," he continued. I looked up at him, trying not to snuffle. "You wouldn't have hurt them, would you," he said more than asked. I shook my head earnestly.

"I'm sorry I frightened you. I don't like to scare little girls." He softly touched the top of my head. "You okay?"

I nodded. We walked down the stairs together, into the bright sun. That day, the day Stan saved the baby birds, was the day I began to trust him.

I THINK NOW how unusual a man Stan must have seemed to my mother. Strong yet gentle, authoritative but sensitive, emotionally tuned in. He could speak softly, and wasn't afraid to defend and support the weak . . . the baby birds, the injured fawn, my mother.

But their relationship was not the only revelation that night in the motel. It was only part of the coming clean.

"Before I met your mother," Stan continued, "I spent some months counselling an alcoholic man who'd been highly placed in a Vancouver organized crime syndicate. The Mafia." I nodded again, wondering where this was going. Stan said this man was trying to dry out, and was experiencing shame and regret for the life he'd led and the people he'd hurt. He'd talked about his crimes, looking for absolution or comfort.

"He never finished his counselling. He was assassinated. By the Mob." Stan was watching for my reaction. I said nothing.

He continued. The man's associates had seen a change in his behaviour and become suspicious. They'd had him followed and realized he was talking to a counsellor, breaking *omertà*, the code of silence. They'd decided he was divulging information about their illegal activities to Stan. The punishment was immediate and merciless.

I looked at Stan's hand, flat on the table as he spoke, the index finger tapping against the hard surface, an unconscious staccato, telegraphing urgency.

It was a compelling if horrifying story, but what could this possibly have to do with us, I wondered. I stayed quiet as he continued. With the suspected rat out of the way, the Mob had then come after Stan, believing he was a threat because of what he'd learned from the repentant and now-dead mobster. The Mafia had decided Stan knew too much.

Mom picked up the narrative. "Remember I went to work at the church when you were in grade two?" I did. I recalled the novelty of packing sandwiches into a new tin lunch can decorated with the bright colours of some long-since-forgotten cartoon characters. She'd recovered from the depression, been feeling stronger and well, and needed to supplement the support payments from my father.

"I didn't have much training, but I had an understanding boss," she said, smiling at Stan before returning her attention to me. I remembered how she'd handled the phone, learned to crank out the Gestetner copies of the bulletins for each Sunday, and mastered the details of administering a small office, assisting Stan with his work, taking notes and minutes.

"One day Stan and I went together to a meeting at another church. We were in Stan's car, on our way back to the office," she recalled. They were driving along a quiet street near a stretch of woods.

"A car came out of nowhere and was trying to run us off the road." Stan tried to outrun the other car. In its front seat were two grim-faced men "determined to keep up," she said. Neither she nor Stan recognized either of them. In an attempt to lose them, Stan had darted down the back alley of a residential neighbourhood. It ended abruptly in a garage. He turned around just as the car was coming around the corner toward them.

"The man in the passenger seat had a gun pointed at us."

"A gun!" I saw images of chase scenes from television cop shows. This stuff didn't happen in real life. At least not our lives.

Stan was slowly nodding, his eyes on the table as Mom spoke, lost in the memory of that frantic afternoon. Stan had driven over a curb and a lawn to avoid the other car and they'd managed to get to a busier road, to somehow lose the other car, and return to the church office, thoroughly shaken.

"Did you call the cops?"

Mom and Stan shook their heads.

"This was beyond the local police."

"What do you mean?" I was incredulous.

Stan said he'd learned from his sessions with the mobster that at least a few city police officers were in the pocket of organized crime. He thought calling the police might be the worst thing they could do.

It was, Stan said, an attempted "hit," or at least an attempt to scare or warn them. An organized crime syndicate in Vancouver had put contracts out on both of them, he said. It was no longer just Stan in danger. The Mafia was after my mother too.

"We've all been on the run ever since."

It was the language of movies and bad TV dramas. The Mob, organized crime, hits and contracts. It couldn't be real. I couldn't take it in, couldn't believe it.

They saw the skepticism in my face.

"I know, this stuff is stranger than fiction," Stan said. "We knew you would have a hard time believing it. But we felt you were old enough to know now."

"You always said you wanted to know," Mom added.

"It's crazy," I mumbled. A feeling of dread was creeping in, making my heart beat hard.

"But why Mom, why our family?" I aimed my question at Stan.

He said the Mob's concerns about him and what he knew intensified when my mom started working for him.

"She was just a church secretary!" I interrupted.

Again they exchanged looks, and Stan reached over for Mom's hand.

"It was because Warren was also involved in organized crime," Mom said. "I'd had no idea until Stan told me that your father was deeply involved."

It was a sucker punch. My dad, a mobster.

In reality, I didn't feel as though I knew my dad very well, didn't feel I had the tools to accurately judge this new information. But at that moment I remembered a day when Dad had taken me to Stanley Park. I was little—three, maybe four. I don't know where Ted was; it was just me and my dad. I was wearing a dress and white stockings. I was trying to walk along the top of a cement curb, to hold my balance without touching the grass on one side or the path on the other, when I tripped and fell onto my knees. As I got up I looked down with dismay. My stockings were covered in mud. I wasn't hurt but I was afraid of how Dad would react. Even then I knew he didn't like messes. I recalled my relief, my gratitude even, when he simply rubbed the worst of the mud off with his handkerchief and said it was okay, not to worry. I'd often thought of this memory. It was a talisman, a small proof of some unexpected gentleness.

Mom was looking at me with concern. She said that my father's Mob connection was initially shocking to her but eventually came to make sense. It explained some of his business associates who seemed dodgy, the sudden appearance of luxury goods she thought to be beyond even Warren's means. A new car for her birthday for which he'd paid cash, a new cottage just across the Washington state border, and the strange request he'd made when she was pregnant with my brother.

"He wanted to fly me to Mexico with a private nurse and have Ted born there," she said. He'd told her he wanted to be able to put Mexican businesses in Ted's name, which the baby's joint citizenship would allow him to do. He said that would create great opportunities for Ted later, "but really, what kind of Mexican businesses was he talking about?" she asked, her mouth pursed, still outraged all these years later that he would have used his unborn child to support some money-making scheme.

They told me that when Mom went to work for Stan, the Mob saw it as a threat, this alliance of a man they perceived as an enemy with the estranged and presumably vengeful wife of an organized crime figure.

"They never even considered it was a coincidence," Stan said. "They thought it meant your mom was feeding me information, things she'd witnessed or picked up during her marriage, names of associates or details about what they were up to. And they figured I was reporting it back to the authorities."

So there were death contracts on Stan and Mom. I looked at one, then the other. They still looked like the people I'd always known and trusted, but this story made them seem like strangers, people I only thought I'd known.

FOUR

MY MOTHER LIKED to tell the story of how my nose was crooked when I was born, pushed to one side during the rigours of delivery. She described how in the days after my birth, when she breastfed me, she would gently push my nose straight and hold it as I fed until after a few weeks the cartilage relented and took on its proper shape.

When a baby latches on to its mother's breast and suckles, it receives life-giving nourishment and comfort. At the same time, the mother's brain releases a powerful dose of oxytocin, the so-called love hormone, which is said to be nature's way of ensuring a baby's survival. The feelings of bliss and deep connection produced by the hormone and associated with the baby contribute to a strong bond that ensures the mother protects and nurtures the child despite the demands and stresses of parenting.

For me as a child, that bond was reinforced by a thousand little acts of reassurance and care. All the meals cooked, the school pickups, the piano and swimming lessons, the sideline cheering at the baseball field, the unfailing empathy for cuts and bruises or spats with friends. These seemingly small threads of parenting wove a blanket of safety and trust.

So at twenty-three, that trust never having been broken, I continued to sit and listen to the story being laid before me in the Sussex motel room.

Stan and Mom described the Mafia as not actually a single entity but a many-tentacled octopus, a collection of inter-connected yet sometimes opposing syndicates or organized crime groups—local, national, and international. Sometimes there were shared interests among the groups; other times they were in com-petition, or even at war. The orders to "get" Stan or Mom didn't always come from the same group. Sometimes the threat wasn't an attempted hit. There'd been attempted kidnappings of me or Ted, or other family members, intended as a way of getting to Mom or Stan, or of controlling them. Sometimes they were just coming after something Mom had in her possession. Once, a list of businesses had been found hidden in the stuffing of a chair that had been custom-made for the Patterdale Drive house in North Vancouver, before the divorce. "Money-laundering businesses with names and account numbers," Stan said.

It was washing over me, too much to take in.

"So do you see why our life was so strange, so secretive?" my mother asked, almost plaintively. She was anxious for me to understand, to accept.

As unbelievable as it was, the story did explain many things. Why a phone call could send us packing and hiking into a remote mountain cabin at a moment's notice. "That was the time we got word there was a carload of men heading from the airport to our house with orders to make me disappear," Mom said.

Or the time I came home to find her emptying out the fridge, throwing bottles, jars, and other containers of food into a trash bag. "We'd been tipped off that someone had slipped poison into some food in our fridge, but it wasn't clear which food, so it all had to go out," she explained. At the time she'd told me the food had gone bad, but even to a nine-year-old that seemed implausible. Does mustard go bad?

The reason Ted and I couldn't tell anyone about normal family activities when we were growing up, or even the most innocuous details about our daily lives, was that any information could potentially offer opportunities for the "bad guys" to get at us. For our safety, Mom said, we'd had to keep our movements as secret as possible.

"But how could me telling my friends what we were doing for summer holidays tip off mobsters trying to kill us?" I asked, trying to discredit the story, as if finding cracks in the tale, finding some evidence to deny it, could somehow return our lives to normal. "It's not as though Robin or Gay or Margaret were reporting back to the Mafia!"

"Not intentionally," Stan said. "But they could be standing at a bus stop when someone walks by, then stops and says, 'Hey, aren't you Pauline's friend?' They strike up a conversation and why wouldn't your friend talk to someone she thinks knows you. And who knows what she might disclose or how that could be used?"

It was chilling, the idea of the Mob sending spies to pump my friends for information about my family's whereabouts. And crazy. I shook my head.

"We know this is hard to believe," Stan said, softly. "But it's deadly serious."

It was ridiculous, I thought, like a cheap paperback thriller. And yet, if it was true it would explain the times we disappeared, leaving everything and everyone we knew behind, without explanation. I'd never been able to imagine what could prompt that. It would also justify all my mother's unexplained tears and her secretiveness. It was, I reluctantly acknowledged, a story that made the puzzle pieces slip into place.

But one thing didn't make sense.

"How could you know what the Mob was planning or reacting to?" I challenged. "How would you know what they were plotting or thinking? Who was tipping you off about the threats and the people coming for you . . . for us?"

Mom looked pained. She lifted her shoulders and then dropped them, trying to release some of the tension. "Here's where this is going to start to bend your mind," she warned. *Really?* I was already reeling. It could hardly get any more bizarre. But it did.

They explained that we had protection from security people who watched over us and kept track of who was trying to get close to us, or following us, or posing some threat.

"Security people," I repeated. "What kind of security people?" I felt a sick understanding that they were telling me we were being watched, followed.

The first time the Mob came after him, Stan said, a man with a knife had jumped him as he was coming out of the church late one night. He was trying to fight the guy off, already had some defensive cuts on his hands, when he became aware of another person entering the fray. It was a big guy, who was apparently coming to Stan's rescue. He quickly overpowered the knife-wielding man, who turned out to be young, in his early twenties, frightened, and strung out. A third man appeared from around the corner of the church, handcuffed the attacker, and led him away.

Stan was puzzled. He thanked his rescuer, saying that he didn't even have his wallet on him, that he could have died in a futile robbery attempt.

"It wasn't a robbery attempt," the man responded. He told Stan the attacker had been hired to come after him.

Stan and the stranger went back into the church office. That's when Stan first learned he was now a target of the Vancouver Mob. His rescue that night was his first introduction to members of a shadowy government agency, under military orders and tasked with fighting organized crime. Even Parliament was unaware of the agency, the man told him. The chain of command led directly to the Privy Council.

Mom was right, this was mind-bending. I was a journalist, I knew how hard it was to keep anything that big a secret on Parliament Hill, or anywhere else for that matter. There were leaks, people talked.

"You couldn't hide that kind of an operation," I interjected.

Despite my disbelief, Stan continued. It was a small, tight organization in which leaks were not tolerated. The agency comprised a cadre of undercover security people who gathered intelligence, provided protection for people under threat, including my family, and who—when necessary—would fight or even kill as part of a government-sanctioned but secret war on what was seen as the growing domestic threat posed by organized crime.

My mind conjured up drug dealers and illegal gambling or prostitution rings being busted, Hells Angels clubhouses being raided. But as Stan described it, that was just the low-level stuff. This agency's war on crime extended to the boardrooms of some of the country's biggest corporations, he said, sometimes to the offices of politicians and even, on one occasion, a cabinet minister. More than once it had involved rescuing warehouses of women or children who were to be pressed into prostitution. The agents had recently raided a state-of-the-art underground facility where designer drugs were developed to be more potent, more profitable.

Stan said in the midst of this darkness there were sometimes signs of grace. Arresting the bad guys was essentially rescuing them too, unburdening them of their horrific duties. And sometimes they came to see it that way and were relieved. He described many of the foot soldiers of the Mafia as victims themselves, people who were vulnerable, who ended up on the street to escape abuse, who came to be controlled by the Mob because of and through their addictions.

"Like the guy who tried to stab me," Stan said. The two agents who'd saved him from the knifing happened to be there because they'd been following a mobster and witnessed him hiring the kid with the knife. The agents then followed the kid, first to a flophouse on skid row, in Vancouver's Downtown Eastside, and then to Stan's church.

"He was willing to do some dirty work in exchange for some heroin." Stan shook his head sadly. "What a life of misery he must have led."

In the weeks and months that followed, one of the agents stayed in touch with him. Slowly they discovered just how big a threat various organized crime bosses around the country were coming to consider him and Mom. It wasn't clear why, but they were thought to be responsible for some important raids and arrests because the busted operations had links to my father and to Stan's client who'd been assassinated. The intelligence team the agent worked with learned of new and widening plots, sometimes to grab Stan or Mom, to find out what they knew and what they'd done with the information. Other times there was an order to eliminate them. But the intelligence team couldn't figure out the root of the threats. The team realized something bigger must be going on than could be explained by the remorseful confessions of an alcoholic mobster to a minister. What that was, they didn't know. But the continuing, even escalating threat to our families was clear.

As I listened, my body was tight with tension. I wanted to run away, to walk out of that motel room and try to forget everything I'd heard. Maybe I could go to Australia, I thought, and lose myself, escape the danger. But wasn't that the catch when you were on the run from the Mob, at least according to movies and books? You could run but you couldn't hide.

"I have to go to the bathroom," I said, standing up.

"Are you okay?" Mom asked.

"No, no, I'm not okay," I replied in a voice that did not sound like my own.

I went to the bathroom and stood with my hands on either side of the sink, head hanging down, and began to shake uncontrollably. Involuntary muscle spasms made my teeth chatter.

When I came out again a few minutes later, I could see the concern on their faces.

"Why did I have to take my jewellery off when I met you at the gas station?"

"So it could be checked," Mom said.

"Checked for what?"

Stan sighed, understanding the impact of his response. "Listening devices."

I was not only followed, by good guys and bad guys, but possibly my conversations were monitored, my belongings bugged. My most intimate moments and conversations recorded. And now some unseen agents were looking for evidence under the stones of my rings and in the workings of my watch.

"Did they find any?" I asked.

"No, they're clean. You'll get them back in the morning."

FIVE

THE YEARS WHEN my mother and father were still together are a disjointed slide show of scenes and scattered moments: a rainy afternoon watching *Star Trek* and deciding I would marry Captain James T. Kirk when I was old enough. Our St. Bernard dog dragging Ted, still a toddler, on a sled after a big snowfall. The things-to-do box—a shoebox filled with craft supplies, old buttons, Styrofoam balls—that Mom would pull out of a closet for me on days when I needed something to do.

There are photographs that either hold or mould my sense of those days. An attractive smiling family of four, smartly dressed and posed in the landscaped yard of a beautiful suburban home. Enviable, and yet there's something about the studied smiles, the positioning of arms and hands, that telegraphs dysfunction. Something is not quite right here.

We lived in the house on the side of the mountain until the year after Dad moved out. Then we moved to a new neighbourhood in Lynn Valley, still in North Vancouver. It was a swinging neighbourhood, less affluent, but filled with young middle-class families. My mom was invited to a block party shortly after we moved in. She came home to relieve the baby-sitter earlier than expected and never socialized with the people on our street again. It was a little too swinging for her.

The men on the street were pleasant enough, stopping by if Mom was working in the garden to see if she could use any help. The women mostly ignored her. Looking back I realize she was something of a novelty in those days, a divorcee and a young, good-looking one. Divorce hadn't become common yet and there was a fascination about a woman who was not sexually naive and yet was single. Her presence may have stirred equal parts interest and resentment in some neighbouring homes.

Our new house was a strange, modern affair, with the family room, two bedrooms, and a bathroom on the main floor; and the living room, dining room, kitchen, and Mom's bedroom and bathroom on the second floor. The back door from the kitchen opened to a dizzyingly long set of stairs down two storeys to the backyard. In the high fence around the backyard was a doorway with a bolted gate opening to the wilds of the canyon park and the whitewater of a rushing river gorge, where children strayed at their peril, and where I once, defying rules, went exploring and became lost for a few frightening hours.

We stayed there for a couple of years, grades two and three for me. During that time I started piano lessons and got a kitten, Frisky, who became my best friend. I wore my favourite outfit three days a week—plaid hot pants with a purple net vest—and otherwise honed my seventies fashion sensibility. Ted made a friend up the street and the two of them spent a summer trying to dig a hole to China, in the sandbox in the backyard. I don't know if they really thought they could dig through the core of the earth and come out the other side, but no adult told them differently. It kept them busy. We adopted a dog from the local animal shelter, but his penchant for escaping the fenced yard, chasing buses, and biting small children meant he had to be put to sleep a few months later. A new dog, Pixie, followed and would be with us for many years and locations to come.

The next move took us to a small, homey storey-and-a-half stucco house in an older part of North Vancouver. There were tennis courts and a high school right across the street and I thought how wonderful it would be when I was a teenager to roll out of bed late and wander over to class. We had a huge old cherry tree in the backyard that I loved to climb. I would take a book up to the crook of two large branches and disappear, looking out over our garage that opened to a back lane. In late summer I could eat cherries as I read, spitting down the pits, aiming for Ted if he was nearby. Mom and Ted grew giant sunflowers in the garden out back, in between the tall pink hollyhocks and blue delphiniums along the side fence.

Ted and I had second-floor bedrooms, up the wooden staircase and under the eaves. I loved the angles of the ceiling, tent-like, making me feel enclosed and protected.

I learned to cook in the little kitchen with the bow window looking out to the backyard. Mom never tried to inhibit my experimentation, even though the popcorn kernels I put in a beef-and-pasta casserole dish stayed unpopped and nearly broke one of her teeth at dinner one night. I was sure they'd pop up in the heat of the oven and look pretty in the glass dish, I told her. She laughed appreciatively. One entire Saturday was spent constructing a castle out of cake, inverted ice cream cones, and miniature marshmallows. I don't remember what it tasted like, only the sweetness of accomplishment as Mom focused the camera and I posed alongside the iced turrets and towers.

That was the year we started doing a lot of camping with the Searses. Stan and his wife, Sybil, had an old camper on a half-ton. We rented a tent-trailer at first, but before long Mom traded her station wagon for a Volkswagen camper van with a pop-up tent on top. I think of it now as the quick-getaway-mobile, but back then I was charmed by the little fridge and stove, the compact organization of the cubbyholes and cupboards. We spent many weekends with the Searses, whose two sons were grown and didn't come along. We visited provincial and national parks around B.C. Sybil and I both loved to swim. While Mom and Stan set up the campsite and Ted buzzed around them in a whirl of excited activity, Sybil and I would head for whatever body of water the park boasted—lake, river, ocean, pool. I don't recall our conversations for the most part. She didn't try to draw me out; she just let me talk or not, as I wished. But Sybil had a quiet, accepting way that invited conversation. Standing in a lake with little fish swimming about our legs, I would tell her about school, my friends, what I was reading.

I was in grade four. I loved my teacher; she was strict, but glamorously beautiful, her long dark hair curled out and up at the ends, her wide-legged pantsuits the height of fashion in 1973. She drove a white convertible Volkswagen Beetle and I hoped I would grow up to be a blond version of her someday. How could Captain Kirk resist me then?

That was the year Mom instituted Wednesday family night. We'd have dinner in front of the fireplace in the living room, and then take turns reading to each other. Eric Knight's *Lassie Come Home*, E.B. White's *Stuart Little*, Farley Mowat's *The Boat Who Wouldn't Float*, and our favourite, W.O. Mitchell's *Who Has Seen the Wind*.

It was an idyllic little bubble of time, a respite during which it appeared we were finding our balance as a family after the divorce. I think of the year we spent in that little house as the happiest of my childhood. But I look back now and in hindsight it's as if I can see storms brewing on the horizon. I realize how chaotic life must have been for my mother during that time. Stan had told her about the Mafia threat a year or so earlier. In addition to the terror she must have felt at the idea of being a target of the Mob, my parents were embroiled in a legal war over our dad's access to us, and over support payments. The courts had ordered limited and supervised access. Dad wanted more. Mom was trying to preserve the limits, trying to protect us from what she saw as the potential danger of allowing her children to spend time with an alcoholic man she'd been told was involved in the ugliness of organized crime. Affidavits were flying as Dad's old friends attested to his sobriety. That volley was countered by the expert opinions of a child psychiatrist consulted by Mom. And on it went.

Meanwhile, my mother's father and sister, who both lived on Vancouver Island, had pretty much stopped coming to visit, once Warren was out of the picture and Mom had instituted a new "dry" house policy. The party was over and the partygoers stayed away, I heard Mom tell Stan.

This was also the period in which Mom's dual life was beginning. The single mom and church secretary was also sometimes secretly running for her life, trying to protect her family, from both the threats and the knowledge of them.

It must have been unbearably stressful and on some level Ted and I must have felt and reacted to the reverberations. This would have been the time when we were first cautioned about "family privacy," and told not to tell anyone where we were going on those camping trips, or who we were with.

Yet somehow my mother managed to maintain a veneer of normalcy that included Sunday dinners, piano lessons, getting up early to help with math homework before school, and playing catch with my brother in the yard after dinner most evenings.

AS I SAT SHAKING in a New Brunswick motel room as a young adult, I tried to match my childhood memories with a shocking new narrative of what had actually been going on in our lives in those years. At some point I ran out of questions and challenges, and they relented and stopped offering up additional stories as evidence. I was exhausted, and finally we went to bed. Mom and Stan went together to the adjoining room. I lay in the bed across from the kitchenette, unable to sleep, my mind spinning. I imagined them lying down together, and was both fascinated by and uncomfortable with the idea of my mother in bed with Stan.

But it was their revelations that swirled as I lay, eyes wide, listening for steps outside the motel door. And if I heard them, would they mark the watchful rounds of a protector or the furtive approach of an enemy? Or just some other guests of the motel making their way to their room? New questions, new implications crowded my mind. If it was true, what about Ted, who'd gone to live with my dad in Vancouver? Was he safe or was he being drawn into some organized crime scheme, to be implicated and controlled? Who were these people following me, both the good guys and the bad guys? Was Terry at risk because he was my boyfriend and lived with me? And how could I go back to my life after this weekend and carry on as usual? Could this be some crazy made-up story? Why would the two people I most trusted want to deceive me, and why would they tell me such a traumatizing tale if it wasn't true?

The questions writhed within me. I thought back along the years I had known Stan. Camping trips where he'd spent hours with Ted and me, showing us how to plug a crabapple on the end of a sharpened stick, take up our best major-league batter stance, and fling the fruit into the river. Or the hikes he took us on, supposedly looking for bears. I thought of the times, as a teenager, when I'd been angry with my mother, rebelling and acting out, and he'd been the buffer, listening to me rant about her, vent my rage, and then, in his calming, reasonable voice, mediating between us. He never simply took her side. He was my advocate too.

I thought about his public life, as a minister. He'd taken on unpopular causes, fearless in defending and supporting the poor, the homeless, the indigent and addicted.

One December, when I was still in university and working part-time at the newspaper, the editor-in-chief had called me into his office. "This Stan Sears," he said. "You know him, right? Your family goes to his church?" I acknowledged we did. He said he was concerned that Stan was publicly complaining about a Christmas program the newspaper was sponsoring to gather toys for poor kids in the city.

The next time I saw Stan I asked him about it. He said he'd seen some of the collected toys and they were hard-used cast-offs. Those children, who had nothing, should receive new toys for Christmas just like more fortunate kids, he said. They were children. It was Christmas.

Stan had shown himself, over and over in my life, to be courageous and honest, caring and principled. I admired him. I could not imagine him lying to me.

And then there was Mom. Ted and I had always teased her about what we called her extreme honesty. When the cashier at the grocery store gave her too much change, she gave it back. She said cheating on her taxes, even a little bit and even if you didn't get caught, was wrong. When ten-year-old Ted had charmed the owner of the local hardware store into giving him a geranium plant, which Ted in turn gave to Mom for Mother's Day, she'd made him go back and pay for it out of his allowance. She wouldn't tell my friends I wasn't home if they called and I didn't want to talk to them. What we tried to sell her as innocent white lies, she saw as the slippery slope.

I kept coming back to the same conclusion: she wouldn't lie to me, and would never deliberately do anything to hurt me.

In the end I dozed off and had an hour or two of broken sleep before Mom was tapping on the door from their adjoining room. It felt strange, awkward as I called out for her to come in, wondering if Stan would be behind her, if he'd be wearing pyjamas, if we'd all have breakfast together in our housecoats. In the end, we did have breakfast together. I was relieved we were all dressed.

They must have decided I'd heard all I could take because they spoke brightly of what a beautiful day it was, and suggested we take a day trip to nearby Fundy National Park.

We retrieved my car from the gas station and then headed east on the highway. The sky was a thin, cold blue, but there was warmth in the late-February sunlight coming through the windows. I drove slowly, uncharacteristically watching the speedometer to stay within the speed limit. I settled into the shared pretense that we were just sharing a happy jaunt, that everything was just fine.

We soon left the Trans-Canada and turned onto a secondary highway that led to the park. We talked about Mom's courses in Halifax, and my work at the paper. I told them about the latest renovation work on my old house, and described my efforts to learn how to tile the bathroom. Sometimes we just drove along in silence, looking out the windows, lost in our own thoughts.

"The guys say you're a good driver," Stan said during such a moment, smiling at me from the passenger seat. Mom was in the back.

"Guys?" I asked, confused.

It was the agents who were following us, protecting us, he said, in a car somewhere behind. And with that, the flimsy pretense of a pleasant drive in the country was gone. The reality of the previous night's disclosures flooded in.

"How do you know what they say?"

He said he had a receiver hidden in the lining of his wallet that vibrated. Messages could be sent to it, like Morse code. He would feel the pulses in dots and dashes and decipher them. Simple ones he could do in his head, he said. Longer or more complex ones he needed to work out on paper. He made a joke about the ear on his butt.

"What kinds of things do they tell you?"

He paused, as if trying to decide whether to tell me. After a moment he listed types of messages. Trouble coming. Someone following you. Get to a busy public place. Don't go out. And other "operational" messages. He didn't elaborate further.

I felt a wave of anxiety, and once again my heart was pounding at the possibility this was all true. I began watching the rearview and side mirrors, looking for the source of the message, trying to figure out which car was following us.

"You'll never be able to tell," Stan said when he caught me eyeing the mirrors, scanning the traffic behind us. He said that for my protection and theirs, the men were trained to stay invisible, to me and to anyone else who might be watching or following me.

For the rest of the afternoon, I felt wooden, self-conscious. We stopped for lunch at a little café, and visited an art gallery and some craft shops in the village just at the edge of the park. But the entire time I was distracted by the feeling of being watched by invisible eyes, even though I wasn't sure those eyes were real.

As we turned to head back to the motel in Sussex, Mom was in the front passenger seat, Stan in the back. He leaned forward, placing a hand on Mom's shoulder, but speaking to me.

"The guys say not to rush, and we shouldn't get back for at least another hour."

We took an exit and found a place to stop for coffee—which turned out to be strong and old, served in small Styrofoam cups. We sat in the car to drink it. I wanted to know why we couldn't go back to the motel now. Stan said he wasn't sure yet. He was waiting for another message. He wondered if the guys had spotted someone suspicious in the area and were checking them out.

"Someone, like a mobster?" I asked. I sounded ridiculous to myself. Stan shrugged. Mom was quiet.

Eventually Stan got another message: "Safe to come back." Nothing more.

After dinner that evening, the conversation turned back to what was on all of our minds. I don't remember all my questions, but Mom and Stan must have decided I needed some more convincing.

"Do you remember the time we went bowling in Portage la Prairie, when you were in grade six or seven?" Mom asked. I immediately remembered the cavernous old bowling alley with maybe a dozen wooden lanes, mostly empty on a weekday early afternoon, and the clatter of the pins falling and the automated return of the balls rolling up the conveyer to bump into a lineup of other balls. When it was my turn I always chose the ones with the blue swirly patterns. The air was smoky and top-forty tunes from a local AM radio station played from overhead speakers. Ted planted his feet wide apart and rolled the balls between his legs, jumping in joy or frustration as they either knocked a few pins or guttered and rolled ineffectually into the darkness. He couldn't sit still, couldn't wait to take his turn, he was so excited and unsettled by this unusual field trip.

Out of the blue, we'd woken that morning to Mom making a picnic, packing up the old blue cooler with egg sandwiches and carrot sticks, a quart of milk, and our plastic camping cups. She'd told us we were taking the day off. I objected because I had a quiz, and plans for after school with friends. Couldn't we go bowling some other day? I couldn't understand why a parent would insist on playing hooky.

That and many of the other odd, unplanned "getaways" we'd had periodically were actually times we'd been warned to go into hiding while a threat was dealt with, Mom now told me.

Suddenly old memories were surfacing. One afternoon in Vancouver, when I was probably eight or nine, Stan arrived at the door. We'd just arrived home from school and were sitting in the living room. The next thing we knew we were being told to hurry to the bathroom, where Mom had run a tubful of water and was sprinkling something into it.

"Wash your feet," she instructed. "And make sure you do a good job between your toes."

"Why?"

"There's cleaner on the carpet that's bad for your skin."

I didn't remember anyone cleaning our carpets. But Ted and I sat on the edge of the tub, rubbing away at some unseen contaminant. When I looked at him to see how he was reacting to this, he just shrugged, made a silly face, and scrubbed some more. Ted always rolled with these strange events, saying little.

After we'd washed, Mom gave us plastic bags to put over our socked feet when we walked to the back door, where she passed us our shoes and herded us back outside. We all left and went out for an unplanned dinner and movie. Just another odd episode in the Dakin house. At some point we learned to shrug, comply, and forget about these strange occurrences. There didn't seem to be any way to make sense of them. Why fuss?

I asked Mom and Stan now, was that really about rug cleaner?

"No," Mom answered. "Stan came to tell me there was poison on the rug." Someone had broken in during the day and sprinkled it along the front hallway. It was some kind of paralytic that would be absorbed by the skin of our feet. Once we were incapacitated, they would have no trouble grabbing us.

"Why? What would they have done with us?"

"Well, in that case they wanted you all alive," answered Stan. "We found out because our agents picked up the guy who broke in and put the poison down, as he was leaving." He wouldn't tell what he'd done, but he still had the bag the powder had been in. Stan said it was quickly tested, identified, and he rushed over to warn Mom and deliver an antidote with which to wash our feet.

Other memories from the theatre of the bizarre were surfacing. A time we'd had to leave home suddenly at night and were told the furnace was malfunctioning. Another arrival home from school, this time when we lived in Winnipeg. Mom met me at the door with instructions to pack an overnight bag.

"We're going for a sleepover at the Searses'," she said, her falsely bright tone an attempt to belie the stress around her mouth, the tension in her body that made her movements jerky as she gathered what she needed for the night.

It seemed odd. Since when did adults have sleepovers? And on a school night. The rule had always been no sleepovers on school nights. But I packed pyjamas, toothbrush, a book, and Fella, my black-and-white stuffed rabbit-fur creature that might have been a panda or bear cub. Whatever its species, it had been hugged fur-bare on many of its parts, like the Velveteen Rabbit. I was too old for a stuffed animal, but sometimes Fella came along, staying hidden in my bag.

When we got to the Searses', we had dinner together: Mom, Ted, me, Stan, and Sybil. The adults seemed distracted and strange. The conversation was liable to break off mid-thought. Not much fun for a sleepover. We finally settled in for an early night.

I was in a spare room on the main floor and had read myself to sleep when the noise started. In the basement below me I could hear what sounded like blows, a scuffle, grunts, the sounds of something crashing into walls, maybe into furniture. I felt electric jolts of fear and wanted to yell, but as in a nightmare, I was unable to make a sound.

I sat up and turned the bedside light on, but it didn't help. The fury of sound continued. I was frozen in the bed when Mom came in to comfort me, but her own jitteriness convinced me my fear was entirely justified.

Stan and Sybil stuck their heads through the doorway. "It's okay," Stan said, before heading down the hall to check on Ted.

"It's the dog," Mom said. "He's all upset."

It made no sense, didn't jive with what I was hearing, but at some point the noise stopped, and somehow, eventually, I must have fallen back to sleep.

In the morning I tried to ask what had caused the racket in the basement, but was brushed off with the unlikely dog story. It was as if the whole thing had been a bad dream and I gave up, storing the memory in a growing mental file labelled "Strange and Unexplained."

I hadn't thought about it in years, until we were sitting in that Sussex motel room.

"That time in Winnipeg when we slept over at the Searses', there was all that crashing in the basement," I said. "That . . . ?"

"That was the night the Cosa Nostra came for us." Mom looked at me steadily.

"The Italians," Stan confirmed. "We had to be together that night so our coverage could double up." He described how intelligence had been intercepted that indicated something serious was headed our way, a serious attack by pros from the old country. There'd been enough warning to get us together so our security people could mount a united response to the threat.

"What you heard that night was a lethal fight," Stan said. They'd come in through the basement windows, two of them armed to the teeth. Our agents were there to meet them. It was a terrible fight and we lost one man, he said. "But they lost two."

He was telling me that people had died protecting us, coming after us, I thought numbly.

But why were the Cosa Nostra after us? Stan said a list of names and businesses involved in money-laundering had been recovered after raids in Vancouver and Montreal. Those businesses had links to the Italian Mob. And some of them were discovered to be in my mother's name, set up that way years before by my father. My mother had been unaware of these businesses, but the Italian crime bosses, like their Canadian counterparts, were convinced my mother knew everything and because of her friendship with Stan, believed she was preparing to either double-cross them or offer that information to the authorities.

"Why would Dad put those businesses in your name?" I asked Mom. "And how could you not know about it?" She said he'd always put the house, the cars, the cottage, everything in her name, ostensibly for tax purposes. At some point she must have signed papers for business ownerships too. Or maybe he'd forged her signature, she speculated.

Another question from my sleepless night occurred to me. "What about Sybil?" I asked. Sybil was Stan's wife of forty-odd years. How could they betray her? Sybil and Mom were friends. I thought of all the camping trips, the birthday celebrations, the Christmas, Thanksgiving, and Easter dinners we'd shared with Stan and Sybil. I pictured her in the last house they'd lived in before they'd moved away to retire, back to B.C. Her tidy kitchen, the meals she prepared for Stan, for all of us. The living-room table with the family photos of their two sons, a granddaughter, and a variety of dogs they'd had over the years. I thought of her quiet, calm presence. Did she know about all this?

Yes, and no, they said. She knew about the Mob threats, the running, the security people who protected us. She didn't know Mom and Stan were in love. They'd agreed they could not hurt her by telling her. And besides, Stan said, he no longer lived with Sybil. He'd gone inside.

"Inside?" I asked. But instead of answering he held up his hand with an urgency that made me quiet.

"Pen?" He aimed this at Mom. She pulled a small notepad and pen out of her purse and started to write down numbers as he said them aloud. I looked at them questioningly, but Stan was intently focused, appearing to be listening to something.

"He's getting a message," Mom whispered. He was deciphering the signals pulsing and being received through the wallet in his back pocket.

When the message was apparently done, he took the pad from Mom and started striking out numbers and writing letters beneath them. Then he looked up at us. He seemed upset, and ran his hand across his mouth.

"What?" My voice sounded loud in the small room.

He told us the motel's cleaning lady had been attacked when she came into my room to clean earlier that day. A man was lying in wait for her. He'd hit her several times and then run out of the room, leaving the woman unconscious and bleeding.

"One of our guys we'd left behind to keep an eye on your car and the rooms saw him, chased him, and picked him up," Stan said. The attacker was already being transported to a cell somewhere in the shadowy secret security world.

"What did he want?" I asked, shaken. Stan said he'd told an interrogator only that he was looking for the Dakin women but realized he'd made a mistake. Then he stopped talking. Stan said the good news was that the attacker hadn't been able to contact anyone before he was grabbed. So maybe we were safe, for now. The bad news was that the cleaning lady was in rough shape. Our agents had gotten her to a hospital and were now trying to contain the situation, convincing her family not to contact local police. Trying to hush it up.

As for the man who'd hurt her, "They'll find out more once they get him inside," Stan said.

"You said you'd gone inside too," I reminded him. "What the hell does that mean?"

I wasn't sure I really wanted to know.

SIX

INSIDE. IT CONJURED up fragments of a le Carré spy novel, and storylines about operatives seeking some elusive place of safety and respite from the dangers of their lives of intrigue. It summoned images of families left behind—sad-eyed wives and children, abandoned for their own protection. Yet such drama did not fit. This was Stan Sears, the steady, respected minister in the clergy collar. The guy who loved hockey, whose guilty pleasure was Zane Grey westerns. He fed his dog pieces of wieners kept in the fridge just for that purpose, and ate apples with a knife, slowly and deliberately cutting bite-sized slices, lifting them to his mouth on the flat of the blade. An ordinary, likeable man. A man with a side to him—actually an entire life—I had apparently never known.

The motel around us had grown quiet. It was late. The bright lights at the restaurant out front had been dimmed earlier. The world had narrowed to the little table we three were sitting around, drinking yet another cup of tea from cheap brown mugs.

We were all thinking about the cleaning lady, unwittingly caught up in our drama, and suffering for it. *Really?* I thought. *Really?* But there was still more to come.

"Inside?" I asked again.

Stan explained that for his safety, and the safety of Sybil, he'd gone to live in a remote, secret community, with the technology and security staff to ensure it remained hidden from organized crime figures and their enforcers. He said there was one disastrous time when its location had been betrayed. Many had died, either attacking or defending this place.

"It sounds like war."

"It is war. But we had a lot of guys there on furlough so we outnumbered them. Luckily. We had losses too, but none of the black hats got away."

"Black hats?"

"You know, bad guys. Organized crime soldiers. The O. That's what we call them. The O."

"The O?" I said, sounding to my own ears like a mindless echo.

"*O*, for organized crime."

I was asking the wrong questions, but it was hard to slow my rushing thoughts, to cut through the distracting details.

"What . . . how many people live there, inside? Who lives there?"

"A few hundred," he said, "at the one where I live." Stan's voice was measured, deliberately understated. He had been looking down at his mug, but peered up at me from underneath his bushy eyebrows with concern, watching my reaction. He looked down again as he turned his mug around and around on the table.

"There's more than one? How can you keep them secret? Where are they?"

There were several across the country, he said. The one where he lived was in a valley between two mountains, not far from Hope, B.C. We had camped near there once, he said. I remembered the lush, dark forests blanketing the round-topped mountains at the eastern end of the Fraser Valley, where the Fraser and Coquihalla Rivers meet. A broodingly beautiful place, where waterfalls cascade down mountainsides after it rains. A place where night comes early as the late-day sun disappears behind the mountains. Towering mountains, at once protective and impassive, whose long shadows creep steadily across the valley, consuming the light.

I tried to imagine, somewhere in a valley deep between those mountains, a hidden community. If true, thought the journalist in me, it would be a huge story. I pictured cement cellblocks with tendrils of creeping vine obscuring the facade from view, twisting about the bars of small windows high up on a wall.

"You live in a prison?"

"No, I live in an apartment in officers' quarters. Some staff live in cedar cabins—you know, log houses. The people we pick up, the O, they live in cells. But it's a pretty humane prison."

Stan described a compound—a village, essentially—where people targeted by the Mafia were stashed away for safety, with the criminals not far away. The prison, he said, was part of an underground penal system entirely separate from the regular federal correctional system. It was reserved specifically for people arrested for and linked to organized crime.

"I live with the rest of the staff, and I help run it," he replied. "We call it the Weird World."

I RECALLED, FROM high school English class, Shakespeare's Weird Sisters, the sinister foretellers of Macbeth's fate. "Double, double, toil and trouble . . ."

That night I could not have imagined how much toil and trouble lay ahead. The Weird World would be the focus of my thoughts and imagination, even my longing, in the years ahead. But on that night, I struggled to grasp and believe the concept of its existence.

"We call it Place of Hope," Stan said. "PH." I could not imagine what the gangsters who ended up there, or in one of the other prisons hidden in remote, beautiful wild places, could possibly have to hope for. For that matter, what hope could there be for the staff or the rescued in such a place?

"Where are the others?"

There was another in the northern prairies. A third in Nova Scotia, in the hills of Colchester County, Stan said. Each of them was close to some place we'd lived, I thought to myself.

"Why don't we ever hear about them, about the people who are sent there?"

He said that a military tribunal, not within the regular justice system, tried the prisoners. It was overseen by the most senior military staff, its funding hidden within military budgets. Politically, only the Privy Council was aware of the existence of the Weird World.

It was weird in another way too, Stan said. Its prisons and homes, its security and undercover work were run with a philosophy radically different from any counterpart in the wider world.

"These guys, women too sometimes, aren't all just bad guys," Stan said. They were often victims themselves, he said, used and abused, suffering from addictions that were cruelly used to lure them into crime.

"They're the unloved, ignorant of any other kind of life." Stan's voice was soft. He looked at me steadily, appealing to me to understand, to think beyond simple good and evil, crime and punishment.

For these sad but dangerous characters, an arrest was essentially a rescue from lives of crime and brutality, Stan said. At PH and the other "homes," yes, they were incarcerated and held for life, without the chance of ever leaving, but they were treated humanely, some for perhaps the first time in their lives. For some that inspired regret, and even repentance. Hardened criminals—often responsible for killings, kidnappings, pimping, human trafficking, or smuggling and selling drugs—were brought to their knees by simple kindness.

Stan's eyes lit up as he told me many of the Weird World administrators and staff were, or had become, Christians. These were people, he said, who wanted to create institutions where prisoners could be rehabilitated, offered counselling and psychological care, made whole.

"Some become new people. They are given new life."

"Like 'The Organist,'" Mom said. They shared a smile. Again, I felt the strange prickle of discomfort, exclusion, at this new intimacy between them.

"Who is The Organist?"

It was Mom who answered. He was a Black man who'd been picked up in Vancouver, part of a plot to grab Ted and me. Ted would have been in grade one, I in grade three, and Mom would have been working as Stan's secretary at the church.

"The idea was to use you two as bait," Stan said. "To lure your Mom into a trap where she could be forced to tell what she knew. And then they'd have killed her."

"Knew about what?" I felt as though I was missing some fundamental piece of information, and that if I could figure it out, it would be the linchpin to understanding this impossible story.

"About the Weird World. The O know we pick up their people and then they disappear. They'd literally kill to know where they go, what happens to them. To prevent them from talking. And they want to know what your mother knew about Warren's business dealings and associates, about what she had told me." Stan took a deep breath, and blew it out abruptly, making his lips vibrate noisily. Any other time, it might have been funny. He was trying to relieve the tension. It didn't work.

"You were talking about The Organist," I reminded him.

"Right. When he was taken, arrested, he was grateful," Stan said. "Well, maybe not the first night, but pretty quickly."

I don't remember all the details of his tragic story. Unloved, abused, angry. It seemed there was almost a script for how the vulnerable became hardened enforcers, doing the dirty work for the people who made money from crime. The cannon fodder of the underworld.

But he was another prisoner who had changed. Stan was nodding slowly. "He earned our trust over many years. Now he's part of your coverage, protecting you. He puts himself in harm's way for you."

I tried to remember if I'd ever seen a Black man who might have been following me, watching me. No one came to mind. I silently vowed I'd be watching closely for him from now on. In my world, in the overwhelmingly white, Anglo-Saxon city of Saint John, he would be relatively easy to spot.

"He's called The Organist because he learned to play the organ in the chapel at PH," Mom said. "He still plays when he's inside, when he gets a furlough from covering you." She talked about it as if she'd been there, knew him, had heard him play the organ. But of course she hadn't. Still, through Stan, she'd become immersed in the details of that world.

Around us, the motel was still, other than the occasional pinging of the electric baseboard heater under the window and the almost imperceptible movement of the curtains, gently stirring in the rising heat.

I felt full, full to choking on this improbable tale. And yet the story continued. There was a sense of urgency, that a lifetime of events must be boiled down and imparted in this one weekend, in this claustrophobic little motel room, we three huddled around the Formica table.

Stan continued to tell me stories of killers, extortionists, drug kingpins, and human traffickers who raged and threatened after their capture but over time became contrite. They were, some of them, transformed by their relief that they were no longer forced to be part of a world of unimaginable and unrelenting violence and horror. He said they were astonished to find they were being offered forgiveness and new, more meaningful lives. Some worked on the farm, or in the kitchen, even in the administrative offices. Those who embraced their new lives were called lifers, an ironic reference that had nothing to do with their life sentences, or the fact they would never again live outside the hidden, electronic walls of the Weird World.

I was torn. It was a compelling ideology of forgiveness, reconciliation, and renewal, Biblical in theme and tone. But the Christian language and narrative felt oversimplified, uncomfortable.

Repentance aside, it was clear that no one left the Weird World. Not the mobsters who'd been picked up. Not their victims rescued from lives of indescribable horror. The door to that world swung in one direction for them, Stan said. They could never be allowed back into the wider world for fear that the Mob would find them, torture them for information about the Weird World and its leaders, turn them, and press them back into service, or kill them.

The exception was Stan, and the security people he worked with, who came and went as necessary, but were, he said, always relieved to return to their mountain valley refuge.

"It's a place we feel safe, and where we can be ourselves, not caught up in the ugliness of the outside world," he said.

Weird. Yes, definitely.

"There's another reason we're telling you all this now," Mom said, interrupting my thoughts. As I looked over to her, I could see she was now holding Stan's hand. She reached across with her other hand and laid it on my arm. There were tears in her eyes.

"I've decided to go inside too. Things were quieter for a few years. I thought it might be over. But the threats have started again. We don't know why. Maybe if I'm out of the way they'll leave you and Ted alone." She looked down to her lap.

"And . . . I want to be with Stan," she continued, more quietly. "And there's work for me to do inside."

I felt a bubbling panic well up in my chest. I was to be left alone. My mother would disappear, never to be seen again. I wondered if this weekend had been arranged as a goodbye. Maybe this was the last time I would see her. When we left this motel room maybe she would drive away and disappear behind the impenetrable walls of the Weird World. Was I to be left alone on the worldly side of that barrier with this horrifying, unbelievable story? I was an adult, but barely. I felt unprepared, unable to be so entirely alone. Yes, there was Ted, on the other side of the country. Terry was at home expecting to become my husband. I had friends, colleagues. But the prospect of losing my mother this way seemed unbearable.

"When shall we three meet again? / In thunder, lightning, or in rain?" Shakespeare's Weird Sisters chanted shrilly and ominously in my head.

SEVEN

"NOTHING MAKES US so lonely as our secrets," wrote Swiss physician and counsellor Paul Tournier. As children, my brother and I didn't have the language to express how the secretiveness of our family isolated us. But our shared sense of the strangeness of it was a bond, and we granted each other small affirmations with the shake of a head or the roll of the eye when we were asked to be silent about our family plans or movements.

Still, Ted was more sanguine than I. "Things just roll off his back," Mom often said. While I fretted, Ted shrugged and moved on.

"Don't you think it's weird?" I'd press him. As young children there had been no conversation about the secretiveness but as adolescents splayed in front of the television in the basement family room, we speculated.

"Yeah." He'd nod. "Weird. It's cuz of Dad, the legal stuff." Even then the skirmishes over support payments continued.

But I was sure there was something more, sure it had to do with the locked cabinet in Mom's bedroom. I'd seen stacks of what looked like letters in there one time when I'd gone into her room to talk to her.

By the time we were in university, the demands for secrecy were fewer, and limited to when Mom went to visit her father on the West Coast. "Please don't mention to anyone that I'm there," she'd say. Ted and I would nod, roll our eyes.

Now Ted was on the West Coast, living with our dad. He'd written a few letters, called occasionally. I missed him more than I'd have imagined, and now, with this crushing new secret, I longed to be in the old family room, debriefing it with him.

As I drove away from the Blue Bird Motel I could feel many eyes on me: Mom's, Stan's, and those of the unknown men who were now part of my life, always somewhere in the background, unseen, watching me and anyone who came near me.

The previous afternoon Stan had asked if I would give permission for a tracking beacon to be attached to my car, to make it easier for my "coverage" to follow me without being too close or too obvious. I was torn between wanting to defend my privacy, my fast-dwindling feeling of freedom, on the one hand, and on the other the feelings of fear that finally made me nod my head in agreement to the request. I wasn't completely certain all of this was real, but it seemed better to take precautions.

Stan also gave me a small pocket transistor radio.

"This is in case you find yourself in trouble." He fixed me with an uncharacteristically stern look. "You can use it to call for help. But it's only for life-threatening situations. If you use it people will be prepared to put their lives at risk for yours; they'll come to you, but they may have to expose themselves to do it. Use it cautiously."

It looked like any other pocket radio, the old-fashioned kind kids carried around in the seventies before iPods or even Walkmans. I felt an impulse to laugh as I imagined myself talking into the radio to unseen protectors. "This is agent 007 . . ." I pushed the thought away. Stan was explaining that the guys had modified it to be able to broadcast as well as receive. He showed me how to roll the volume dial to the maximum setting and the tuning dial to a specific frequency, and then flip the on switch to activate the broadcast function.

I slipped it into my bag where, even turned off, its presence broadcast a constant static of anxiety. *I have a spy radio*, I thought. *I have the ability to muster security agents. I am under threat.* A strange brew of power and dread.

Mom reassured me she was going back to school. Her move inside wasn't imminent.

"I don't know when. We will give you as much notice as we can."

AFTER TURNING ONTO the highway, I drove self-consciously, staying at the speed limit, passing the familiar landscape, no longer focused on the beauty of the hills along the Kennebecasis Valley. Everything that had made up my life to this point seemed diminished, irrelevant. The job, house, and relationship I was returning to. I couldn't summon enthusiasm for any of it in the face of the invisible, terrifying events I'd been told were surging around me, the danger my family was in, and the prospect of losing my mother to the Weird World, once the path was cleared for her to go inside. I could not imagine how I would now return to the routines of my life. I worried I would somehow telegraph my fear, that it would seep from my pores in a sickly sheen, the smell of anxiety in my sweat.

Of course Stan and Mom had warned me I could tell no one; as alone and afraid as I would feel, I couldn't talk about it, to anyone. Not even Terry, to whom I was now engaged and who was even now waiting for me at home. The sworn secrecy of the situation cut me off from all support except that of Mom, who lived four-and-a-half hours away, and Stan, who existed only behind an impenetrable wall of secrecy except for his risky and infrequent trips out. There could be no fearful calls. Phone conversations had to appear completely normal in case the line was bugged, they had told me.

Some part of me was unconvinced. But increasingly, as I weighed the possibility the story was a sham, my conclusion was that I had to believe, if only for the risk we faced if it were true. Or at least I had to live as though I believed. If I couldn't trust Mom and Stan, all was lost anyway.

I pulled into Terry and my driveway, alongside the bare, tight-budded lilac bushes that surrounded the front yard, and looked up at our old house in downtown Saint John. It was a big, two-storey, wood-framed place, more than a hundred years old. It had three apartments: the main-floor flat that Terry and I lived in, an upper flat, and a small apartment out back. The house needed a paint job. That was part of the plan. We'd been renovating it since buying it just over a year ago. In reality, I'd been doing the renovating work, removing layer after layer of old wallpaper from the fourteen-foot walls, filling the cracks below, painting, sanding trim work, retiling the bathroom. Terry was supposed to paint the exterior that spring. That was his job, suitably, as he'd at one time worked as a house painter. I sighed as I imagined the combination of encouragement and nagging it would require of me to get him to start and then finish the job.

I'd met him the year after I graduated from high school. He was the friend of a friend's boyfriend, just returned from working in Calgary. He charged into my life, telling me mischievously the first night we met that we were going to be together, that I wouldn't be able to resist him. He was right. I was intoxicated by his flirtatious charm, sparkling brown eyes, and infectious smile. He was smart, funny, and full of energy and surprises. I tended to be serious, earnest. He was like a freshening breeze, blown in from the west, and I was happily carried away.

We spent our first summer taking long drives, going to the beach, and after I turned nineteen that August, dancing at the clubs. He loved to dance and revelled in the beat, the movement, his energy effervescent. The eyes of other women followed him on the dance floor, taking in his slim, athletic body, wavy black hair, and rhythmic abandon. I felt a new, proprietary impulse that deepened my feelings of desire for him.

He lived with his alcoholic father and an older brother, and was looking for work. I lived with my mother and was studying and working. With nowhere private to be alone we parked his battered old Fairlane station wagon in seldom-used wooded lanes, or in lonely cemeteries. "So beautiful," he breathed in my ear, as he held me, and I was convinced by his awe, and fell a little further, allowing myself to be encompassed by sensation and new feelings of tenderness.

The intoxication eclipsed any worries about the lack of direction in Terry's life, at least for a while. He'd work here and there, enough for gas and pocket money. I thought out every possibility, every outcome, measured every risk and every potential benefit. He lived in the moment, with a reckless abandon that was irresistible. He was contemplating going to university but had to upgrade his high school marks first and had missed the application deadline. He'd come home because his mother was dying of breast cancer and he wanted to be closer. He had terrible nightmares about her, he admitted. I held him more tightly, stroking his hair, silently promising I would be there for him. When he gave me a ring, I'd agreed to marry him. He wanted to have babies, and he imagined happiness in creating the kind of family he'd never experienced growing up in his own home. He thought this, marriage and babies, would be the piece that would finally provide the focus to settle into a steadier life of achievement.

Now I sat in our driveway feeling raw and shaken to the core. I didn't know how to walk in the front door and confront Terry with the newly revealed family story that was weighing on me. I felt changed at a cellular level, felt sure it would show, and knew I would be unable to explain.

Gazing at the peeling paint on the front porch, I had to admit Terry's charm had worn thin in the intervening years. He'd gone to university, but dropped out. He'd returned to Alberta for a few months, then come back and started a painting company with a buddy, but contracts were intermittent. Sometime he drove a cab. By this time I'd graduated and was working full-time as a reporter and columnist at the local newspaper. The mismatch was becoming undeniable, my disappointment obvious. He alternated between remorse—coupled with heartfelt promises to buckle down and get it together—and defiant gestures such as heading out the door with no word of where he was going or when he'd be back.

As I opened the car door and walked up the porch steps I could see through the bay window that Terry was on the couch, the television reflecting blue light across his face. I walked inside. He turned to me, smiled. "Hey, you're back," he noted, then turned back to the TV. I took my bag to our bedroom and started to unpack. After a few minutes he followed me in, hugged me, asked how the weekend was, how my mom was. "Fine," I answered in a monotone. "All fine."

He accepted this with a nod, and headed back to the living room. I could hear the canned laughter of some sitcom.

In the following week I was tight, humming with tension, constantly looking over my shoulder, fearful at the approach of any stranger. The feeling of being watched was overwhelming. I went to work and then hurried home and holed up. I was afraid to go out at night. I told myself I was in no greater danger than I'd been in before hearing about the Mafia threat, but it was no comfort.

One evening, when Terry was out, I went to the kitchen to make a lunch for the next day and realized we were out of bread. The corner store was less than a block away but the thought of going outside in the dark was terrifying. I paced from the kitchen to the front window, pulled the curtain aside a crack to peek out into the night, let it fall back. I went back to the kitchen and looked at the bread-less collection of lettuce, sprouts, cheese, and mustard on the counter.

Suddenly I was angry, an eruption of rage at my own fear, my feelings of entrapment, my helplessness. I felt shamed by my loss of confidence and the circumstances that had made my world such a small, frightening place. I rushed to the front hall, grabbed my jacket and keys, felt for money in my jeans pocket, and stormed out the door, heading for the store.

That surge of anger took me down the driveway. As I approached the street I peeked out past the tall lilac hedge, trying not to think that it made a perfect hiding place for some-one waiting to jump me. Then I walked fast, my hands jammed into my pockets, head down but eyes sweeping the street around me, searching the dark alleys between buildings, the shadowed doorways. Just before the corner, a white, windowless cargo van was parked facing me. I felt my heart leap. I slowed. Instinctively I felt the potential danger, the sinister presence of the van. People could be hiding in it, poised to throw open the back double doors and grab me. Or maybe it was the good guys, my security people, and the van their watching post from which they were protecting me. That felt scary too. The thought of what they'd look like, how they'd risk their own safety for mine, sent another surge of adrenalin coursing through me.

The street lights reflected weakly on the wet asphalt, refracted and distorted in pothole puddles. Bare tree branches reached out and retreated in the wind gusting up the hill from the blackness of the harbour. There was no one else in sight. I couldn't decide if that was a cause for relief or worry. I took a deep, shaky breath and darted to the other side of the street, practically running, grateful to reach the brightly lit corner store and hear the bell on the door as I opened it, almost falling through the doorway in my haste. I looked up to the startled expression on the face of the man behind the counter, and smiled weakly at him. I wondered if he would try to protect me if someone were to rush inside behind me with a gun or a knife.

I made my way across the worn floorboards of the store to the rack of breads. I selected a loaf of whole wheat, and then loitered, wandered up and down a few aisles, hands shaking, trying to still my pounding heart, stalling to avoid going to the cashier and then back out into the inevitable night.

When I got home I called my friend Bruce, who often came by to mow our lawn, since we didn't have a lawn mower. "Do you have a hedge trimmer?" I asked him.

The next afternoon when I got home from work the hedge had been cut to knee height. There would be no fragrant mauve blossoms to intoxicate me this spring. But no longer could someone hide within the now brutally trimmed branches.

I don't recall much about the following weeks. I was numb, and stumbling through my days in a cloud of distraction. "What is it?" Terry asked a few times. I could feel his growing worry and frustration with my anxiety, my uncharacteristic reticence. On several nights I came close to telling him. But in the end I would shake my head, say I was just worried about Mom, alone and working so hard at school in Halifax, and he would let it be.

There were frequent, unsatisfying phone conversations with Mom, who was calling to make sure I was coping with the new information. "I'm okay," I assured her. What else could I say? But I likely didn't sound okay. There seemed so little to talk about; the only topic I was interested in was forbidden on the phone. We made plans to be together at Easter. She would come to stay with us over her holiday break from school.

In the meantime, Terry had started to pressure me about setting a date for a wedding. Perhaps he felt me slipping away. Being unable to tell him my secret made the inadequacies of the relationship starkly clear. We continued to go through the motions of domestic life, I continued to go to work, to feign interest in my assignments, but all the while I was thinking that my mother would soon disappear forever and I would be left alone in a life that no longer seemed safe or even desirable.

In the months that followed I must have figured out a way to separate my daily life from the world that increasingly took over my mind, my emotions. I was increasingly unhappy at work. In the face of Mafia plots to target me or my family, what interest could covering council or school board meetings possibly hold?

And some big decisions were forming as I dragged myself through the days, back to a home where there was little respite or comfort.

It was a dark time and much of it is now indistinct. I recall the feeling that I had to make the most of what time I had with Mom before she disappeared inside. We went to Bermuda later that spring, the two of us, and stayed with her friend from school who was doing an internship there. Back at home I continued the renovations and distracted myself by learning to tile the bathroom. I lost myself in measuring, cutting, nipping, and gluing the tiles, slipping them neatly into place in unerringly straight and reassuringly predictable lines, covering the grungy old walls with this new neat, shiny clean surface. Then grouting, filling in all the empty spaces between, and when the grout was dry, washing away the residue. It was precise work that demanded close attention and was both time-consuming and comforting. I could not stop. What started as tiled walls around the shower enclosure expanded to tiled half-walls around the entire room. I dreaded the completion of the project.

From tiles I moved on to shingles. As the weather improved, I began building a wall on one side of the front porch, enclosing the railing and creating new privacy beside the entrance where I often imagined someone hiding around the corner, waiting for me. Line by precisely measured and levelled line, I hammered cedar shingles. The rhythmic blows of the hammer diverted my thoughts from the worries that always threatened to swamp me.

Through the spring and early summer I sanded and painted, finishing our apartment and then moving on to the one at the back of the house when those tenants moved out. It smelled of dirty laundry and stale food; a yellow nicotine hue unevenly stained the walls. I compulsively scrubbed and painted my way through it, replacing the grime with a new sheen of bright paint, taking satisfaction from the transformation, and from my ability to take charge of this space. Because outside those shiny, new walls I perceived chaos and danger, or at least its ever-present threat.

EIGHT

IN THE WEEKS and months after the motel meeting in Sussex, as I struggled to work through all I'd learned, I also felt surprised by a sense of affirmation. As awful as the scenario might be, this explanation could mean that at least my family wasn't just odd or crazy. This story offered a workable—if extraordinary—explanation for the way our lives had unfolded, a justification for our disappearances. It addressed many of the mysteries that had plagued Ted and me: why we kept moving, why our mother was so determined to keep us away from our father, why we had to be so secretive.

There was also the emerging concept of being part of something bigger, something with implications far beyond my small life. It was frightening but also intriguing, removing me from the humdrum of daily minutiae. I think my mother felt this too.

As time went on, I was increasingly drawn into the drama of the Weird World, especially during the times when I would visit

Mom, or Stan would come out from PH to visit Mom in Halifax. Often I would join them for a weekend. During these times together we usually took road trips, never remaining long in one place. Stan said it was safer for him to stay on the move when he was out, preferably in uncrowded areas. That made it easier for his coverage, his security guys, to spot anyone following or watching. If faces that seemed familiar showed up nearby, the guys would check them out, running licence plates through police databases. Sometimes we'd be told to move on again, and find a new motel farther down the road.

I never saw the guys, at least not that I was certain of. Sometimes on the highway I'd think I had picked out a familiar car that had been just ahead or just behind earlier in the day, or the day before. But their job was to be invisible and I decided they were remarkably good at it.

Stan began bringing me letters every time he came out, messages from inside. He would hand me a packet of letters in plain envelopes, each marked with a series of initials indicating the names of supervisors and security staff in the inside communities who'd checked and okayed the contents, or been involved in transporting the letters. Usually they were hand-written or hand-printed; occasionally, typed. A few times I received letters from people through the regular mail system, but mostly, as with all contact and information from the Weird World, Stan was the conduit. The mailman bearing messages on his forays from the protection of PH.

In the early days each new letter was accompanied by a story. Some of the letters came from people I'd known as a child in Vancouver, or people who'd known me but of whom I had little or no memory, only recognizing their names—people who had since been implicated in some organized crime plot, picked up and imprisoned, never to return to their outside lives. Like us they had disappeared from life in Vancouver, only much more permanently. Stan would tell me how these people had come to be inside, and how their lives had changed as a result of being freed from the tyranny of the Mob, whether they were its conspirators or its victims, or more often both. He explained many of them carried a heavy burden of guilt when it came to Mom, Ted, and me, because they'd played some role in attempts to harm us or betray us in some way. Some had simply been aware of threats and regretted not warning us.

One of the first letters was from a couple by the name of Crow. She was my godmother, and had been close friends with Mom. He was Ted's godfather and had worked with Dad. It was the *Mad Men* era: there were cocktail parties, patio gatherings, events at the golf club or the winter club. But the friendship ended soon after Mom and Dad separated, a victim of the legal conflagration that was my parents' eventual divorce. The Crows had signed an affidavit on behalf of my father saying he was clean and sober, and fit to see his children. Perhaps they hadn't known, hadn't realized, but nothing could have been further from the truth; at that time Dad was drinking heavily. Mom saw the affidavit as a betrayal.

The Crows signed off their letters to me from inside as "the Caw-Caws," a joke meant to hide their identity from anyone who might intercept the correspondence. They were different now, they had changed, Stan told me. They were decent people who'd become caught up in something they couldn't get out of. One becomes entangled with the O by small but increasingly less benign degrees, he explained.

"When you finally realize what you're a part of, it's too late to get out," he said. Unless, as the Crows did, you end up in the

Weird World, a one-way ticket out. Stan described their anger and then—surprisingly quickly—their relief to be picked up and taken to a safe place where they were treated as prisoners, yes, but also with compassion and caring. Eventually, Stan said, they'd expressed deep shame and written to Mom to apologize. They'd been able to give tips and useful intelligence to our security people and, through that, felt they had partly made up for past treachery. Eventually they had built up new lives and become trusted in the Weird World. Now they lived in staff quarters and had administrative jobs.

In their letter to me, the wife recalled me as a chubby blond toddler. She apologized for their part in forcing us to run from Vancouver. She signed off with a sketch of a crow in flight.

I thought of the last time I'd seen her, when I was a fifteen-year-old visiting Dad in Vancouver for the first time since I'd left six years earlier. We'd spent an afternoon visiting at her home. She'd tried to talk to me about Mom, asking me how she was, but some loyalty prevented me from saying much. Mom had asked me in her most serious voice, as she was driving me to the airport, not to talk to anyone "out there" about her or what she was doing. "Not about my work, my friends, vacations. Please just don't talk about me to anyone, even people who were my friends." The intensity of her request, her seriousness, annoyed me. I grudgingly agreed, even though I could see no reason for such secretiveness and thought she was being over-sensitive or silly.

Among the letters Stan delivered was regular correspondence from the man who called himself The Organist. He'd been a dentist, and he confirmed the story of how he'd once come after our family with instructions to grab Ted and me. He'd been picked up years before, when we were still in Vancouver. He too apologized, and told me how he'd found some peace and a happy life at PH, working outdoors, caring for animals, and building and repairing things. When I opened the first letter from The Organist, Stan reminded me this man was sometimes part of my protection, my coverage. The Organist told me he understood my life was difficult, stressful. But he said I was lucky to have people like Stan and Ruth who loved me. He wrote that that was something he'd never had as a child.

Some of the staff at PH, whom I'd never met, wrote to say they understood how terrified I must feel, how sorry they were that I had to live with that fear. They tried to reassure me that Stan and the others were doing everything they could to protect us. They called me Miss P, mostly.

Someone who signed off as LtYCR wrote, "P, it seems like only yesterday I sent you a small gift of moccasins." I remembered those moccasins, their smell redolent of buckskin and fire smoke, soft with a fringe around the top and brightly beaded. They were under the Christmas tree the year before we left Vancouver, when I was nine. When I'd asked who they were from, Mom had said simply, "A friend. Someone you don't know."

"He's the boss inside," Stan said, interrupting the memory I was connecting to the letter before me. "A wise man." He was a First Nations man who had risen in the ranks of the military and been tasked with building the anti–organized crime task force. "He recruited me," Stan said.

I recalled other mysterious presents from unknown friends.

"Who always left the box of oranges?" I asked now. "Someone from inside?" Mom nodded, smiling as we both remembered the mysterious annual box of Christmas oranges that would appear as if by magic on our doorstep in mid-December. We'd come home from piano lessons or hockey and there it would be. No card. Ted and I would nag Mom to tell us where it came from.

"Just a friend, someone you don't know," she would always reply.

"And the Christmas angels too?" She nodded again. I still have the ceramic angels, a small choir of cherubic figurines each playing an instrument. Every Christmas they came out to be carefully unwrapped and placed on the mantel or the top of the piano. It seemed these people who'd existed outside of my awareness had in some sense known me, cared about me, been moved to send gifts to me, and now seemed excited to introduce themselves by letter.

These letter writers all said they hoped I would be safe, cautioned me to be careful, often warning me that strangers who tried to get close to me in the outside world might have nefarious intentions. None of those who had been taken inside against their will, imprisoned, or caught up in a sweep spoke of longing for their previous lives. None wrote of the children, parents, partners, or siblings left behind, still outside. The impression, from what Stan said and from what they wrote, was that the Weird World had allowed them to wipe the slate clean, start again in a kinder, more humane world. But important losses were the price of that.

Most of these people said they had become Christians since being taken inside, repenting, being forgiven, making amends. Lifers, Stan and Mom always called them—people who'd found new life as a result of a life sentence. They liked the irony of that.

Eventually I burned most of those earliest letters. Mom, Stan, and I stood beside a bonfire in a remote wooded area outside the city, feeding pages into the flames. Mom, who was receiving many more letters than I, and had been for years, had done this many times before. We were asked to do so as a security precaution, even though they contained no full names, no identifying information, and the writers had been told to disguise their hand-writing. But I kept many of the letters that arrived later, as did my mother. Those letters were a rare link to a secret world, small pieces of evidence, and we resisted letting them go.

I imagined the excitement our replies must cause. In most cases, Stan said, we were the only contact those people had with the outside world. Often I would get a reply expressing surprise. "I certainly admit I was surprised to hear from you," wrote The Organist the first time I responded to him. "It wasn't necessary for you to write." He went on to tell me that he had taken up painting, and that there was a lot of snow in the valley at PH.

Even as I vacillated between belief and moments of doubt about the reality of these communities, I was fascinated to read the small details, to receive the hand-delivered mail that crossed a chasm between worlds. I was eager for hints, images, a sense of that place out of reach to me but still very much linked to my life. Always, though, I searched the lines and references for bits of proof that might further convince me these people were real, or inconsistencies that would prove that they weren't. Even as time went on and the shock wore off, a large part of me resisted this awful, ugly world spawned by crime, greed, violence, ruth-lessness, and pain, no matter how idyllic the descriptions might be of morning light illuminating the snow on the mountaintop.

Those letters also revealed more about Stan's role in the Weird World. "He is a big chief here," wrote my godfather, Roy B. Apparently Roy and his wife, Jeanette, had been wrapped up in some Mob plot with my dad and ended up as "guests" at PH. I recalled travelling to Ontario the summer I was seven, to spend a couple of weeks with Roy and Jeanette and their daughter, Karen, who was my age. It was my first time flying. I went by myself, watched over by cooing stewardesses who thought me cute in my specially purchased travel pantsuit and matching handbag. Uncle Roy had picked me up at the Toronto airport and taken me to the family cottage on Georgian Bay, a bucolic place where we swam in the clear warm water every fine day, and curled up on old couches in the screened porch with comic books, puzzles, and novels when it rained.

Despite this, I was desperately homesick, with a ferocity that clawed at me and made me fight back tears at bedtime. It was better when Roy was there, but he spent most of each week working in the city. Returning on the Friday after the first week, he brought me a book, *Adventure Stories for Girls.* "Daaaaaahhhhling," he wrote on the inside flap, our inside joke that made Karen peevish with jealousy, her mouth pursed as she glared at me. "Daaaahhhhling girl, how was your day?" he'd drawl to me at dinner each evening, and I'd giggle.

"Dear P," read Roy's letter from inside. "Finally your godfather can write and be honest with you. Hard to realize you are an adult. No longer a little blonde girl, lost in a sense because of your Dad."

He said he heard from Mom sometimes and he was grateful for her forgiveness and hoped I could also forgive him.

> *The days you once knew me I was one horrible person, deserving of the most severe punishment that could be given out. Now while not forgotten I am forgiven and can be real and liked and even loved . . . I am now respected here. Isn't that wonderful after what I was?*

Now, apparently, Roy was not well. He'd fallen down some stairs, he wrote. No longer confined to a cell, he was now accepted as a reformed lifer at PH, but was not the vibrant, charming man I remembered, Stan said. Jeanette was now a cook at PH. Roy and others said in their letters that within the prison there were many who hated Stan and wanted to kill him, but a lot of others who loved him for his gentleness, his forgiveness, and for the prayers he said with and for them as they contorted with pain and shame over past lives and deeds.

I knew that gentleness, that compassion. As a teenager in constant conflict with my mother, I was always happy to see Stan's car in the driveway when I came home from hanging out with my friends, especially if it was past my curfew. He buffered the tension between Mom and me, joking with us to soften her sternness, which I now know was rooted in fear for me. He intervened on my behalf if I was late or had done something we knew would upset Mom. He was always happy to see me too, interested in what I was doing, willing to overlook my teenage foibles. Over the years I had come to think of Stan as a father figure, and now that I was a part of the inside circle, aware of his secret life, trusted and included, and spending so much time with him, this feeling intensified.

"I feel silly still calling you Mr. Sears," I said one evening when he was out with us. It's what I'd called him since that first meeting at his church. I don't remember which anonymous, interchangeable motel room we were in that evening. They were mostly dated, well-worn places with kitchenettes and decorated with a nautical or woodland theme, kitsch pottery, and cheap photographs or prints on the walls. As we surveyed the latest accommodation, Stan sometimes joked that the government of Canada was really springing for the Ritz. He always paid for these rooms, cash. One room for him and Mom and another for me, covered by some budget in Ottawa as part of our security detail, he said.

On this night it was somewhere in Cape Breton. It was fall—must have been early November because only a few desolate leaves still clung to the branches that dipped and bucked in a cold wind. The tourist route was largely empty and beautiful in its barrenness. As we'd driven that day, we'd remarked on the stark beauty, the way the dark-bellied clouds scudded so quickly across the grey choppy waters of the bay. It wasn't a vacation. I knew we were at risk and that at any moment we could be told to run; being with Stan made us targets. But there were moments of sweet contentment, pleasure at being together, savouring the natural beauty around us.

All my life I had dutifully referred to Stan and his wife as "Mr. and Mrs. Sears." This was a nod to my mother's sense of the respect due to adults, and a reflection of my young age when we'd first met. It had just stuck. It seemed increasingly awkward and strangely formal as our families had grown closer and as Ted and I grew older, but no one had suggested an alternative. Until now.

"What would you like to call me?" Stan asked, smiling. "Stan? Or something that reflects that I think of you as my daughter?" I nodded, feeling pleased. "Dad" didn't seem right. That's what I'd always called my father, we agreed. We settled on Papa. We smiled at each other, feeling silly and pleased, and he hugged me. "Papa" felt strange for a while, but the sense of belonging and connection it contained felt right; a case of the name catching up with the relationship. Those repetitive, softly puffing syllables on my lips were a balm for the years of feeling father-less. He began to call me his "other girl," Mom being his first. I thought about Sybil, his wife, with a sense of guilt. Stan had assured me they were no longer together; he'd bought her a home with a garden near Gibson's on the West Coast. She was happy, he said, and knew Stan was inside living a new life. She had no idea he and Mom were in love, and they'd agreed there was no reason to tell her, to hurt her.

Papa bought me small presents. A small, woven Mi'kmaq basket, a pewter lapel pin. He knew I loved lobster and we sometimes drove the twisting road to Peggy's Cove, outside Halifax, and the restaurant with the freshest lobster and the gingerbread cake with real whipped cream. He seemed proud to tell the waiter, "A nice big lobster, pound and a half at least, for my daughter." Then he'd nudge me playfully.

As I remember it, Stan came out to spend time with us often, every few months, but I know my mother didn't feel that way. She missed him, worried about him, and apart from his presence, I think she missed the conduit to information he offered about what was going on around us on the unseen side of the curtain, and what the current threat level was.

He would call her, always from a pay phone. He was just coming, or going, from PH, he would tell her, and had stopped at a phone booth. "I only have a few minutes," he usually said. There were no phone calls from inside. Sometimes he had a message from the people protecting us, a warning or instructions to take a particular precaution. More often it was just a chance to say hello. If I was around when he called, I tried not to listen as Mom's voice lost its worried pitch and became tender.

When they had time together, they would count the days and too soon begin to mourn the coming time apart. A day or so before they had to say goodbye Mom's face would become sad, and Stan would tell silly jokes to cheer her up, or sometimes just envelop her in a hug, whispering in her ear. He would leave notes for her to find after he'd gone, little jokes or love messages in her housecoat pocket, on a shelf in the medicine cabinet, or on her dresser.

The notes, the letters, those tenuous connections became increasingly important. On the second or third trip Stan made out to visit us after I'd been brought into the picture, the packet of letters included one from Linda, and another from Tom. My half-siblings from my father's first marriage were already teenagers when Ted and I were born. I'd spent time with both on the trips to see Dad in my mid-teens. Tom was a great bear of a guy—friendly, funny, always in some sort of trouble that would cause his wife (the first of three) to look at him with disappointment. He fed me drinks when Dad wasn't looking, and one evening he took me up Grouse Mountain to see the view over North Vancouver from the Cleveland Dam. He pulled out a joint, lit it, and passed it to me. On the way back down the winding road he drove so fast I couldn't keep my dazed head erect. Letting it fall back against the headrest, I hallucinated I was in a cartoon with velocity streaks waving behind us as we hurtled down the sharply twisting Capilano Road. There was a moment when I acknowledged my mother was justified in her worry about this visit. But as I allowed my head to loll and my eyes to close, I could hear Tom laughing, always laughing, and thought it was nice to just let go.

Now as I looked at the letters from Tom and Linda, I shook my head. My new understanding of the world was crashing into a barricade. Ted was living in Vancouver. He regularly golfed with Tom. He'd seen Linda when she'd visited Dad from Oklahoma City a few months earlier. They weren't inside.

"This can't be," I said, my voice sounding flat and measured despite the frantic flapping of doubt and alarm filling my chest. What could these letters mean? It must all be just a crazy story after all, complete with forged letters.

I waved the envelopes at Stan.

"These can't be real."

NINE

IN OUR LIVES, people were not necessarily who they seemed to be. So said the man who Mom thought was Stan, as he settled down on a bench beside her at Ted's Little League baseball game one afternoon.

"I'm not who I appear to be," was how he'd replied to Mom's warm hello. Years later as she was telling me this, she recalled how Stan—the real Stan—had recently grown a moustache. The man wearing Stan's clothes, walking with his gait, smoking the same brand of cigarettes, also had a moustache. Somehow she had fixated on that. But surely, I thought but didn't say, growing a moustache was the easiest part of the impersonation.

"But what about his shape, his face . . . his scar?"

"All exactly the same," she said. "The only thing that was off was something about the way he talked. I didn't pick it up at first. It was eerie."

Winston Churchill famously had a double during the war.

A political decoy. In the 1990s, an American undersecretary for the U.S. Army claimed other international leaders had doubles. Manuel Noriega, Fidel Castro, George W. Bush, Osama bin Laden. A doppelgänger—from the German, literally "double-goer"— could be sent into particularly risky situations, or used to distract from the actual movements of a world leader, to draw eyes away during critical operations.

These were among the examples placed before me as I sat with the letters from Tom and Linda in my hands.

"They're doubles," I repeated dully. "The brother Ted golfs with isn't really Tom?"

I don't recall the entire explanation. I was distracted by the frantic thoughts in my head, once again measuring and questioning my trust and belief in the people I loved so completely against the outrageousness of what they were telling me. My mother and the man I had come to think of as a father. Good, reliable, loving people. Educated, respected. They were not people who would make this shit up, I thought desperately.

But I kept coming back to the same wall. This idea of doubles was impossible, unreal. Wasn't it?

"Why?" I asked. "And how could you even do that?" I thought of Stan's scar, Linda's bright blue eyes, Tom's unique nose. I couldn't imagine how they could be replicated in a believable way.

"Sometimes plastic surgery, if they're going to be in place for a long time. Sometimes moulds or prosthetics, coloured contact lenses, heavy makeup," said Stan, describing how talented makeup artists, part of the Weird World team, could transform similar-looking people into dead ringers. How doubles were trained for months to mimic the gestures, expressions, and tics of their marks. How they practised speaking like them, behaving like them, and learned about their lives in intimate detail that, once they were in place, could make the difference between a successful operation and disaster. It was a high-stakes game. The intelligence and inside information gathered by a double could be critical.

"If they're detected, they're usually killed, probably tortured for information first," Stan said.

It was espionage. Nabbing and replacing key people involved in organized crime to infiltrate their operations, learn their plans, and sometimes use the information to intervene or protect targets.

"But why Linda and Tom?" I understood that with Dad's connection to the Mob they were likely to have become involved. I'd been repeatedly warned that Dad had at various times tried to involve Ted and me, putting businesses or properties in our names without our knowledge, the idea being we would be given more explicit roles and initiated as we got older. But it was implausible that Linda and Tom could be such key figures in that world that, once they were arrested and imprisoned, they would be replaced by doubles. Linda was a real estate agent who'd moved to Oklahoma and started a security company. Tom hadn't even finished high school. I knew he hung out with some tough people—bikers, maybe Hells Angels. It didn't surprise me that he would have connections in the drug world. But he was the jovial guy with the little stereo shop on Marine Drive in North Vancouver, installing high-end sound systems in people's homes. Not exactly nefarious work.

"Apparently he was very good at bugging homes and offices," Stan said. He let that sink in.

"And Linda?"

"She had skills too," he replied.

They were soldiers, and did what they were told, Stan said. Or had until they were picked up. Now they lived inside; they had for some time. And they were writing me letters.

I opened Linda's first. The left-slanted, rounded script looked like Linda's writing:

Once I was a very poor and miserable half-sister. I would have used you for whatever I could get from you. I can understand why your mother was once afraid for you to know me better. As I think of the past I'm glad you didn't know me better.

Linda and I had reconnected briefly during one of my summer visits to Vancouver, when I was fifteen and had decided to visit my father despite my mother's clear reluctance. Linda and her husband had flown in from Oklahoma City, and Dad and I had picked them up at the airport. Dad was on the wagon and on his best behaviour. Linda and I sat in the back of the car on the drive back to Dad's condo. We noticed we were wearing the exact same colour of nail polish. "I guess we really are sisters after all," Linda said. Wishing for connection, I took it as a sign that despite so many years of separation, we did share something besides a portion of our DNA, even if it was only a predilection for a particular shade of pink.

She'd taken me for lunch and shopping that week, bought me an outfit, a flowing patterned skirt and blouse. When I asked her if she liked it, she said it wasn't her taste but it looked fine on me. She'd asked me about school, boyfriends, Ted, Mom. I thought she'd been expressing interest, trying to connect. Now I was to believe she'd actually been digging for information to pass along, some tidbit that might have been useful to someone in some unimaginable way.

"You likely know the story of why I am here," her letter continued. "It is not a pretty story but I thank my God I am a new person and wouldn't trade life in this world for anything out there."

Stan said that Linda had been picked up in a raid on a prostitution ring, and was discovered to be involved in running it. Part of her role was identifying and luring new recruits, he said.

Linda was now working as a nurse at PH, she wrote, adding, "You will see a different T [my brother] than you had known or heard about. We have had some good visits together."

Tom's letter was brief. "I guess I have been awkward all my life but just now I feel more so than ever," he half-wrote, half-printed on a sheet of yellow paper. He'd learned to write after being arrested, Stan said. That was after the addiction treatment. He'd been involved in drug trafficking, money laundering, a little strong-arm stuff. When he arrived at PH, he was strung out and spent time detoxing, often restrained because of his violence toward staff. He too had changed apparently; he described his new home as "a world that had to be created because of greedy people like I once was," and continued: "Well I've said it! I am glad, I'm glad to have ended up in this secret unknown world (unknown to most). Here I have learned what real life is and how to share it with others."

I folded the letters and placed them back in the initialled envelopes. Father, siblings, godparents, so many friends and family involved and now in a prison.

"Your mother was caught in the thick of it." Stan seemed to have read my mind. "The three of you were surrounded."

Suddenly it occurred to me that the Tom and Linda doubles would be looking out for Ted, not a threat to him. But, like everything else with the Weird World, it wasn't that simple.

"We're not the only ones that use doubles," Stan said. "Sometimes the O grab our people and put their own in place. Sometimes we take theirs too."

Double espionage. It was too complicated, too unlikely to imagine.

"So you're not sure who's around Ted, who's actually who?" The thought was unspeakably creepy. I wanted to call Ted, tell him not to trust anyone, to run, to once again disappear. But he was enjoying his life and would say I was crazy. Maybe I was. Maybe we all were. Maybe this was just what it sounded like, a preposterous story. But now I was a part of it.

I began asking Stan and Mom who had doubles, whose doubles they were—ours or theirs—going through the list.

"Does Uncle Roy have a double?" I demanded. I hadn't seen him since that summer I was seven. Another relationship that had been lost when we disappeared the first time.

"No. But he did at one time, after he was first taken."

"What about the Crows?"

"Yes, both of them."

"When I visited them, when I went to Vancouver, were those doubles?"

"No. They were picked up later, maybe two or three years after."

I was trying to pin it all down, map it out. I wanted an understanding of the lay of the land, but the topography was heaving and the answers did not reassure. I had increasingly come to accept Stan's story of Mafia threats, but this latest layer threatened to undo my belief.

I said I was tired and would head off to bed in my room next door. They both hugged me. "It's been a lot to put on you," Mom said. "I'm so sorry. Are you okay?" I nodded, unconvinced myself but unsure what anyone could do about that. Stan put his hand on my head, and looked at me steadily, trying to read my state of mind, and finally nodded back, and promised we'd take a break from all this the next day. We'd have some fun.

There would be more revelations to come, but mercifully not on this night.

THE NEXT DAY we continued on our trip around the Cabot Trail. It was 1989 and the tourist trade was still undeveloped and quiet in the off-season, the vistas beautiful at every turn. Stan said there was talk of a new facility on the East Coast, perhaps here, on a cove in one of the hidden valleys in the vast unpopulated areas north of Highlands National Park. At a scenic lookout, we pulled into the gravelled parking area, got out of the car, and walked to the guardrail at the edge of a steep descent down the mountain to a sparkling sea far below. Stan pointed up the coast to a series of high bluffs whose blue-green folds against the horizon were progressively hazy as they marched into the distance.

"There, probably forty kilometres up from the only road that goes up there," he said, describing how scouts from the Weird World had reported back that the entrance to the bay there was sufficiently discreet, and there would be a place for a short landing strip farther inland between the hills. I wondered if Mom could go to that facility, when it was built, instead of PH, so far away. But even as I thought it, I realized it would not matter. Once she stepped into that world, unlike Stan, she would not come out again. Geographic proximity would matter not at all.

Often while we were together, Stan would receive messages on what I jokingly came to call his butt receiver. Mom and I would know something was up when he'd pull out a small note-pad he kept for the purpose and start transcribing and decoding. I was always surprised how much he would tell us about what was going on. Sometimes it was a threat around us, but often it was word about an operation somewhere else. That

Cape Breton trip was no different. It was the second or third day when Stan began to jot in his notebook, his face becoming grim. We'd stopped for lunch, a picnic in the car at a lookout.

"What is it?" Mom finally asked. She would become tense, alert when messages started to come in, engaged as if some new crisis were inevitable and she'd been waiting for it. This day it had nothing to do with us.

"They've found a death ship," Stan said. They'd been tipped about a large yacht adrift off the East Coast. "It gets worse," he warned. He was getting reports from the security officers who'd boarded the ship and found dozens of dead, dying, and injured people. Most appeared to be illegal immigrants who'd been in the United States. Survivors were telling the agents they'd been kidnapped and imprisoned aboard. Something had frightened the kidnappers and they'd abandoned the ship the previous night. It had then drifted into Canadian waters just southeast of Nova Scotia.

"Human slave trade?" Mom asked. Stan shrugged and continued to write in his notebook. He was receiving more information. We waited.

He groaned. Mom reached for his hand.

"Their organs were being harvested." The horror I felt at the images this summoned was reflected in his voice. "Once they had the organs, they were left to die." Stan looked as though he might cry. My mother put one hand over her mouth and her other arm around his shoulders as he described what survivors on board had told the officers. Some days earlier, they said, they'd been drugged and taken to the vessel, where a team of doctors in surgical garb was waiting. They were put in a holding room in the belly of the ship and every hour or so armed men would arrive to take several away—for medical checkups, they'd been told.

But something had happened the previous night and the doctors and gunmen had suddenly left on a motorboat. When the security guys arrived they found gutted bodies in piles, dead or unconscious, and some people still on makeshift surgical tables screaming or moaning, the doctors' grisly work of harvesting incomplete, the anaesthesia, if there had been any, now worn off.

I imagined men and women with gaping wounds where their vital organs had once been, those organs presumably meant for people on organ transplant lists, patients desperate enough and wealthy enough to buy them on the black market, not knowing or caring where they'd come from.

"There are quite a few survivors," Stan reported, "but they're not in good shape, and the guys are short-handed." He looked at Mom, then me. "We need more help." He asked if we would go to help care for those still alive. The boat was being brought into port in Yarmouth, on the southwestern tip of Nova Scotia, he said. Port officials there would be told it was a rich American on vacation who wanted privacy. Because of the need for secrecy, local emergency officials couldn't be alerted. Would we go and do what we could for those immigrants?

We headed for Yarmouth, hundreds of kilometres away, stopping at a store in a town along the way to buy sheets, scissors, antibiotic ointment, antiseptic, and water. It all seemed completely inadequate for what I imagined we would find. We took turns driving; whoever wasn't at the wheel ripped sheets into bandage widths and rolled them up.

I was frightened, repulsed, and filled with anticipation. This was it, the proof I craved that the Weird World and its legions of security personnel were real. I would meet them, and perhaps my coverage too. It was all hands on deck, after all, in a time of crisis. I prepared myself for the grisly scene, the emotion, and felt flickers of excitement at the thought of the curtain between worlds being pulled aside for my gaze.

But then, it wasn't.

Several hours after we began our headlong rush for Yarmouth, Stan got word calling us down. The decision had been made to divert the ship to Saint John, New Brunswick, across to the other side of the Bay of Fundy, where backup security and medical staff from inside were being flown to for assistance. There was to be no proof this day, I thought, and I was both relieved and deflated, and suddenly, once again, very tired. I lay down across the back seat of the car, amid the rolls of white sheet strips, and watched the sky and trees whip by out the car windows, a dizzying slide show of branches, poles, highway signs, clouds, and patches of distant blue sky. I felt Mom's concerned glances at me as she drove, and closed my eyes, feigning sleep. I didn't want her to see my frustration and resentment.

I remember the hum and vibration of the road as we turned and headed back toward Halifax that late afternoon. It could not numb my growing impatience with the invisibility of the forces at play in my life. Stan was continuing to get messages on the butt receiver, but I was no longer interested. Determinedly not interested.

I thought about what my life had become. Brief interludes of normalcy punctuated by these times of heaving chaos. I was spending more time away from home, away from Terry. As I became more deeply engaged with the Weird World, unseen though it might be, it was harder and harder to transition back to so-called normal life. That life seemed increasingly meaning-less, trite. How to care about my everyday tasks and pleasures, or the people I shared them with, when the backstory, hidden to all around me, consumed more and more of my consciousness?

It was life writ large, with high stakes and unimaginable consequences. How could covering the local news for the paper, or
making plans to catch a movie with Terry, compete with that? It
wasn't that I had stopped loving my friends, no longer cared for
Terry, but it was as though I perceived them all through the
wrong end of a telescope, distant and small against the pan-
orama of this new secret life. I had accepted that I couldn't tell
anyone about it, but that was creating a chasm across which I
struggled to retain and sustain my connections with my old life.

I felt increasingly desperate, isolated. I thought about rejecting Stan and Mom and their story, running away and refusing
to have anything more to do with them, and seeing what would
happen. Or I could do something even more extreme. I began to
consider an unimaginable, irreversible course of action.

TEN

I HAVE BROKEN THE spoon rest Mom gave me. It's an ugly ceramic thing, shaped like three bunches of celery and painted in a pale green that fades to white at what would be the root of the stalks. For some reason there are crude roses painted on either side of the bottom edge. It was a cheap, Depression-era piece of crockery that had been my grandmother's. The only mark on the back was a hand-painted, barely legible word, *Japan*. Now I've dropped a heavy pepper grinder on the ugly spoon rest and it's in five pieces. I put the pieces in the garbage can, not without some hesitation.

Mom gave the spoon rest to me the first time I visited her in Halifax after the revelations in Sussex. After she told me she was going inside. We were in her kitchen. I was leaning on the counter by the sink, generally getting in her way. I was ruminating, unsettled. Wanting to be close by her but not sure of what I wanted to say. I longed to beg her not to leave me behind, outside, alone and afraid.

"So what would you be taking with you?" I asked, looking around her modest apartment. "Would you sell everything or take it all?" I tried to make it sound conversational, but my tone was challenging.

"No, I'd just take my clothes, books, a few keepsakes, the photo albums." She looked over at me, trying to gauge my mood, my intent.

"What about the piano?" Somehow Mom had always managed to bring the piano on our many previous moves. It and a few favoured pieces of furniture would arrive sometimes many weeks or even months after we reached our destination.

"Honey, I'd have to leave everything behind. I couldn't give any indication that I was going anywhere. That would be dangerous, especially for you." She said it with a hint of impatience in her voice. I should know this. I'd been briefed.

This was a fraught time. The O apparently had a sense that Mom was getting ready to make some kind of move and there'd been threats, Stan told us. A letter left on Mom's windshield, and found by her coverage, said if Mom disappeared there would be hell to pay for those she left behind—me, Ted, and her father, Cliff, who was now in a nursing home in Nanaimo on Vancouver Island, with Alzheimer's. Our security had been intensified. It was chilling to think of someone skulking around the parking lot outside Mom's apartment building, slipping the warning under a windshield wiper and then sliding away into the nearby bushes, having delivered the terrorizing threat.

The threats meant that Mom's plan to join Stan inside was on hold. The intelligence people said that if she disappeared, those she left behind might be targeted as a means of drawing her out. But she and Stan continued to dream about being together. Whenever Stan came to spend time with Mom, they would talk about the little log cabin that was being built for them at PH, Place of Hope, in the lee of the mountain, by a stream.

"The front door is here," Stan would say, trying to sketch the house that was being assembled thousands of kilometres away. "And there's a window about here"—rough pencil stroke— "where you could put a bird feeder and see a bit of the sunset when you're doing the dishes."

"When *I'm* doing the dishes!" Mom replied, with mock outrage. "*You're* the dishwasher in our home." She crossed her arms against her chest, trying not to smile. Stan laughed, coming toward her. He put his arms around her, and kissed her cheek. "You're right," he said softly against her face. "I'll do our dishes. I'd do a million dishes if it meant you were there helping me make them dirty." Mom's smile faded. She hugged Stan back. "I want to be there too," she said sadly.

It was unclear when that might happen. Stan told us the intelligence people in the Weird World were desperately trying to find the source of the threats, but they kept uncovering new complications, loose ends that must be tied up before Mom disappeared for the final time, to ensure that her exit didn't unleash a deadly response.

"What will happen to it all?" I asked, looking at the heavy wooden coffee table and cabinet that had been in the den on Patterdale Drive in North Vancouver. "You'll just leave it for your landlord to deal with? That doesn't seem fair." I knew I sounded peevish.

HERE IN MY own kitchen, I am drawn back to the garbage can. I reach in and pull out the three larger pieces of the spoon rest. I have to dig around for the little bits. And here they sit now, by my laptop. Ugly and embossed, suffused with memories. The spoon rest sat on the stove in every kitchen we ever had. When Mom said she was going inside, I wanted to have something that would always make me think of her, happily making a Sunday dinner, rolling out the pastry for butter tarts at Christmastime, taking care of her family.

I first remember it in the kitchen on East 24th Street in North Vancouver, where she allowed me to conduct culinary experiments with sometimes dubious results as I learned to cook, when I was nine. That summer of 1974 was the last time I thought of my family as having any relation to normal. The events that followed made Ted and I know that we were different, somehow apart. Ted would sometimes, in the years that followed, refer to "normal families." Not in a critical way, but in a straightforward acknowledgment that we were not one. We had no explanation for this. It was just a feeling we shared.

School had just finished, grade four for me and grade two for Ted. It was late June, and we packed up the Volkswagen camper van with all our camping gear, games, and books, the bicycles strapped to a rack on the back. We were heading out on vacation to the prairies, and ultimately Winnipeg, a trip halfway across the country. The Searses were coming, in their old camper, and we talked about the stops we would make along the way to visit Mom's old aunties in Saskatchewan and Manitoba, before we turned around and headed home in time to go back to school.

But it was a vacation from which we would never return.

The morning we left, the sun was struggling to break through misty, low clouds as we pulled away from our little stucco house. We drove over the soaring Port Mann Bridge, which straddles the Fraser River, and then along the Trans-Canada Highway toward Abbotsford, and beyond to Chilliwack. Blue sky finally gained the upper hand. I marvelled at the near neon-bright greenness of early summer fields lit up by the sunlight now flooding the fertile river valley. Ted and I sat in the back with the foldaway kitchen table dropped down before us, alternately playing cards and watching the landscape flash past out the windows. The Searses were ahead of us in their old camper, which swayed atop an equally old blue-and-white half-ton truck. We followed the back of that camper through British Columbia, Alberta, Saskatchewan, and into Manitoba over the following weeks. We convoyed through southern B.C. and the Interior, stopping by mid-afternoon most days. Mom would hoist the pop-up tent on the top of the camper van to make the bed where Ted and I slept. Ted and Stan would search out firewood and soon have a blaze alight in the firepit, feeding it green branches to make smoke to keep the bugs at bay. If there was a lake or river nearby, Sybil and I would head off for a swim.

It felt like a grand adventure. We stopped at roadside attractions, thrilled by the whimsical castle and fairytale figures at The Enchanted Forest, between Sicamous and Revelstoke. At Glacier National Park, Stan took us on an evening bear-hunting expedition. We giggled as we traipsed through the drizzly forest in our rain boots, the dripping branches illuminated by the weak light of our coal-oil lanterns held high—altogether making enough noise to ensure any bear nearby would give us a wide berth.

That night, while Ted and I slept, the bear we'd sought found us. It reared up on its hind legs to sniff at the camper, which it gently rocked with its weight. Mom, still awake and reading, pulled back a curtain and saw its snuffling shadow. Hastily letting the fabric fall back, she held her breath until the bear lost interest and swayed away into the dark. The next morning she showed us its massive muddy paw prints on the side of the camper.

At Banff we camped at Two Jack campsite in the national park for a few nights, going into the town to trek up and down Banff Avenue, duck into the shops, and stop for ice cream. The second afternoon, Stan took Ted and me horseback riding, on a trail that wound through forest above the startlingly turquoise waters of Lake Louise. I felt completely happy, perched on the strong back of my lovely chestnut-coloured horse with the dark mane, tail, and muzzle. Stan was ahead and frequently turned around to smile, to check that we were enjoying this treat he had planned for us. I often wondered what it would have been like to have him as a dad and felt envious of his two sons, now adults, and the experiences they must have had growing up.

From Banff we wound our way south to the Badlands of southern Alberta. Ted excitedly named all the dinosaurs as their life-sized likenesses rose out of the desert to greet visitors to Drumheller, where archaeologists were steadily unearthing dinosaur bones from earlier millennia. That night at the treeless campground, Mom and I lay in our sleeping bags on the picnic table beside the campfire to watch a dramatic prairie lightning storm dancing and flashing on the horizon, slowly making its way in our direction, but still so far off that no thunder was audible. There were no clouds above us. The stars seemed close and bright against the darkness of this vast space, away from the competition of city lights, and with no mountains or trees to block the panoply of the sky. We watched for shooting stars, finally drifting off as the campground became quiet. Hours later, fat raindrops pulled us from sleep and sent us running for the camper. We stumbled and laughed on the way.

Sometimes the drive felt long. Ted became practised at assembling an expression of irresistible longing to accompany his appeals. "Boy, I'd really love some ice cream," he'd intone sadly as we approached an ice cream stand. Or "I'm so thirsty. I really wish we could get a root-beer float," as an A&W hove into view. It became a family joke, and Mom and I would mimic his woebegone features until he laughed.

In Saskatchewan, as we headed east from Regina, we began so see familiar names on highway signs, names we'd heard all our lives: INDIAN HEAD, WOLSELEY, GRENFELL, SUMMERBERRY.

We spent a couple of days in Grenfell with Auntie Dot, my mother's favourite aunt. Mom had lived with her for a time as a teenager, while Grandmother Jessie, Dot's sister, was dying. Dot and Uncle Herb still lived in the same house, with their adult daughter, Grace.

Ted, Grace, and I picked vegetables from the back garden for supper that first day, and then sat on the back porch shelling peas, the smell of nearby sweet-pea blossoms thick in the late-afternoon heat. That evening after supper around a massive old dining-room table, we all sat in the formal living room for what seemed like an interminable time while the adults caught up, trading stories about people we didn't know. Our ears perked up for stories about Mom, Penny, and Murray when they were young.

Then we headed to the village of Summerberry. It's no longer even a dot on a Google map, but if you search it by name, Google will produce a seemingly arbitrary flag along the Trans-Canada Highway, probably not far from where my grandfather's gas station and garage once were. If I switch to street view, I can electronically scoot along the dusty road that swings north off the highway and follow it down an incline to where the village was. I compare the image on the computer screen with the painting that hangs on my dining-room wall. My mother commissioned it after she'd left the prairies and was living in Vancouver. At the time the village had begun its decline, the young people were moving away. But the three grain elevators still towered over the town, the skating rink, and the little rust-coloured house along the dirt road where Mom and her family had lived. I glance back to the Google image. It's almost all gone now—a ghost town, except for a few houses that remain along what would have been the main street, and the sturdy yellow-stone school that still stands.

I remembered Mom's stories, how there was a village well that she was sent to each day to fetch buckets of water if the cistern at home had run dry in the hot summer months. How this was the place she remembered as home, when her mother was still alive, even though there were other places before and afterwards.

It was after the war that her family had moved to Summerberry. The small garage that Grandpa Cliff had bought with his military severance was just up the highway. The dirt road leading into the village, sprayed with used engine oil in the summers to keep the dust down, rolled down the slight dip in the prairie, past that small red house Cliff and Jessie rented on the edge of town. Across the road was the ice rink, where teams from nearby towns came for curling bonspiels through the winter. The rink was also where Mom learned to figure-skate, and where she performed each year in the local ice carnival, losing herself in the music and the graceful arabesques and Axel jumps, camel spins, and fan spirals, the highlight of each winter for her. Her face would light up as she told Ted and me about those happy parts of her childhood.

In the summer she played baseball—any position would do. And on days when the blinding high-noon sun seared the fields and dusty roads, and the grasshoppers' whirring filled the air, she would lie under the caragana hedge and watch the clouds endlessly form and re-form in the brilliantly blue sky.

A house, a giraffe, a turtle. The sky was an ever-changing and ever-entertaining picture book and she its avid reader.

In the later afternoons she would walk in the fields on the edge of the town, making the noisy grasshoppers start and jump ahead of her. She would sing to the prairie at the top of her lungs. She was shocked to learn, years later, that the whole town could hear her.

For a while her maternal grandmother, Maggie, lived with the family in the little house. Maggie had immigrated to Canada from Scotland as a young girl. Her life had been hard. She was grumpy and demanding in her old age, and she shared Ruth's small bedroom with her.

Ruth, Jessie, and Maggie kept a small garden, and at the end of each summer would spend steamy hours in the kitchen canning, pickling, and preserving, lining the shelves along the basement steps with gem-coloured jars of the summer's bounty for the winter ahead.

When she was in grade twelve, Mom made a best friend. Marlene has told me how sensitive and serious Mom was as a girl, how she applied herself diligently to her school work, her chores, her piano practices. There is evidence of this. Her school report cards, carefully saved in their yellowed envelopes, were lined with As, and remarks about her hard work, her earnest application.

In the year she was in grade ten, that changed. For the first time there were some Bs and even a C. But at home, there were more worrisome problems. Her mother had been diagnosed with breast cancer. Jessie was taken to Regina, where she had a radical mastectomy. She came home, weak and in pain, missing one breast and much of the flesh of the corresponding upper arm, where the doctors had removed lymph nodes, muscle, and tissue, trying to excise the disease.

Somehow Maggie disappeared from the picture around this time or shortly after. Did she die or move to an old-age home? That part of the story escapes me, if I ever knew it. But this meant that Ruth now had more responsibilities—cooking, cleaning. Penny was still a small child. As my grandmother, Jessie, slowly faded away, overtaken by the cancer that had not been caught, the family didn't talk about it, or about Jessie's looming death. Eventually the decision was made that Jessie should go to stay with one of her sisters. The process of dying was deemed too distressing for her husband and children. The demands of caring for the children must also have been thought too much for Cliff. The two girls were farmed out to aunts and uncles. Penny went to Uncle Lou's farm, where she learned to ride and take care of the animals. While she missed her family and home, she had no sense that this wasn't just an extended vacation. Murray, four years older than Ruth, may have been away at university by that time. Mom went to stay with Auntie Dot, and ever after remembered her as kind and loving in a practical prairie way.

These stories came to life as we visited the places where Mom had grown up. Late on our last day in Summerberry, Mom took us to the little cemetery across the highway. This is where her mother is buried. Mom approached the large metal gate that marked the entrance, with Ted and I trailing behind. The evening sun slanted in against the grave markers, mostly unpretentious upright rectangles of mossy stone or simple slabs with only a last name. The markers had sunk into the ground, many of them tilted from decades of heaving frosts and many of them obscured by overgrown grass and shrubs. We finally found Jessie's grave in the southwest corner.

Looking across the unkempt cemetery, Mom recalled a man named Mr. Piggott, who had once kept the burial ground neatly mowed. "He must be gone now," she mused. We wandered through the graveyard. Dusk had crept up on us. An occasional breath of wind rustled the grasses and we could hear the lonely whine of tires on the adjacent highway.

I was first to go back to the car and when Mom and Ted followed they found me crying. I wasn't sure why. I had never known Jessie and could hardly miss her. But perhaps I missed having had a grandmother; maybe I mourned for my mother, and the upheaval of her motherless and largely loveless teenage years after Jessie's death. Perhaps I wept for all of them, recalling the many nights in my childhood when Penny would call Mom crying, angry even as an adult that she'd never had an opportunity to say goodbye to her mother, having been kept on the farm and away from the funeral by well-meaning aunts. On those nights Mom would wave me away as she tried to comfort and contain her younger sister's sorrow. The family was never the same after my grandmother's died.

When she was gone, Grandpa Cliff moved the family up the highway to a one-roomed building near his garage. They took their meals in the grill of the service station, where my mom worked after school and on the weekends. She wasn't paid, other than a bit of pocket money once in a while. It was simply her duty, to help support the family. She came home from school every day at lunchtime to prepare a hot meal for the family, slipping out of class early so food could be ready when her dad closed the gas station for the noon hour.

She felt it was her job to hold the increasingly fractured family together in her mother's absence, taking care of Penny, and her father too. But soon he moved a "housekeeper" into the home to help out. Pearl was married, but maybe thought she was onto a better situation, despite the children she didn't much like. It soon became obvious that she and Cliff were sharing a bed as well as the household workload.

Once, when I was in my mid-twenties, Mom and I took a day trip to Mahone Bay, on Nova Scotia's South Shore, stopping at a diner along the way for lunch. The smell of fat from the deep fryer was strong as we walked in the door, and she made a funny sound. I turned to look at her. Her face was contracted in an expression of repulsion.

"Are you okay?"

She nodded. And then, recovering herself: "Let's find something nicer."

As we drove away she haltingly began to tell me about her final year of high school after her mother's death. The smell of fryer grease evoked that year in Wolseley—a grieving girl trying to fit into a new place, her long hours behind the lunch counter at the garage, her clothes always reeking of deep-fried food.

Years later her friend Marlene recalled meeting Mom that year. "Ruth joined our grade twelve class, swelling the numbers to an even dozen," she told me in an email. "This was the first time I'd met Ruth. Red hair, freckles, erect posture with head held high, she courageously joined the new class. She wore a rust twin sweater set and a plaid skirt. She wore it on the first day and every day thereafter for the entire year. I remember being so impressed with this new girl who, at the tender age of sixteen, could wear the same clothes without apology or complaint."

ELEVEN

A HEAPING TEASPOON OF fine, dark cocoa, mixed with a rounded spoonful of sugar, plus just a bit more. Add a small amount of boiling water to make a thin paste. Add canned milk, maybe a third of a cup. Mix until it's smooth. Then fill the mug with boiling water. I can picture my mother mixing, stirring, sipping. She often made cocoa at bedtime, or any time comfort was required. Sometimes I have made it for my children, and always as I mix and stir it reminds me of a night I couldn't sleep, in late July a few days after we'd arrived in Winnipeg, the last stop on our summer holiday in 1974.

We were staying at the home of an old friend of Mom's, Gary, whom we never saw. He and his wife and their children were away, letting us borrow their house. It was a nice neighbourhood with lots of other kids around and a park just down the street.

At some point in the last day or so, Mom had told us the Searses were going to be staying in Winnipeg, that Mr. Sears had a new job at a new church. I was sad about this. I'd come to think of them as family and secretly wished Mr. Sears was my dad. Maybe that's why I woke up that night and couldn't get back to sleep. Or maybe there'd been a bad dream. I finally got out of the bed that belonged to one of Gary's children and made my way down the stairs, through the front hallway and into the adjoining kitchen. Mom was sitting at the table. She looked up in surprise.

"How come you're up so late?"

I told her I couldn't get back to sleep.

"Would you like a cup of cocoa?"

When it was ready and we were both sitting at the table she said there was something she needed to tell me. Something she was obviously worried about. I could see she was trying to decide how to begin. She opted for directness.

"We're not going to go back to Vancouver," she said. I could feel her willing me to be calm, to take this news bravely. In those first moments I felt only disbelief. "We're going to live here now," she continued, in case I wasn't following this remarkable leap.

I pictured our little North Vancouver house on East 24th Street, and my room with my bed tucked under the sloping ceiling, where my cat would curl up beside me while I read.

"What about Frisky?" I demanded. "What about all our stuff?" I pictured my drawers and shelves full of clothes, books, toys I wasn't quite old enough to part with. I thought of my friends, the familiar neighbourhood where Ted and I were allowed to walk to the grocery store to each buy a can of pop as a treat on Fridays.

"I'll be going back to get Frisky, and pack up some of our things," she said.

"Why?" It was the real question I finally managed to get to. There was no satisfying answer, no answer that I remember at all. I was left with the impression it had to do with my dad, that she'd decided we needed some distance from him because of the chaos his drinking and the ongoing legal battles between them were causing in our lives.

There were good grounds for this impression. Dad was supposed to visit us on a regular basis but often didn't turn up. I would get quietly sad, Ted would become angry and agitated. I thought of one such Saturday, when we had finally stopped waiting, accepting that he was not coming. Ted had gone upstairs and pulled the heads off my dolls. We had very different reactions to the feelings of disappointment and rejection; Ted's were focused outward in acts of destruction. Mine were focused inward but were similarly destructive.

So we were to have a fresh start, in Winnipeg. Mom enrolled us in the day program at the park up the street, and while we spent the summer days on escorted trips to museums, pools, and theatres, she looked for work and a place for us to live. We objected, cried, complained about the unfairness of it. But there was no third party to appeal our mother's decision to and we soon accepted it, or at least gave up our protests.

At some point in August she went back to Vancouver alone to retrieve the cat and to pack some of our things that would be stored and shipped to us later. She told us, firmly, emphatically, not to talk to anyone—not anyone—about where she'd gone. We stayed with a family that lived up the street, across from the park. I don't know how Mom had met the mother, or why the woman agreed to add Ted and me to her already large household for a week. It seems strange now that Mom would have left us with near-strangers. Perhaps Gary recommended them. I think now it was an act of desperation.

It was disorienting, being in a new place and suddenly living with a family we'd never met before. The woman was kind. Her children—there were at least three or four of them—were a blur of rambunctious comings and goings. In the midst of the busyness of park program days and the evening household chores, meals, lunch-making, and television-watching, I didn't have much time to think about what was happening. At night, when the house and its many inhabitants became quiet, I would wonder at the transformation of our circumstances, the dizzying feeling that Ted and I were lost and alone, with no orientation to our surroundings. Just weeks before, we'd waved goodbye to Ted's friend Randy, telling him we'd see him soon, watching him grow smaller out the back window of the camper van as we set out on vacation. The excitement of that adventure was gone, eclipsed by a sick feeling of uncertainty. Now we were essentially homeless, my small blue-flowered suitcase tucked under a strange bed, my mother having left us with these unfamiliar people. In the mornings the woman, whose name I can't recall, would survey my eyes swollen from late-night crying and give me a quick hug and a sympathetic smile as she handed us our bagged lunches and hustled us out the door to the park.

Mom finally came back. I was much relieved, having wondered whether in this new realm of the unexpected she might not return. She arrived with the cat in a carrier, a few more suitcases, and the promise that some other belongings would soon follow.

We moved into a rented characterless duplex that had pink and brown siding and sat on a windswept, treeless corner lot. Grant Park was a neighbourhood with low-rise apartment buildings and small one-storey or storey-and-a-half bungalows, most of them built as wartime housing. Just a few doors away on our street, Ebby Avenue, were two shacks that were the source of endless fascination. They were tiny dilapidated dollhouses patched together from mismatched building supplies, with corrugated metal roofs.

"A troll lives there," the neighbourhood kids assured us, pointing to the larger of the shacks. "And the woman next door is a witch!" they said, shifting their derisive fear to the smaller hovel. In fact, it was an ancient Ukrainian woman who looked as though she'd been transported from a previous century in her long skirts and aprons. She spoke no English. She spoke to no one except the ruddy old Ukrainian man who lived in the shack next to her. But she did yell, unintelligibly, shaking her fist at the children who mercilessly harassed her. They would stand at her gate calling her names and ripping leaves and branches off a nearby tree to dump in her yard for the excitement of watching her come out of the house to heave everything back over the fence onto the sidewalk, screeching with the outrage and injustice of it.

Ted and I wondered at the oddness of this new neighbourhood and the ugliness of the duplex that was now home, its only redeeming feature being the laundry chute that ran from the hall outside our bedrooms on the second floor to the unfinished basement far below. It became a favourite source of fun to send Barbie, Ken, and GI Joe careening down the chute's metal innards on extreme imaginary adventures. Then we'd run to the basement, assess the damage, and repeat.

Mom had found a job with the provincial hydro office a short walk away, and our new school was kitty-corner, just beyond the skating shack and what would become an outdoor skating rink once the weather got cold. Practically speaking, life was knitting itself together again in a new and different pattern.

Soon school started up and we met new friends. On my first day when the teacher asked me to tell the class something about myself, I said I couldn't wait to see a prairie blizzard, like those my mom had told me about. There was a lot of laughter, some groaning. Most of these kids had been in classes together since their first day of school. I could sense, if not fully understand, the well-defined social strata—who was cool, who the tough kids were, the A students, the ones into sports, and those at the bottom of the heap who were essentially invisible. I felt like an interloper, suffering from the suspicion and resentment that accompanies the extra attention paid to the new kid. I signed up to be a sidewalk crossing guard, longing to wear the bright orange webbed vest with the shiny metal closure awarded to the kids considered to be responsible enough for the assignment. It seemed a coveted position and a good way to gain a place and become a part of things, accepted.

There was a lot of curiosity about me but it didn't translate into social invitation. I began to make up stories about the wonderful things my family used to do together, the spectacular trips my dad had taken us on, the exotic places we had been, hoping this would make me more interesting, desirable as a friend. It was really wishful thinking, longing for a different life that included a dad and adventures from which we all came home together. My stories backfired disastrously when some kid in my class thought to ask Ted about our family trip to Bora-Bora. "Huh?" he replied, mystified, debunking my tales of travel.

I came back from lunch that day to the triumphant scorn of my classmates. "Liar," they sneered, and I could see the giggles and glances directed my way. Mom had to come and pick me up early and take me home weeping and snuffling. I don't know what my new teacher—the gentle giant Peter Suderman—said to the class that afternoon, but by the time I skulked back to school the next morning, feeling shamed and afraid, they'd lost their blood lust. Some were even kind. Now I imagine him, a man who clearly loved his job and was respected by even the toughest trouble-makers, trying to instill some empathy for the newcomer.

Eventually I settled in, and when winter descended, I spent every free hour after school—afternoons, evenings, weekends—with the neighbourhood kids at the outdoor rink. We'd layer up in snow pants, hats, double mittens, and scarves wrapped around all but our eyes, and circle the ice, playing bumper cars or crack the whip. The cold was like nothing I'd ever known, but we'd stay out until the moisture from our breath had frozen our scarves to our faces and our eyes were streaming from the wind. We'd rush into the adjacent skating shack with its old stove in the middle and huddle with arms and legs stretched toward it, warming fingers and toes that burned from the cold and then tingled excruciatingly as they defrosted and all feeling returned.

We continued to see the Searses, at their new Winnipeg church that we also attended, and to share Thanksgiving, Christmas, and Easter dinners together. We went on a few week-end camping trips, and Sybil (Mrs. Sears) took me snowshoeing that first winter—teaching me to avoid tripping by stepping with my legs apart—along a long band of deep snow bordering the Assiniboine River, not far from where they lived.

By the time the school year ended, Mom had bought a house in another neighbourhood. I was excited to move this time, and not just to escape Ebby Avenue. The new place was a decaying but grand old pile in a once-genteel area that had the mixed quality of a neighbourhood in decline. The house of the violin teacher and her ancient father next door and the house across the street where the university professor and his young family lived were stately and in good repair. But the massive three-storey house several doors down, inhabited by hippies and all their combined children, dogs, kittens, and macramé-hung houseplants, was a study in dissipated splendour.

I immediately loved our house on Dorchester Avenue, with its generous front yard and the streetscape tunnel of old trees arching together overhead. Our house had been owned by the same family for decades, and many of their antique treasures had been left behind in the attic and the garage when the old man was finally taken off to a nursing home. Ted and I scouted the cubbyholes and crannies, coming up with an ancient bathroom scale, old magazines, a wicker baby carriage with ornate wheels, and decades of spiderwebs and dust. There was a collection of seventy-eights from the 1940s and '50s that we would play, and Mom would sing along, mimicking the saccharine warbles of some songbird while Ted and I laughed. For a while she seemed happier, more relaxed, even though there was much to do in this new home.

Mom had bought it as a "fixer-upper bargain," and the reasons for the description became more apparent as she began calling contractors to begin the long-overdue repairs and renovations. One suggested she undertake them with a match and a can of gasoline. Most thought this single mother was in over her head. They would shake their heads as they handed her long itemized estimates with large figures at the bottom. She must have had misgivings, questioned the wisdom of taking on this project. But eventually, by a stroke of luck, she found Bill, who became a fixture around the house. He was a jack of all trades—honest, with reasonable fees. He was an aging, chain-smoking slight man who wore his hair plastered to his head with some oily substance. He didn't say much. I thought him taciturn at first but soon realized he was shy. Once he warmed up, he seemed happy to have Ted and me watching him hammer, cut, paint, and generally bring our old house back into repair. First there was a new roof, then teleposts in the basement to prop up the sagging floor joists. The unused kitchen chimney where a wood-fired cooking stove had once exhausted its smoke came down in a sooty pile of bricks and mortar. The hole was patched up and new cupboards arrived. Bill painted the house exterior a deep blue-grey; inside, Mom spent evenings stripping wallpaper and filling cracks in the walls and ceilings. Bill took down a few dead trees around the property, tore down the rotting garage, and built a new back fence. Mom planted gardens, and we began choosing new wallpapers and paint colours. The transformation was slow but steady. As the house lost its sad, neglected appearance, I was losing my lost, dislocated feeling.

Soon Mom, with Stan's help, found a new job working in the national audiovisual department of the United Church. Ted and I started at a new school a few blocks away. I was once again the new kid, but this time I wasn't reeling from the shock and sorrow of a surprise move. Grosvenor School was a handsome old building, my teacher strict but ready to laugh. Once again the other kids were curious about me, the newcomer, but they must have soon decided I was harmless, not a threat. I was beginning to form some tentative friendships. I'd saved my money for a five-speed bike, which gave me freedom to explore. I spent entire days pedalling through Winnipeg neighbourhoods, alone or with kids I met. It was as though the secret move from Vancouver, the bizarre dislocation, was a memory I didn't quite trust, a bad dream I'd emerged from to find myself in a new life.

But the new routine and normalcy didn't prevent a new feeling of detachment. Something in me had gone quiet and watchful. It began to seem as though I was observing myself as if from a distance, whether I was going to school, talking to other kids, or riding my bike, and increasingly I could feel no point in any of it. As the fall progressed, the effort required to get out of bed, to show interest, or to take pleasure grew, until each task seemed a mountainous obstacle, overwhelming and threatening.

I went to school, I came home, ate supper, and watched *Welcome Back, Kotter* or whatever else was on TV. I went to piano and swimming lessons, continued to go through the motions of my life, but a dark uneasiness I couldn't name grew and gnawed at me. I found myself crying over things that didn't seem, even to me, that they should be so upsetting. I would head out the door in the morning feeling as though I was forcing myself toward some terrible fate. As I approached the school, a weight of hopelessness would descend, slowing my feet, making my eyes swim with tears, curling around my heart and squeezing its chambers.

One morning I stopped, turned around, walked home, and sat on the step by the back door. I could *not* go to school. Mom came out on her way to work and found me hunched over my knees. She sat down beside me, put her arm around my shoulders, hugged me.

"What's wrong?" She was concerned, alarmed, wanted to know if someone had hurt or scared me. I shook my head. I had no words to answer her. I didn't know why I felt so sad, so unable to do what I was supposed to do. Why I couldn't stop crying.

She got me some tissues. "I'll drive you to school and we can talk about it when I get home tonight," she said, glancing at her watch. She was now late for work.

"I can't," I said, shaking my head, but I allowed myself to be led to the car. When we arrived at the side door of the school a few minutes later, the tears had started again and she relented. I went to work with Mom that day, and sat reading in a corner behind shelves of film reels, ashamed of my tears and embarrassed by the curious looks of the other women in the office. It was the same the next day. We began the morning acting as though I would head off to school as normal, perhaps believing a good night's sleep had made things better, somehow dissipating my fear and sadness. The first hour's hopefulness faded as the time to leave approached. I made it out the door, partway down the back lane. But by the time Mom was leaving for work, I was back, defeated and appealing to her not to make me go.

On the third morning, with new determination, perhaps born of frustration or desperation, she drove me to the school, explaining calmly and reasonably that I had to get an education, she had to work, that there were no other options. When I refused to get out of the car, she came around to the passenger door and reached in for my arm, then gave it a soft tug. I pulled it back. She reached in again, this time putting both hands under my arms as though to lift me out. I braced my feet against the floor of the car. By now I was sobbing as she pulled.

"No, I can't, I can't." Suddenly she stopped, and I settled back into the seat.

I think we were both shocked by the physicality of the interaction. Mom straightened up, looking stricken, then, after a moment, quietly closed the passenger door, walked around and got into the driver's seat. We sat there, the only sound my sniffles.

"What are we going to do?" she asked finally, rhetorically. I had no idea.

TED WAS ALSO struggling. Before starting school, he'd been diagnosed with what was then called hyperkinetic disorder but is now known as attention deficit hyperactivity disorder (ADHD);

at the time, it was a lot less common than it is now. Studies by American, Canadian, Swedish, and British researchers have shown that mothers who experienced stressful life events or anxiety during pregnancy are more likely to have children that develop ADHD symptoms. This is especially true for boys.

Ted was prescribed Ritalin, so one of the first orders of business when we arrived in Winnipeg was finding a new doctor to prescribe and monitor the medication. It was one of those times that the universe relented and granted a gift, on this occasion in the person of Dr. Richard Snyder at the Child Development Clinic of Winnipeg's Health Sciences Centre. A tall, red-headed, gentle man, he became Ted's doctor and advocate, and an important support for Mom. When I stopped going to school she called him, and he quickly connected us with Marion Robinson, a child psychologist at the clinic. She was small, with dark pixie-cut hair surrounding a face that smiled easily. I dreaded my first appointment with her. When I walked into her basement office, she gestured to a chair and asked if I'd like to sit there. I nodded, feeling awkward, and sat. She smiled, asked me a few easy questions. Yes, I was eleven; yes, I had a brother; yes, I lived with just my mom.

We began to talk about school, and she smiled sympathetically, with small nods of encouragement. I felt the heat of dreaded tears, but she didn't act as though it was odd or shameful that I cried as we talked. I told her about our recent moves, the new schools, teachers, and friends. We talked about my dad, my mom, Ted. We agreed to meet every week. In the meantime, she said I did not have to go back to school, not right away. We would find another option until I felt better. I was so relieved, I cried again.

"You're just a little leaky right now," she said, smiling, passing the box of tissues.

The diagnosis was clinical depression with school phobia. The treatment included medication and a new volunteer position, spending my days helping out at the nursery school at the Child Development Clinic, just down the hall from Marion's and Dr. Snyder's offices. Some of the children there were sons and daughters of staff at the hospital. Others were outpatients who were being observed and treated. It wasn't always clear which were which. Pam and Sue, the women who ran the program, must have been briefed because they welcomed me without question and treated me as part of their team. Now, as an adult, I realize how remarkable the situation was, how lucky I was to have been embraced by all of those supportive people who didn't seem to see me as the weepy, broken girl I felt like. They treated me as though I were capable and they were glad for my help.

Every morning I caught the bus to the Health Sciences Centre. Marion would often drop me off on her way home at the end of the day. During lunch hours I would eat with the clinic staff in the cafeteria. They were friendly, accepting, interested in how I was enjoying being at the centre. Several afternoons a week I would go to another wing of the clinic to meet with a tutor, a kind lady who gave me small assignments and made sure I was keeping up with the grade six curriculum. It went on like this for about six months.

The day I knew I was finally getting better was a bright afternoon at the end of winter, a harbinger of warmer days to come. I was sitting on the front steps of our house. The sun had new strength and the snow was melting fast. I could hear dripping, running water, was sure I could hear the snowbanks shrinking, rotting from within, giving up their icy moisture. The sun reflected off the wet cement of the front path and made me squint. Winter was releasing its grip, the frozen world was coming back to life, and I felt the anticipation and excitement of it amplified by the months of feeling so flat. I imagined warmer weather, getting my bike out, living as a normal kid again. I was happy, I realized.

During the months away from school, spending my days at the Child Development Clinic, I had come to love Marion and the children and staff at the nursery school. They treated me with remarkable care and respect, and provided me with a refuge, a place where I felt secure and supported, and an opportunity to get back on my feet. Now it was time to return to the life of an eleven-year-old girl.

I started back to school gradually, with the co-operation of the teacher and principal. A few mornings a week to start with, and by early June I was there for full days. I was embarrassed, and squirmed my way through the questions about where I'd been and why. For the most part, everyone was kind. It was only a temporary return to Grosvenor School. The next fall I would start grade seven, junior high, at Grant Park High. My sixth new school in seven years. This time I felt prepared, and even excited.

TWELVE

REMEMBRANCE DAY, 2014. I'm waiting to hear the gun salute from the Grand Parade, just across the Halifax Common and over Citadel Hill. I think about my father on this and every Remembrance Day. He survived the war but, like many young soldiers, came back with unseen scars.

I really didn't know my dad very well. There were long periods, years, when I never saw him. And yet there is much I know about him. Warren Augustus Dakin was a soldier. He was many other things, but at least in his later years, it was his time at war with the Regina Rifles that he most often recalled. His best stories were war stories, set in bombed-out villages or along muddy riverbanks in Europe.

He lied about his age to join up and was only seventeen when he began basic training. I have a picture of him heading off to the camp in Alberta where he learned to march, shine his shoes, and take care of his rifle. In the photo, he's standing on the outside step of the Regina train as it leaves, holding on to the doorway with one hand and waving jauntily with his other arm, probably to his parents and his younger brother and sister. He seems taken with the adventure of it. His parents must have felt quite differently. It hadn't been very long since they'd received the dreaded knock on the door. Their oldest son, Tom, a pilot on loan to the Royal Air Force, had been shot down and killed over France.

Dad always said his father's dreams had been invested in his brother Tom. Their father, also named Warren, was a urologist and surgeon. He had trained at the renowned Mayo Clinic in Rochester, Minnesota, Dad would proudly and frequently repeat. Tom had also had an affinity for medicine. He'd volunteered in his father's urology clinic, and hoped to become a doctor too. After the bitter loss of Tom, my dad knew he was not going to step into that role; he often joked he wasn't much of a student, and had only finished grade eleven before leaving for the war. But if he couldn't be the doctor his father had hoped for, he could pick up the military service where Tom had left off.

Once in Europe, he quickly climbed through the ranks as most members of his battalion were slaughtered. He narrowly escaped the same fate, but lost hearing in one ear when a tank exploded next to him and his Regina school buddy. For the rest of his life, he retained images of his friend's body coming apart in a hail of limbs and blood beside him, even as he himself was lifted by the force of the explosion and thrown through the window of a nearby storefront.

When the war ended, but before the battalion headed for home, Warren and a friend went AWOL, away without leave. They gathered a few bags of German pistols that had been seized from the enemy and hopped on a train to Paris, where they sold them to American troops wanting souvenirs as they headed home. The proceeds financed a month of high living in the City of Light, including betting at the tracks and visiting a gentleman's club. Dad would laugh gleefully as he later told the story, but they faced harsh discipline when he and his comrade ran out of money and crept back to their battalion, which by then was readying to head home to Regina. They were court-martialled and assigned to stay on in Europe for several months of mop-up duty in Germany.

When he finally made it home, he became an investment dealer, was transferred to Vancouver in the 1950s, married his first wife, and became a father to Linda, then Tom two years later.

When that marriage ended, he was busy flying back and forth between Vancouver and Toronto, where he sat on the board of an investment company. It wasn't long before he noticed my mother, who was working the Vancouver-to-Toronto route as a stewardess for Trans-Canada Air Lines.

They made an attractive couple. In their wedding picture she is wearing a smartly tailored, pale pink suit perfectly fitted to her slim figure, with her matching hat of dyed feathers jauntily askew. He, fifteen years her senior, looks dashing in his wedding suit, his stance and smile conveying an aura of self-assured success. He must have seemed irresistible to a prairie girl who grew up during the dregs of the Depression era and wore the same skirt and sweater, spot-cleaned and neatly pressed, to school every day. But eventually the charm wore off, and two children later, the marriage had unravelled, a boon to the lawyers who would feed on its remains for years to come.

THE DATE ON the cassette tape is Saturday, January 19, 1974. I would have been nine, and Ted seven.

There's a repeated clicking sound on the tape, and three voices. Dad is describing the workings of the lighter that Ted is flicking, over and over. Pontificating really, interspersing his description with warnings about the dangers of lighters and lighter fluid. Ted is dutifully asking questions. I'm telling a story in between about how we went to Mr. Sears' cabin and he had coal-oil lanterns.

"Coal oil, that's something else," Dad says. "This is butane, or methane." It's his instructive voice. A voice determined to be calm even though the adult listener in me can tell that Ted playing with the lighter is clearly getting on his nerves. And he's not that thrilled to hear about Mr. Sears either.

This is one of our supervised visits with Dad, in our living room. On this day he arrived promptly and sober. On the tape, he's on his best behaviour, expressing rapt interest as Ted and I drone on about our piano lessons, swimming lessons, and the lighter.

We're on our best behaviour too, the human equivalents of performing seals, going through our paces, pulling out tricks designed to please. At least, this litany of school and extra-curricular activity successes is what we imagine will please. In truth, Dad sounds a little bored.

The court judgment of less than a month earlier said the respondent, Dad, "shall be permitted to visit with them in their home for one-half hour periods on alternate Saturdays." It said the petitioner, Mom, "shall be entitled to be present on all occasions of access."

The recordings of these visits are testament to the fear they invoked in my mother. She didn't trust him around us. I'm arrested by the sound of my own voice on the tape. So matter-of-fact, steady, monotone almost, as I tell my dad I've skipped a grade in piano, and show him the stars in my piano books. I'm selling myself, looking for approval, approbation.

March 2, 1974, and Dad is late. Mom has started the recorder just before the allotted time. It's quietly recording the banal conversations of a Saturday afternoon. Now I listen as our life plays out . . . bits of conversation between Mom and me. Library books are due; it's time to put the Valentine's cards away—do I want to keep mine? I hear our dog, Pixie, brought back to life on this magnetically coated plastic tape cassette, the jingle of her collar and tags as she jumps up onto the couch beside me, behind which the tape silently circles against the recording head.

I have no memory of this day, of the conversation about someone who had a baby I thought was so cute. "I don't think anyone could have a cuter baby," I say.

"I had babies I think were even cuter," my mother responds.

Pixie barks. Dad has arrived. There are some shuffling sounds as he comes in and finds a place in one of the big chairs, or perhaps the couch.

We're telling him about our upcoming summer vacation to Saskatchewan. We're going to visit Wolseley and Summerberry, where Mom grew up.

"That's a wonderful trip," Dad says. "Regina, that's where I was born. A lot of people out here in B.C. don't know how pretty the country is in Saskatchewan."

From the vantage point of so many years later, I want to tell him that it might be a wonderful trip but nothing will be the same again afterwards. I want to warn him that we won't ever be coming back.

But of course the tape rolls on without my latter-day warning; another visit stifled by the confines, or as the courts and my mother saw it, the safety, of the living room. Dad gamely asks what we've been up to. "Have you been swimming or skating?"

Thirty minutes of sometimes awkward chit-chat. It sounds like work. Ted and I dutifully conjure up questions to keep the conversation going, to give Dad an opportunity to impart his wisdom on topics ranging from the benefits of practice in sports to the price of oil and gas.

The sound on the tape is sometimes distorted, muddy, showing its forty years of age. There are silences, which Dad also feels compelled to fill. He hums old war songs, tells lame jokes.

"Come over here and let me see how your muscles are," he tells Ted. Ted is happy to submit to the showy squeezing of his upper arm.

Somewhere in the background, silent and invisible but anxiously listening, is Mom. The operator of the tape recorder.

The disappearance to Winnipeg unleashed a new legal firestorm between my parents, once Dad, or his lawyer, eventually found out where we'd gone. He was furious. Understandably so, I now think as a parent.

He visited us once while we were there. By then we were living in the big old house on Dorchester Avenue, and it was the spring that I had started to recover from my depression. Dad and Thora had been to Florida on vacation and stopped over in Winnipeg on their way home. Dad came to the door alone at an appointed time. Mom was obviously tense. Her voice and words had become formal, brittle, as she attempted to control her feelings at having my dad in her house.

We all sat down in the living room, the family of four. I tried to remember the last time we had all been in a room together. It was fascinating and frightening, sitting on the couch beside Ted, watching silently to see how Mom and Dad would behave toward one another. Ted was unusually still, focused on this rare tableau: the family talk.

These parents were like strangers, to themselves and to us. They tried and failed to stay calm, make their points. They engaged angrily, then remembered Ted and me, sitting wide-eyed on the couch. They regrouped, and tried again. I could smell the will it was requiring of them to impose a veneer of reasonable adult behaviour over the rage, the fear, even hatred perhaps. The living room was swirling with it. Ted and I didn't really understand the discussion. And really, neither did Dad. Because what was driving this disastrous family meeting, what had brought us all to this place, was not being discussed: the fact that Mom had disappeared with us because we were on the run from Dad and other members of the Mafia. Of course Ted and I didn't know that yet. We thought it was about Dad's drinking. And at least on the surface, it was.

"You were drinking when you had the children, before we left Vancouver," Mom accused. In the last few months before we disappeared, Dad had graduated to unsupervised visits. He'd taken us to the planetarium, to parks, a circus, and a few times to the condo where he lived with Thora.

"I was not!" Dad huffed. He looked over to us. "You believe me, don't you?"

I was silent. Ted was squirming beside me. "Well, you had something dark in your glass one time," he said reluctantly.

"What were *you* drinking that time, Ted?" Dad leaned forward toward him.

"Coke."

"I was drinking Coke too." Dad looked steadily at Ted for a moment. "Do you believe me?"

Ted nodded, and Dad looked triumphantly at Mom. But she was unconvinced, accusing him again of not having turned up when he was supposed to visit because he'd been drunk, and of drinking when he was supposed to be taking care of us.

This time Ted jumped in, anxious to end the conflict, to defend his dad.

"How do you know, Mother?" he asked. His voice was thin, tremulous. "You weren't there."

Mom was determined to prevent us from being flown to Vancouver for court-ordered summer and holiday visits with Dad, and she had support from the doctors and specialists— Marion, Dr. Snyder, and others. They'd concluded that Dad's drinking, his insistence on enforcing his access rights regardless of the effect, was making the situation more stressful and upsetting for us. They'd talked to Dad on the phone and written letters to him, telling him to stay away, at least until we were both more stable and strong.

"While Mr. Dakin had access to his children," Dr. Snyder wrote in a letter to a colleague he was consulting about Ted, "his visits and attentions toward them were unpredictable and inconsistent. This state of affairs compounded Ted's hyperkinetic state."

Dad, furious at being denied access to his children, had applied to the courts, asking for enforced visitation. His eighty-two-point affidavit included point seventy-six—"That I love my said children and believe they love me."

The doctors asked him to be patient.

"Dr. Penner and I subsequently recommended that Mr. Dakin refrain from any contact with his children for at least six months and we would review the situation on a regular basis," Dr. Snyder wrote.

Dad had grudgingly agreed, but now here he was, in our living room.

And then I realized this was my fault. I precipitated this awful meeting. I had secretly sent Dad a letter the previous

Christmas. I didn't tell him where we were—he'd found that out some other way—but I said I missed him. "If somebody gave me a penny for every time I thought of you, I'd be a billionaire by next week," I'd written in my immature hand on notepaper embossed with blue and red curlicues along the top edge. It's a letter he kept until the day he died. I can't remember now if it was true, if I ever really missed him that much, but it felt as though it should be. In truth, life was less bumpy living far away from him. But surely I missed my dad.

Sometime before Dad's visit to Winnipeg, Mom had said she needed to talk to me. She handed me a photocopy of my letter. I was stunned. How did she come to have it? I was afraid she'd be angry, but she wasn't.

"Your dad sent your letter to his lawyer, and he sent a copy to my lawyer," she said. She was calm, serious. "He wants the courts to order visitation."

The deal was that I could ask for time with Dad when I wanted, she said. But now I was angry. He was using my letter to get what he wanted. It was supposed to be private.

It would be years before I saw him again, before I forgave what I then saw as a betrayal. As a parent now, I see complexities and points of view that weren't available to me at eleven.

After Dad's Winnipeg visit, the turmoil took some time to subside. It was like the receding waters of a tsunami that had swept in, shaken us up, and left a field of emotional debris behind. I always thought that visit and the subsequent legal battles were to blame for the constant low-level hum of anxiety and worry that became the norm at home. It was, at times, palpable. Mom was distracted, working hard to settle Ted, who must also have been sensing and responding to the uneasiness. In truth, there was much more going on that Ted and I knew nothing about.

We began having more frequent surprise holidays, as we'd occasionally had in the final year we lived in Vancouver. I'd wake up and get ready for school, but when I got down to the kitchen for breakfast, Ted would happily announce that Mom had said we were skipping today.

"We're going to take a drive, get out of the city. I thought we'd go to Portage la Prairie, maybe go bowling," Mom said.

Portage la Prairie was a town less than an hour west of Winnipeg. There wasn't much there, but there was a bowling alley. These day trips—and sometimes weekend trips—were framed as getaways, a break from routine. More than a decade later, I would be told they'd been designed to get us out of harm's way. When Stan would get word from the Weird World's intelligence team that there was some threat, we would disappear until it was taken care of. I don't know if we ever went away just for fun and no other reason, but we did get to see a lot of the Manitoba countryside in the months that followed.

I don't recall exactly what time of year it was—early spring or perhaps late fall. Sunset was early. The fields were brown, the sky hard. We were driving to the small town of Sainte-Anne, about forty-five minutes southeast of the city. But this was not a jaunt or a lark. Stan was in the hospital there, seriously injured. Sybil was in the front seat with Mom. I was in the back with Ted. We'd been making this trip regularly for a couple of weeks. Not every day, probably. But often enough that it had become routine. Sybil didn't drive. We were taking her to visit Stan, who was groggy with painkillers and looked small and shrunken in the bandages wrapped around his chest and his head. It was frightening to see him so reduced, incapacitated, and weak.

He'd been horseback riding with a friend and was thrown by the horse, Mom told us. He'd broken seven ribs in eleven places and hit his head. Something had startled the horse, he told us as he lay, grunting and wincing with distress if he tried to move, struggling to breathe past the pain in his chest.

"It was gunshots that startled the horse that day," he told me much later, on the night of revelations in the Sussex motel room, knitting all the strands of the story together for me, in very different colours and textures than those I had perceived as a child. A hit man, hiding in bushes, had fired several rounds, aiming for Stan. One of the bullets had hit him in the chest, knocking him from the horse. He'd nearly died.

"Again," my mother commented dryly, but that was much later, when many horrors were being revealed.

On those cold nights at the little rural hospital in Manitoba, we would visit with Stan for a few minutes and then Mom would usher Ted and me down the hall to the waiting room so Stan and Sybil could talk. We did our homework in the waiting room, or watched the television. Ted and I would fall asleep on the drive home, rousing ourselves only long enough to climb the stairs, brush our teeth, and fall into bed long after our usual bedtimes.

Stan would eventually heal enough to be sent home from the hospital, although for months to come he moved gingerly.

The summer after his accident we set out on another camping trip. This time we headed for the Maritimes, where Stan was from. I learned later we were once again on the run, disappearing for a while to allow the security and intelligence people to deal with the latest threats. But at the time it was framed as just another summer adventure. Once again our little caravan set out. This time, behind Stan and Sybil's camper, we were towing a tent trailer. Mostly we kept moving, staying only one night at any campground, and then packing up and heading out early the next morning.

That changed when we got to Algonquin Provincial Park, west of Ottawa. We stayed there for several days. It was beautiful, with the huge pine-tree canopy overhead and the lake for swimming. Strangely, it's one of my best camping memories, even though something odd was happening while we were there. Something that had Sybil and my mom worried.

Stan was acting strangely. He spent those days sitting on a chair by the campfire, in turn looking confused, suspicious, and agitated.

"Who are you?" he asked me as I approached him, wondering what was wrong. Who was I? What did he mean?

"I'm Polly," I answered simply, using my childhood nickname, unsure if I should elaborate. He didn't reply. Just stared at me a long time, questioningly, before turning his gaze back to the fire.

"What's wrong with Mr. Sears?" I asked Mom that night. "He's acting really weird."

Mom said he had a virus, wasn't feeling good. He should be better in a few days.

"Weird," I repeated, but didn't object further. Weird was often just par for the course.

More than a decade later, as Mom and Stan were describing the dangers we had survived, this was one of the stories they asked me if I remembered. It wasn't a virus, they said. Stan had been darted, poisoned, the night we arrived at Algonquin, by some thug who'd turned out to have been following us since we'd left Winnipeg. When Stan went to the bathroom to wash up, his assailant had been in the bushes nearby, and the last thing Stan remembered for several days was a stinging pain in his neck.

"It scrambled my brain," Stan told me. "I didn't know who anyone was, where I was."

One of the undercover security people protecting us got him back to the campsite and left him by the fire, where Sybil found him shortly after.

I remembered him hunched in a lawn chair, feeding logs into the fire, looking afraid and depleted, his eyes following everyone who came near with suspicion.

Mom said that soon after Stan had started acting strangely, she found a note under a rock on the step of our tent trailer. It wasn't signed, but it said that while our guys hadn't been close enough to prevent the darting, they'd caught the attacker and they were having the poison analyzed. She and Sybil were to keep Stan quiet, not to take him to hospital.

The next morning there was another note, she said, with a small bottle. An antidote. They were to make sure he got a pill every four hours. He would be fine in a day or so.

This story was remarkable not just because of the ever-present but invisible threat it implied, but because it was a rare time when contact with the Weird World wasn't filtered through Stan. To me, as an adult, this seemed significant. Up to that point, knowledge of the dangers, the directions, and any communication with our protection or the intelligence gatherers inside had come to us through Stan. That was for the safety of those in the Weird World and those who protected us, he said. Even as I changed my life to accommodate the story, the threats, there were still times I wondered if he could be making it up. Could he have brainwashed my mother? It was a guilty thought. If I logically weighed out everything I knew of Stan, I could not imagine it. It was easier to believe the Mafia was after us than to believe he would deceive us. And I couldn't figure out what he could possibly have to gain from such a ruse. As for my mother, she valued truth above almost all else.

"You can make a mistake, you can do something wrong, but just don't ever lie to me," she had always told Ted and me. "We can fix anything but a broken trust."

She would not lie to me. I knew this without question. My circling thoughts always returned to the same conclusion. It had to be true.

And there was the incapacitated Stan in the lawn chair, and during that emergency there had been contact without his intercession. It was evidence I relied upon again and again.

AS WE CONTINUED our camping trip through Ontario, Quebec, New Brunswick, and into Nova Scotia, a part of me wondered whether we would go home again. Whether this was another secret move that would result in my starting school again—grade seven—somewhere new that fall. It was a worry I didn't share, just a niggling thought that would visit me in my bunk in the tent trailer at night, with the quiet sounds of the settling campground and the small creatures in the woods around us. I wasn't worrying about who else might be lurking in the forest, but I'm sure Mom, Stan, and Sybil were.

It was on that trip that I discovered the white sand beaches of Nova Scotia, places where I now walk and swim in the summers. Stan also took us to the tiny island of Grand Manan, off the southwest tip of New Brunswick, where he'd grown up. Being back there was obviously awakening memories for him, and our evenings at the campfire were rich with his stories of the characters who had populated the island in his youth. His eyes lit up as he told these tales, mimicking the broad twang of rural Maritimers of the time, and their unique turn of phrase.

"He was right drunk, buddy was," Stan aped and exaggerated the islanders' sing-songy cadence and inflection. "I seen him on the back road and he musta had twenty-four beer into him, he was some unsteady." It was the story of the island drunk of decades before. "The wind, she was blowin' and ol' buddy, he jus' blew down too, onto his back. Lookin' like a turtle, the flipper dipper, all hands and feet wavin' about. His brother hadda come get 'im agin."

Ted and I giggled, loving the contrast between the intellectual, spiritual Stan of the pulpit and the bright, funny Stan of the campfire comedy. The drunken, ribald characters he described seemed to us risqué and fascinating.

He told the story of tobogganing down a nearby hill one snowy afternoon when he was small. Swooping down the slope in vertiginous glory only to slide right into a barbed-wire fence, which sliced through his flesh, opening deep wounds in his face and neck. But for the cold, which slowed the blood flow until the doctor arrived, he would have died that day. How different our lives would have been, I reflect now, if the weather had been a little warmer.

The camping convoy did in fact turn around and head back to Manitoba. By the last night on the road, in eastern Ontario, the nights were cold, and some mornings Ted and I would break ice off the top of the tent trailer as we packed up. I would start grade seven in Winnipeg, at Grant Park High. But as much as I would come to love it there, we would not be allowed to stay long.

THIRTEEN

IN HALIFAX, NOT far from where I live now, there are horses, a small barn, and a fenced riding ring. The horses are just up the hill from the downtown core, overseeing daily rush-hour traffic. For years I walked or drove past the Halifax Junior Bengal Lancers riding school and felt lucky to live in a place where the traffic occasionally had to stop for the horses to cross to the grassy common on the other side of the street. On winter mornings the horses are often playful, running and feinting, jousting with each other in the paddock, gusts of steam puffing from their nostrils. In the afternoons they are dignified, soberly bearing the young equestrians of the after-school riding programs. I have sometimes stopped to watch.

I was never an expert rider, but like many young girls, I suppose, I loved horses, and was always excited about a chance to go riding.

So that was the enticement: a horse of my own.

It was the beginning of grade eight. I was thirteen and still at Grant Park High. I'd just been elected vice-president of my class. I liked my teachers and had some good friends. Boys had become interesting and there was one in particular who inspired me to comb my hair and wear my nicest sweater during the public skates at the rink next to the high school. He worked there and looked carelessly confident as he circled the ice in his official rink jacket, helping anyone who fell, making sure the slow skaters stayed to the right and the hot dogs didn't knock down the little kids. Once—I can't remember how this came about—he helped me tighten my skates, kneeling down to pull at the laces and smiling up at me in a way that made me suddenly aware of how red and drippy my nose was from the cold.

I recall this time as the happy lull before the next change. We were leaving Winnipeg. Secretly. Another disappearance in the offing.

That fall became grim with sick anticipation. The for-sale sign was on the lawn but Ted and I were instructed not to talk about our impending move. This time Mom had told us we were going, entrusting us with the plan but swearing us to secrecy.

"If anyone is asking you can just say we're looking at other houses," she said, pointing to the real estate catalogue. "It's the truth. You just don't say we're looking at houses in another city." The catalogue was from Saint John, New Brunswick, on the East Coast. A small city I'd never heard of until we'd visited it on our Maritimes vacation fourteen months earlier.

I felt it was unfair that, having finally settled into a school where I had a group of friends that I fit into and was happy, I had to move again. Thirteen is a difficult age for girls in the best of circumstances. I contemplated running away, refusing to leave, staging my own disappearing act. But then there was the possibility of that horse. Daydreams of riding and caring for it took some of the fight and rebellion out of me, allowing me to envision at least one happy element of a life in this new place so far away.

As we waited for our Winnipeg house to sell, I looked at the real estate catalogue Stan and Sybil had sent from Saint John. They had moved there a few months earlier. I loved the Searses but wondered why we always had to move every time they did. Ted asked the question out loud, but there was no answer. Mom seemed like such a strong person; why did she rely on them, need them so much? Ted and I talked about this, speculating why our families moved in geographical lockstep, but we couldn't come up with any good theories.

The small, grainy black-and-white pictures in the real estate catalogue showed only exterior shots of houses. There was one we all agreed might be right, a place on a couple of acres, with an ocean view, in a suburban part of the old port city. It was cheap, another fixer-upper, which appealed to me. The photo offered little information but my imagination generously filled in the missing details. And best of all, Mom said it might be a place where I could have a horse. My own horse.

I don't think that the horse was a conscious manipulation, proffered to gain my co-operation for a move I dreaded, and one that would prove the most difficult of them all. I think Mom honestly wanted to find a way to make this move less painful. It was effective. I didn't run away. But I did rebel against the secrecy, on our last night in Winnipeg, Halloween night.

THE HOUSE HAD finally sold. Someone else would be living in this place my mother had worked so hard to restore. Now that it was such a beautiful home, it would become someone else's, I thought bitterly. Again, Mom would not talk about why we were leaving, why we couldn't tell anyone. She was preoccupied and unusually quick to snap at Ted and me.

I sat on the narrow stairs leading up to my attic bedroom, looking out the small window at the landing, at the black branches of the leaf-bare trees that lined our street. It was mid-October and already the air was cold, the sky promising snow. A child of the mild wet Vancouver winters, I found the prairie blasts hard: too cold, too windy, too long. I thought about what it was like to stand at the bus stop on the worst of the January mornings, when the radio warned that exposed skin would freeze within minutes. Now I would not have to experience that again. But another set of goodbyes was approaching and my stomach felt clenched and hollow. I thought about an upcoming school trip we were all excited about. Now my class would be doing that trip, and the remaining years of high school, without me. I was resentful but I tried to think about the horse.

We were leaving for New Brunswick on November 1, driving the vast distance across Ontario and Quebec. In the days leading up to that, I longed to tell my friends that I was going. Every interaction with them felt heavy with unspoken significance, knowing as I did that these would be my final memories of this place, these friendships. Knowing what I could not tell them—that soon I'd be gone. I quietly gathered their addresses, vowing silently to write them all letters someday, to somehow explain my disappearance, to tell them I'd wanted to say goodbye, to ask them to forgive me, not to forget me.

During those final weeks in Winnipeg I sat in school trying to pretend that everything was normal, that the assignment due next week mattered to me when in fact I would never hand it in.

My picture wouldn't be in the yearbook. I wouldn't be at the next dance. In the final week, I wondered what my teachers and friends would be told or would think about my sudden, unexplained absence the following Monday. They would be speculating about where I was, while we would be driving east to some unimaginable new life, new school, new classmates.

"You can write them later," Mom said, seeing my unhappiness. "Once we've been in Saint John for a while, it will be okay to write."

It was unsatisfying. I imagined what it would be like, should be like, if I could tell everyone before we left. There would be a going-away party, like we'd had for another kid who'd moved away. There'd be promises to stay in touch, maybe tears that would match and affirm my own sadness at saying goodbye. I could talk about my horse, try to paint this move in glowing terms I didn't truly feel or believe. Instead, we would creep away and leave nothing behind but questions. Before long it would be as if we'd never really been there.

On our last night in Winnipeg, I slept over at my best friend Wendy's house. She was having a Halloween party. I don't remember much about it, just the isolating effect of the impending distance that would soon be between us. And the constant hum of my desire to tell them, not to let them say goodnight without saying goodbye.

There is a picture of Wendy and me that was taken that night, at either the beginning or the end of the evening, before everyone else arrived for the party, or maybe after they'd all left. We're kneeling backward on her couch, forearms on its back and looking toward the camera. Below her giant sombrero, decorated with embroidery and shiny metallic tabs, she has a painted-on curlicue moustache. I have on a plaid shirt; perhaps I was dressed up as a hobo or lumberjack. My smile seems half-hearted but Wendy's is characteristically wide. We'd met a couple of years earlier when I'd been the new kid in grade five. When we moved up to junior high we ended up in the same class.

It was a friendship that developed slowly. I was intimidated by the fierceness of her enthusiasm for anything that caught her interest or promised fun. She was loud, always funny, and never seemed to mind that her size—she was an overweight kid—was sometimes the butt of jokes. Sometimes she made fun of her own weight, a pre-emptive humour, shutting down hurtful jabs by owning them. Over time I was won over by her sense of fun, her boisterous laugh, and maybe, too, by some undefined vulnerability that I occasionally glimpsed.

After the last of the partygoers left that Halloween night, we settled in front of the television set in her basement family room. On one wall, across from the stairs, was a bar with a shingled front and a mini-fridge behind it, some Naugahyde chairs, a plaid couch and a rug. We'd had many sleepovers here. We were watching scary movies but I wasn't really following along, absorbed by my thoughts, which were occasionally punctuated by the creepy voice and sinister *bwah-hah-hah* laugh of Vincent Price, our favourite horror-show host.

I thought of the day, the month before, when we'd skipped school and walked from our suburban neighbourhood out onto the prairie and found an abandoned white cargo van, its tires flat, its side doors ajar. It was a perfect hideout. We were hunkered down inside, imagining how we could decorate it and provision it with stores of snacks, when we heard someone approaching. We peeked out to see a man coming toward us. Looking back, I think he probably had developmental problems or was mentally ill. He was moving slowly, without any apparent destination, his face slack. Naturally we immediately assumed he was a serial killer–rapist coming for us.

I was frozen with fear. Wendy, deciding the best defence was a good offence, hopped out of the van, put her hands up before her in zombie stance, and began walking toward him in a Frankenstein-like shuffle, all the while moaning maniacally and rolling her eyes, bobbing her head in a frenzy that simulated extreme pain, insanity, or possession by some demon entity.

It worked. The man looked alarmed and, then, appearing to suddenly get a sense of direction, turned around and walked quickly away.

Wendy and I waited a few minutes, until he was beyond some scrub bushes a distance off, and then burst into uncontrollable laughter. We rolled around in the van, clutching our bellies. Every time our hilarity would start to wane, Wendy held her arms out and rolled her head, and we'd be gone again, our cheeks aching with laughter.

I looked over at Wendy now, her face reflecting blue light from the TV, and thought of all our adventures, how I admired her bravery, even recklessness, and how it contrasted with my own cautious approach to life. I remembered how the year before, some kids had dared us to shoplift a roll of Life Savers from the Woolco store at the local mall. Of course we were caught and ended up in the store's security office. There we discovered that the big mirror on one wall of the store was actually two-way, and that anyone in the office could see the aisles of products. I sat there frightened and remorseful, horrified equally by the bullying attitude of the security woman who wanted to search us and by Wendy's defiance, her wondrous sense of her own power.

On that last night, Wendy was completely absorbed by the old horror movie, her mouth slightly ajar, her eyes wide.

I decided I could not, would not, just disappear on my best friend, regardless of my sworn promise of silence.

"I have to tell you something but you can't tell anyone. I mean really. You have to swear."

She pulled her gaze from the TV screen and looked at me, intrigued. "What?"

"I'm moving away tomorrow. We're going to New Brunswick to live."

"What!" she yelped. "Fuck off, you are not!"

I told her we were leaving as soon as Mom picked me up from her house in the morning. I told her I'd write, maybe even phone her. Her face was disbelieving, and I watched her dawning realization that she was losing her friend, her follower, her partner in petty crime.

The next morning as I was packing up my things, I warned Wendy—no showy displays when we said goodbye at the door. She wasn't supposed to know. We said goodbye then, in the privacy of her basement. Breezy see-you-laters followed a few minutes later at the door.

Mom was parked at the curb out front, waiting. Ted was in the back seat watching me, expressionless. I was crying by the time I reached the car. Mom hugged me after I got in. "I know," she said, her face sympathetic, her arms holding me tightly. "I know."

If you know, why are you doing this to us? I silently raged. She put the car in gear and headed toward the highway, past my school where Mr. Gridley would call my name on Monday morning and wonder why I wasn't there, and my friends would go to lunch without me and ask if anyone knew why I hadn't come to school today. Would Wendy tell? If she did, would anyone wonder what was wrong with my family? Would anyone try to track us down? Try to fix whatever was wrong? I wonder now whether any of the teachers or adults in my or Ted's lives in Winnipeg raised an alarm when two children disappeared without explanation.

The November morning was cold and smelled of snow as we headed east on the Trans-Canada. We were all quiet for a long time.

THE DRIVE WAS mostly uneventful. There was one late afternoon, somewhere along the remote north shore of Lake Superior, when we got lost. We'd turned off the highway to look for a motel that was nowhere to be found. In that pre-GPS time, Mom pulled to the side of the road and unfolded the map. In the fading daylight she strained to find the road, her finger running over the creased paper.

"It's not here," she said. Her voice was carefully controlled and I could sense her worry. Alone with two children, lost, and miles from anywhere, with snow in the forecast. She turned around and headed back to the highway, and we continued until we found a place to stop, a few hours later. I don't remember much else about that drive, except that the landscape looked so different than when we'd driven this way on vacation in the summertime—now it was bled of colour, bereft of tourist traffic, with short afternoons and long evenings that we spent in unremarkable motel rooms.

We arrived in Saint John on such an afternoon, with little light to see the details of another motel that would be our temporary home until Mom could find us a new place to live. We drove partway down a frighteningly steep driveway.

"This is it," Mom said. We were road-stunned and didn't reply. She disappeared into the office and came back with a key. We drove the rest of the way down the drive and around the back, where the balconies of the two-storey building looked out to what the next day's light would reveal to be Saints Rest Beach and the ocean, a few kilometres away.

We began taking our bags, the cat in his cage, and the dog into the motel room. It was a large rectangular room with a living room, kitchenette, and a separate bedroom off the back. The lighting was poor and the furniture out of date and worn. The decor was like that of a summer cottage, or maybe the apartment of university students, with the couch, chairs, and table still serviceable hand-me-downs but no longer desirable.

"Who's going to sleep in the bedroom?" I asked, walking over to look through the doorway into the space just large enough for its three-quarter bed and a three-drawer dresser with a speckled mirror above.

"Ted will," Mom answered. "We'll share the fold-out bed in the couch. It's bigger."

I couldn't help it. I felt my lower lip begin to quiver and my eyes fill. *No, don't be sad,* I thought. *Be angry.* How had we come to this, from our beautiful old house on Dorchester Avenue in Winnipeg? We'd just finished fixing it up and had hardly even had a chance to enjoy it. I'd loved Grant Park High—my teachers, my friends. I had lots of friends, even a best friend. Why did we have to leave that? I couldn't understand the vague, opaque explanations, couldn't even remember them. Even the Winnipeg winters were better than this shabby place. And we didn't know anyone here except the Searses.

Mom was watching me. "It's just temporary," she said softly. Ted had been opening and closing the kitchen drawers and cupboards, assessing their contents. He stopped to look at us. "I'm sorry, Polly, I know you're upset." Mom's voice was sympathetic. "It will get better."

"They've got a waffle maker," Ted pointed out, trying to be helpful. "And you can have the bed."

"It's okay," I muttered sullenly. It was anything but okay.

MY NEW SCHOOL was a hulking brick pile fronted by a small parking lot. It had business-like double front doors. Metal on the bottom, shatterproof glass reinforced with wire on the top, as though the building was braced for something.

The first day I walked across the parking lot and through those unwelcoming doors wondering where all the other students were. I had butterflies, and a queasy I'll-be-the-new-kid-again feeling as I went up a short flight of stairs to the main level. Before I reached the top, I was met with the raised eyebrows and consternation of the vice-principal. No, no, he told me after establishing that I was a new student who'd registered the previous week. Students use the back door, he said. "Out you go!" He pointed the way, his expression conveying his astonishment at my presumption to use the front door.

Feeling foolish and unjustly reprimanded, I walked around the block to the back of the school, past a group of kids smoking on the sidewalk. Their eyes followed me. They fell silent as I made my way down the hill from the sidewalk and across the asphalt yard toward two large back doors interrupting the imposing brick face. Above them were sandstone panels with letters raised in relief. BOYS, read one; GIRLS, said the other.

I felt in equal parts affronted by this old-fashioned delineation and yet awkward at being alone in a schoolyard populated by clots of kids, talking in groups. This first day, at this adolescent age, the taking of social measure was more acute. I was excruciatingly aware of the eyes on me, the curiosity and talk about me as I made my way toward the doors.

"Hi." The voice, somewhere to my right, startled me. I looked up. A girl with long blond hair and a friendly face was smiling, waiting for a response.

"Hi," I returned, relieved to be talking to someone, no longer trying to figure out how to stand, how to arrange my features so as to not appear awkward and afraid and alone.

"I'm Heather," she said, and introduced me to a boy named Mark standing next to her, and a few others.

"How long do we stand here?" I asked.

"Until the bell rings," she said. And just then it did. Everyone headed for the doors, except the smokers on the sidewalk. They hung back, drawing final deep pulls from their cigarettes, disdaining the bell, making a show of their refusal to be rushed.

Throughout the day, during my hallway travels between classes, at lunch, and after school, I was watched or approached with intense, excited interest.

"Where are you from again?"

"Winnipeg."

"Why did you come here?"

That was the most common questions, with the emphasis on the "here." Apparently it was extremely unusual for someone to move into the area. I was a come-from-away, an interesting species, seldom seen in the west side of that small city, where not much had changed in decades.

Some of the queries were friendly. Some challenging, tinged with suspicion. I thought about my friends back at Grant Park, where I fit. I felt like crying, lashing out at someone. But instead, when I walked past the group smoking on the sidewalk behind the shed of a nearby house, I tried to look tough, nonchalant.

Ruth Main as a young teenager, before her mother's death

Ruth Main in Stanley Park, 1960

Ruth's official stewardess photo, circa 1962

Warren Dakin as a young man

The Dakin family: Warren, Ruth, Teddy, and me, circa 1969

Me at age seven, the year I met Stan

Warren the businessman

Cliff Main, Ruth's father, in front of his garage, early 1960s

Stan Sears, visiting for tea, 1972

Stan and Ted, with the Volkswagen camper van and Ruth seated in the background, during a camping trip to Banff, 1974

*Mom and Ted at my graduation from
the University of New Brunswick in 1987*

Stan gave me away on my wedding day, June 1990

*Sybil and Stan Sears, 1987, just before they retired
to British Columbia*

*Reverend Ruth Main, in front of her church Wesley United Church,
Hunts Point, Nova Scotia, September 1990*

With Stan, Ted, and Elaine in a motel room in Vancouver, 1991

Ruth and Stan, camping, early 1990s

"Smoke?" a girl offered. It seemed a challenge. She was skinny, gangly, with a wide mouth and thick dark hair, and trying hard to seem cool, intimidating.

I accepted the cigarette and a light, trying not to choke on the acrid smoke.

"I'm Patty," she said. "That's Cindy." She pointed to a taller girl with long wiry hair and a pronounced nose that hooked downward. That, combined with the sharp way she was looking at me, made me think of a hawk. I felt like the prey.

"Hi," she said. It was brittle-friendly. "The *new* girl," she commented, determined not to be impressed by my exotic status. She looked over at Patty and smiled. Patty smiled back some type of affirmation I couldn't interpret. There were a couple of boys standing and smoking nearby. They didn't speak, but they were listening. We went through the usual questions—where was I from, why had we moved here.

"Just say we wanted to be on a coast," Mom had said when I asked how I was supposed to answer such a question. "It's true, we've missed the West Coast. Now we're trying the East Coast. Don't you love being by the ocean?"

My mumblings about the attractions of oceanside living didn't seem to satisfy, or were met with blunt skepticism.

"What does your dad do?" followed, from Patty. Surely he'd been transferred, was the thinking. This was difficult. I explained my parents were divorced, he lived in Vancouver. Also unsatisfying for the curious. It just seemed to raise more questions. Yes, my mom worked. No, she didn't have a job yet, she was looking for one.

"Where do you live?"

Nowhere, I thought. In fact, I'd moved from the motel to the Searses' guest room. Ted and Mom were still at the motel. We'd spent the previous week looking at houses. It became clear our circumstances had declined with this move. One house we looked at seemed the epitome of hopelessness and decline—it was an ancient and neglected storey and a half with uneven floors; faded, peeling wallpaper; and three tiny bedrooms that smelled of dirty clothes. As the agent moved through the upstairs hall with Mom and Ted following behind, I hid in the first bedroom and cried, longing for the restored graciousness of our Dorchester Avenue house. How had we come to this?

Mom came back to find me, hugged me, and offered a tissue. She explained we were on a budget, "but don't worry," she comforted me, "we won't be living here!"

By contrast, the tidy one-storey bungalow Mom bought was a relief. It had only two bedrooms, but there was a full basement where she would add another bedroom and a rec room. It was just across the street from my junior high, around the corner from Ted's new elementary school, and only blocks from the Searses' house.

This house would turn out to be where we lived the longest as a family. Mom would plant a garden and some trees. She and Ted would play catch in the backyard in the evenings. We would paint the wide-plank siding a soft grey-blue, and eat casseroles on weeknights and roasts on Sundays in the little dining room off the kitchen.

It was a steadier, more stable time. But I was neither of those things. I began reacting, resisting, and rebelling, unconsciously punishing my mother for what I perceived as many losses.

FOURTEEN

FALL BACK. LOSE light. Gain time. The clocks have been set back an hour from daylight saving time; I have gained an extra hour on this Sunday morning. That one hour seems a poor exchange for the long phalanx of dusky afternoons mustering for the march through the months of shorter days ahead.

When I was sixteen, I anticipated the darker evenings. They offered privacy as my boyfriend Paul and I searched for out-of-the-way places to park his little silver sports car—to be alone, to talk, to kiss, to listen to the radio. *"My endless love..."* we would warble along with Lionel Richie and Diana Ross, looking meaningfully and earnestly into each other's eyes, hands held tight. Paul would drop me home at ten o'clock, or close enough to it that Mom would only roll her eyes as she looked at her watch.

"How was the movie?" she'd ask.

"Fine," I'd mumble, rushing to take my boots and coat off and get to my room before she could ask any unanswerable questions about a movie I'd never seen.

But many of those nights, when I came in the door, Mom would be sitting in the living room, her legs tucked under her in the tall-backed beige chair. Too often her face was tear-stained, her eyes and nose red with weeping. Stan would be in the matching chair a few feet away, a cup of tea nestled in the palm of his hand.

"Are you okay?" I would ask awkwardly.

"Yes, fine," Mom said, making light of her tears. "You know me, just teary," she laughed.

Eventually, I stopped asking. There seemed no point. I would pretend not to see the tears, and Mom and Stan usually didn't acknowledge them either. We would exchange hellos, Stan would ask how school was, I would escape to my room.

Once, after many such nights, Stan violated our unspoken agreement and smiled sheepishly at me. "You're going to wonder what I'm doing to always make your mother cry," he joked. I smiled back. We all knew that Stan was Mom's most constant source of support, he and Sybil. He frequently came by for tea on his way home from church meetings and they would sit in the big matching chairs, talking. Despite the tears I was always glad on those nights to see his car at the end of the driveway. Perhaps I was glad Mom had someone she could talk to, who could comfort her when I could not. Maybe it was the reassuring sense of another trusted adult, backing her up in whatever dire situation she was dealing with.

On the night Stan acknowledged the strangeness of it all, I didn't rush to my room. I sat down on the couch. If Stan was abandoning the pretense, so was I. Because he was right: I did wonder what he and Mom talked about that so often resulted in her tears. The tears that had begun all those years ago in his church. The undefined sorrow that continued still. Often she'd be reading what appeared to be letters. The living room was fraught with some unseen, unknown—at least to me—worry or threat. It created a sense of impending crisis or doom. Something bad was happening but they wouldn't tell me what. In the strange secrecy that surrounded so much of our lives, it seemed wrong to ask. But on that night, I thought maybe Stan was opening the door to my constant unspoken question.

I looked across at them from the couch.

"Why?" I began. I was suddenly aware of my heartbeat.

Mom sighed. "Honey, someday I will tell you, but when you're older." She wiped her eyes. "I promise."

There was to be no explanation this night. I tried to control my exasperation.

"I'm not that young. I'm not stupid, you know," I said, realizing I sounded quite young, and petulant. "I'm only two years away from graduating," I tried again, making an effort to be calm. What could be so awful that they wouldn't share it with me?

"You're definitely not stupid," Stan said. "Not even close."

"And I know you're growing up," Mom added. "But not yet. Someday."

I flounced off to my room, registering my dissatisfaction by turning my music up, trying to drown everything else out and turn my thoughts away from my mother and the damp tissue gripped in her hand. Her ongoing bouts of sadness were increasingly incomprehensible to me because in many ways Mom seemed happier, more relaxed, more settled than at any other time I could remember.

After we'd moved into the little bungalow on Duchess Street in Saint John, she once again began working with Stan at his new church—a soaring stone structure with a tall steeple in a once-grand downtown neighbourhood of large Victorian houses. Most were now chopped up into rooming houses or cheap apartments. Stan had convinced the church to do some outreach in the community. First it was a food bank, actually a cupboard of donated food. At the end of the month, before the welfare, disability, or pension cheques arrived, when money was running short, people would appear at the side door of the church and leave with bags of groceries.

Stan and Mom also talked of an adult daycare, for people with dementia or developmental or physical disabilities, a place that would give such people opportunities to socialize and offer their families and caregivers some respite. The board of the church agreed; funding was found. It was the first adult daycare in that part of the country and Mom, who'd been doing temp work for the first months we were in Saint John, became its director. They were a team, Stan and Mom. They dreamed of a better world. The work they planned and did to help the hungry, the broken, the lonely, drew them together, a bond of purpose and vision.

Mom grew to love the people who came to the adult daycare, and their families, and many of them loved her in return. My high school wasn't far away and sometimes I went there after classes to catch a ride home. I saw Mom's endless patience with Aida, a woman with Alzheimer's whose daughter dropped her off each day on the way to work. Or David, the young man in a wheelchair with the mental capacity of a small boy, whose mother was exhausted from caring for him.

I was proud of my mother's work, of how well regarded she was by the people she worked with and for. But I didn't tell her this. A new distance had developed between us in the years since we'd come to Saint John. I no longer told her everything.

I spent more time away from home, and when I returned I retreated to my room, door closed firmly behind me. Part of this growing remoteness was a natural teenage separating. Part of it was anger. And some of it was guilt. I was doing things I knew she wouldn't like.

In junior high, I'd become a regular at the smoke hole, the patch of sidewalk just beyond the school grounds. I smoked and trailed in late to classes, exhibiting a new and unnatural defiance that was both exhilarating and stressful to me. I went to beach parties down the cliff-ringed shoreline of the cold Bay of Fundy, where we built massive bonfires and drank. I was breaking rules and expectations, unconsciously punishing my mother for taking me away from Vancouver, from Winnipeg, to a place that seemed alien and unwelcoming. In the early days I made some connections but not friendships, just kids to spend time with. The social habitat felt dangerous—a choppy swirl of shifting alliances. I'd observed but was unable to predict the way members of this group could be liked one day and the target of cutting whispers the next. I knew I was vulnerable to this, the come-from-away attempting to find a place in that cutthroat hierarchy.

I began hanging out with Linda, a girl on the outskirts of the group—sometimes in, sometimes out—imagining we would commiserate from the sidelines. Other kids sometimes referred to her as trash, or skank. She had thin black hair, misaligned teeth that made her laugh or smile through a self-consciously raised hand. She had perfected the art of teenage defiance. She lived nearby with her parents, sister, and brother, all crowded into a flat half the size of our little house. Her father was a bully, her mother timid, and the kids ran wild.

I was surprised by my mother's visceral reaction the first time I brought Linda home. "Hi," was Linda's curt response to my mother's greeting. Linda's face was half turned away, her eyes skittering around the room, only glancing off Mom. Her jaw was thrust forward defensively, as if anticipating a blow. Parents didn't like her, she'd told me. My mom was no different. And not without reason. Linda knew and introduced me to a world I'd never encountered before, the wrong side of the tracks, or in this case of the harbour. It was only a bus ride away but an existential leap to a neglected, often dangerous part of the port city. Linda had lived there when she was younger and she'd stayed in touch with some of the kids after her family had found the resources to move to a better neighbourhood.

She took me to a slovenly apartment where four teenaged boys lived with their father, Doug. The mother had run off to Montreal years before. It was the second floor of an old brick building with a wooden addition that sagged alarmingly off the back. It made me think of the dilapidated hideout in the movie *Oliver,* where the treacherous Fagan had housed his young band of robbers. In the kitchen, the fridge was bare except for beer and a crusted can of evaporated milk, a staple used for tea and cereal. There were usually clothes soaking in the bathtub, a forlorn attempt at cleanliness in the absence of a washing machine.

We went there to hang out, drink beer, smoke pot. Doug, who worked as a maintenance man at a nearby shopping mall, escaped to drunken oblivion on the weekends, his sons free to do as they liked in his stuporous absence.

I romanticized this stark world, its inhabitants and all their struggles. I was touched by the way a drunken Doug would show me baby pictures of his sons and cry sloppily, heaving beery gusts of regret to an out-of-place girl listening sympathetically. I was sure that this show of emotion indicated he was a good man beset by bad circumstances; that his boys, who went to school only sporadically and sold joints on nearby corners, three-for-five, were intelligent and misunderstood—they'd just never caught a break. For me it was as though a curtain had been pulled back on a previously unimagined reality.

I'd been sheltered, I realized. Protected, taught to be nice, clean, honest, earnest, responsible. I'd assumed that was, more or less, most kids' experience. Now that life seemed boring, embarrassingly white-bread. I envied the boys their freedom, their self-determination, without any understanding of how few choices they actually had.

Initially I mooned after the oldest son, Dougie, who walked through his grimy neighbourhood with a long-legged and liquid stride, completely unselfconscious, lost in some daydream. He was quiet, thoughtful, and loved The Beatles. We sat on his bed one night, when I was supposed to be sleeping over at a friend's, listening to old vinyl recordings of "Love Me Do" and "Please Please Me," staring out his window across the chimneyed roof-tops. I didn't think about the wisdom, or lack of it, being alone in the house with a drunken man and his teenaged sons. I, who had been schooled to be so wary, careful. I trusted they would do nothing to hurt me and they didn't.

Mom had no idea what I was up to but somehow discerned risk. "You're like Mr. Magoo," she said, citing the nearsighted, heedlessly blundering cartoon character during one of our many fights about curfews and friends. "You're walking blindly, you're naive about dangers around you." *Ha!* I thought. *You have no idea.* I felt a strange pride that now I had a secret life too, and would tell her nothing of it. Years later, Mom and I would jokingly guess how many of her white hairs I was responsible for during that time, but her laughter was rueful as she recalled how angrily defiant I had been, how worried she had been.

At the time, our conflict seemed monumental, unbearable. Something had to give, and as our second Christmas in Saint John approached, I shocked her by saying I wanted to visit my dad. It was meant to be an atom bomb to end the war, meant to signal my options and power and make her back off.

The agreement between my father and the doctors in Winnipeg had been that Dad should leave us alone unless Ted or I expressed a desire to see him. That had been several years earlier. Now, despite her clear reluctance, Mom wrote to my dad and made the arrangements as she was required to do in their legal agreement. There was no direct flight from Saint John to Vancouver, so to avoid my having to make connections by myself, Mom and Ted took the train with me to Montreal and I caught my plane from there.

"Please," Mom said, taking me aside in the busy Montreal airport as I prepared to go through the security gate. "I don't want anyone out there to know my business. Please don't talk about me, my job, Stan, nothing. Not to your dad, not to Penny or Grandpa. It's important." She was pleading, attempting to impress me with the seriousness of a situation she would not allow me to understand. I felt the usual impatience.

"Fine, fine." I turned back toward the security line where Ted was standing. Mom walked the few steps with me. I turned to her again and she smiled shakily, hugged me hard, and then gripping my shoulders held me away from her and looked intently at me. "It's important. Please." I nodded, hugged Ted, and stepped into the lineup. We waved a few times until the line moved and I was hidden behind the security barrier. I busied myself with my carry-on bag so no one could see how close I was to crying as I imagined Mom and Ted walking away and out of the terminal to catch the bus back downtown. I wasn't nearly as tough as I pretended to be. And while I would not admit it, I was jittery at the idea of seeing my dad again after so little contact for so long. Not including his disastrous visit in Winnipeg, it had been more than five years.

HE WAS WAITING for me by the baggage carousels at the Vancouver airport. I didn't see him at first, and felt my breath coming faster at the idea he might not turn up. But there he was, just beyond a half-wall that separated the baggage area from the entrance, rocking up onto the balls of his feet and then back down on his heels, like an excited kid, unable to stand still.

"There you are!" His voice was booming, jolly. "You made it." We hugged, and when my old blue-flowered suitcase slid down the chute I pointed it out and he took it for me, leading the way to where he'd parked his car.

It felt strange to be back in Vancouver, in a car with my dad. I looked over at the way his right hand was splayed, his long fingers spread wide across his thigh while he steered with his other hand. It seemed familiar. I thought of a day when I was small, before my parents had separated and he and I had driven together to our cottage in Point Roberts, Washington, just across the American border. For some reason Mom and Ted were already there. I remembered the bouncy vocals of the Ink Spots on the stereo, and Dad humming along, his hand arranged the same way on his leg, the diamonds in his chunky gold ring catching the light, refracting it against the dashboard. The physical familiarity felt like a homecoming, something to cling to, as did the familiar stuccoed houses along Granville Street, and the crouching mountains of the north shore, as we made our way toward the Lions Gate Bridge. I silently rolled the almost-forgotten street names around in my mouth, savouring them . . . Davie, Nelson, Robson, West Georgia. Past the law courts, the art gallery. Soon we were driving into the green island of Stanley Park. I recalled visits to the zoo, birthday parties at the aquarium, summer picnics near a massive fallen tree that we were allowed to climb on if we were very careful. I tried to take it all in, the views and the memories, and hold it, memorize it. This was home, where I was from. I'd never had a chance to say goodbye to it, had missed it for years in an abstract way. Now the full weight of my longing for the big trees, towering mountains, rich vegetation, the winking harbour, made my throat ache.

I'd been too overwhelmed by this to pay attention to Dad's rolling commentary. He didn't seem to require a response, but as we emerged from the bridge into North Vancouver the tone of his monologue became more urgent.

"I bet you know where you are now!" We were turning onto Capilano Drive. If we stayed on that road it would take us up the side of Grouse Mountain, to Patterdale Drive. The last place we'd all lived together as a family. But we turned off into a condo development my dad's company had built. As we pulled up at the security gate, a man in a uniform appeared.

"Mr. Dakin, how are you?" He nodded as he spoke.

"This is my daughter, visiting all the way from Saint John, New Brunswick." Dad was ebullient in announcing my visit. I watched his face, looking for some sign of what made my mother so fearful of him, so anxious about my visit here. He seemed so benign.

He drove into the underground parking area of one of the tall concrete buildings. As we emerged from the elevator a few minutes later and headed down the hallway, I could see Thora peeking out from an open door.

"Oh, you're here!" She, too, was excited, and pulled me into a hug. "I'm so happy you've come." She was dressed as if she'd come from work, in a skirt and jacket, high heels. She was selling real estate. The condo wasn't large but it seemed luxurious to me. I recognized some of the furniture and paintings—the Kenderdine, a Gainsborough-like prairie landscape that had hung in Dad's family home in Regina and our house on Patterdale; his mother's Royal Crown Derby china with the delicate blue Chinese figures; the silver cigarette box with Dad's initials on it. Again I was reassured by the familiarity.

"We've got you set up in the study," Dad said, taking my bag into an office with a sofa bed, his father's mahogany desk, a TV and stereo. I thought he would leave while I unpacked but he took a calendar from the desk and gestured to me to look.

"Tom wants to have you for dinner. Tom and Dale. I guess you haven't met Dale yet, his wife," Dad said. "Nice girl. I thought we'd do that on Tuesday night. Your godmother wants to see you. And Penny. You'll have to get the ferry over to Nanaimo for a visit with your Auntie Penny." Tom, my half-brother; I didn't even know he'd married.

There were notes on the squares for each day of my visit. It was all planned. I pushed down a tickle of annoyance. "Sure."

Over the next ten days we checked off the items on Dad's list, seeing people I remembered—some clearly, some only vaguely—and visiting Stanley Park, the planetarium, and other childhood haunts. We ate out most nights: a Hawaiian restaurant with hula dancers; a Japanese place where we sat around a teppanyaki grill watching the chef's performance with chopping, flying, flashing knives; and his favourite fish and chips restaurant, Troll's at Horseshoe Bay. From there I caught the ferry to spend a night with Mom's sister, my Auntie Penny, on

Vancouver Island. Dad dropped me at one end and she picked me up at the other.

Penny was glad to see me too. That night we sat in her family room, the fireplace blazing. I answered her many questions about Saint John, our school, Ted, and Mom, in careful terms, trying to satisfy her curiosity without violating Mom's demand for privacy. As we talked, Penny regularly refilled her glass from a large vodka bottle in the kitchen, and soon her questions became more probing, more plaintive.

"Twice, twice." She shook her head. "She just up and moved you kids away and didn't even tell her own sister, her own father. Why would she do that?"

I had no answers. I was unhappy to be put on the spot, and it got worse.

"What about that minister she got so tight with, Sears? Is he still around?"

She knew we'd followed Stan and Sybil to Winnipeg in the first move. Did she know we'd once again followed them to Saint John? I didn't know, and couldn't decide how to answer. But surely that was information she could get from a telephone operator, I thought. So I nodded, feeling sick and unsure. Penny was expressing hurt, anger, and betrayal that seemed reasonable to me, but I had no answers, no comfort for her.

The rest of my time in Vancouver was a dizzying display of the pleasure of a life in which money was no object and the expressed goal was to please and entertain me. I went home with a stylish new ski jacket I'd admired in the window of a trendy shop, along with some other clothes and new makeup, all of which had been unhesitatingly purchased for me from the large wad of cash, mostly fifties and hundreds, that Dad always had in his pocket.

When I emerged from the plane, eager to see Mom after the break, having missed her and Ted, she looked at the jacket and frowned. She must have known how I had been feted and fawned over, indulged and spoiled, the long-lost daughter returned to her father's bosom. It must have been hard to take, knowing I was coming back to her household, where pennies were often pinched in the week before payday. How unfair it must have felt; she did all the heavy parenting, feeding, housing, supervising, driving, counselling, correcting, listening, disciplining, cheering our wins and mourning our losses—day in and day out. And then her ex got to be the fun dad, full of treats, surprises, and gifts, with nary a nag, never a reprimand from his lips. How bitter it must have been to see me proudly wearing the expensive new ski jacket she could never have afforded to buy for me.

But I was fifteen and her frown drained me of my goodwill, made me forget how I'd missed her and how the rough edges of our conflict had been smoothed by distance and time apart. I felt my smile slip away, the old resentment swelling.

"How was your trip?" Mom asked, her smile forced.

"It was great," I said. "I'm going to go back in the summer." Now her smile was gone.

I would go back, and the next year Ted went too.

What I didn't know until much later, what Mom and Stan told me that night in the Sussex motel room, was that every time I came home from visiting Dad, all the new clothes, jewellery, and other gifts were surreptitiously taken from my room and checked by security people, to make sure they didn't contain any listening or tracking devices, poisons, drugs, or other tampering. My father's gifts were seen as threats to my safety. Even if nothing was found hidden in or on them they were still considered corrupting allurements, meant to create an appetite for money and things, to entice me to be a part of my father's business world, a world of organized crime. If I couldn't be induced in that way, they said, it was only a matter of implicating me. Perhaps drugs would be found on me, and Dad would ride to the rescue to make the charges go away. Perhaps it would be pointed out to me that money-laundering business fronts were in my name and I could be turned over to authorities if I didn't play ball. There were many ways to control someone, I was told.

Apparently my dad was going to get me, one way or the other. At fifteen, I just didn't know it yet; all I could see was the glamour, the satisfaction, of being my father's long-lost girl.

FIFTEEN

THERE IS AN image I cannot forget, of a mother as she learns of the death of her adult child. It was captured by a television news crew at an airport in the Philippines, where anxious families were waiting for word of survivors after a plane crash. When the official confirmation comes—no survivors—it is like a body blow from an unseen force. The mother falls down, physically overwhelmed by the shock and sudden weight of grief. As she falls, her features are twisted with pain, her eyes no longer seeing.

It is terrifying to see the moment a life is forever changed. Or hear it.

Mom had already gone to bed. I was awake, reading, and rushed to the phone in the kitchen when it rang, well after eleven.

"Hello?" My voice was sleepy.

"Is your mother there?" It was Stan, but he sounded strange, frantic, wild. "I need to talk to her. Is she there?"

"She's asleep. Are you okay?"

"No. Michael is dead."

The anger, the raw pain, the bewilderment, reached me like shock waves across the phone line. I was horrified by the irreversibility of what had happened, and the way it was undoing Stan, whom I could hear now was breathing as though he couldn't catch his breath.

"Just a minute, I'm going to get her." I felt frantic as I rushed down the stairs to wake Mom.

Michael was Stan and Sybil's younger son. He was thirty and lived in British Columbia with his girlfriend and their new baby. I'd only met him a few times, but remembered a quiet, slim man, his long dark bangs spilling across his forehead and into his eyes, his smile shy but warm.

Michael's girlfriend had come home from work that day to find him dead in their bathtub, their infant daughter in a baby seat beside the tub. He'd been dead for some hours, apparently drowned.

I stood outside Mom's room listening to her voice murmuring as she spoke to Stan, an ageless cadence of comforting sounds. "Oh Stan, I'm so sorry, so, so sorry." And then, "I know, I know." She was crying, and I remembered her saying the worst thing that could happen to any parent was losing a child.

I thought about the baby, crying and no one responding, unaware that her father would never come to her again. I began to cry too.

In the days that followed I was unable to look at our bathtub without imagining Michael sightless and floating. If the shower curtain was closed, I would fearfully pull it back, unable to stand not seeing that it was, of course, empty. I felt ashamed that I was reducing the tragedy of his death to this creepiness, but for a couple of years I could not enter a bathroom without looking over at the tub.

There was an autopsy. The medical examiner determined Michael had had an epileptic seizure while in the tub and drowned.

Sybil seemed to accept the loss more easily than Stan. She was sad but her grief was not angry. Stan's sorrow was sometimes sharp with fury. He wore it in the deepened lines of his face and the heaviness of his stride. It was a long time before his usually irrepressible humour returned, and the stab of painful memory never seemed far off.

I don't remember what I said to him the next time I saw him. It seemed too big a thing for mere words. I thought how lucky Michael had been to have a father who had loved him in such a full-hearted way.

IN SOME WAYS Ted and I had similar experiences with our dad. We were indulged, treated to outings and gifts, our behaviour never challenged. But now when we talk about those visits as adults with our own children, what stands out is the remarkable, even dangerous freedom Dad gave us, along with lots of "walking-around money," as he called it.

Ted remembers being fourteen or fifteen, licence-less, and taking Dad's big Oldsmobile 98 for a spin. Apparently Thora had been away and, after some years of being on the wagon, Dad was drinking. Ted went to pick up some food, and cruised along Marine Drive. We laugh, ruefully, aware of the potential for disaster, imagining what our mom would have thought, and cringing at the idea of our kids being in such a situation.

On my last visit as a teenager, just after my sixteenth birthday, I told Dad I was going to meet a friend from back east who was in town and spend the day with him. I said I'd be back later that night. He didn't ask me anything about Ernie, just offered to drop me off at Stanley Park, where we'd agreed to meet, by the polar bears at noon.

Astonishingly, Ernie had remembered the details and was there. Ernie was older, a handsome stoner I'd encountered at Doug's apartment a few years earlier. What I interpreted as his implacable cool I realize in retrospect had more to do with his near-constant state of smoke-induced buzz than any existential insights into the futility of effort or worry. He rolled with whatever life brought. He'd won me over when he offered to let me stay in the apartment he rented to store his stash, at a time when Mom and I had been fighting. I seriously considered it, what I naively thought of as such a gracious offer. I never thought that if the apartment had been raided, I'd have been seen to be in possession of the stash.

As I approached the polar bear enclosure, I could see Ernie had a friend with him, a giant red-headed, bearded guy whose name I no longer remember. The three of us left the park and headed to a pub they knew of in Gastown, the not-yet-gentrified part of the downtown where no one would check my ID. Hours later we ended up in a low-rent apartment in the east end, where Ernie was staying with several other guys. It seemed like an adventure, a story to tell—hanging with the bad boys in Vancouver on summer vacation. But at some point I realized that I didn't really know any of these guys, other than Ernie, and that it would probably be smart to go home before everyone became too uninhibited. I didn't know how I would get there, though. Ernie offered one of the guys money to drive me. He grudgingly agreed and we all piled into his battered car with the rear struts jacked up for racing. Dingle balls adorned the interior periphery of the windshield, and AC/DC roared on the stereo, attracting stares.

The officer at the security gate at Dad's condo looked stern as we pulled up vibrating with sound, smoke drifting out the window when the driver rolled it down to greet him. He looked concerned when I leaned across from the middle seat, between Ernie and the driver.

"They're just dropping me off," I said. I could tell he was reluctant to let this rabble in. "Mr. Dakin's daughter," I reminded him. He shook his head as he raised the gate to let us pass.

I wondered whether he'd tell my dad about the disreputable bunch that had driven me home. No clean-cut boys these. Part of me hoped he would. I think I wanted Dad to be made to pay some parenting dues. But if anything was said, he didn't take it up with me, simply asking the next day if I'd had a nice time.

Ted continued to visit Dad every summer. I stopped after the summer I turned sixteen. My recollection is that during the last trip I was upset that Dad forced me to stop over on my way home, to visit his sister and her two children in Regina. They were all strangers to me and it felt awkward. Aunt Diane was nice enough, but I didn't get along with the daughter, Janet. I came home from that trip with a bad taste in my mouth, feeling resentful toward Dad.

By the next spring, when I would normally be making plans to go to Vancouver, I had a boyfriend. I asked Dad if Paul could come with me that year and he said no. Strike two. Fun dad didn't get to be party-pooper dad. That was the end of my summer visits, and he didn't visit me, so I would not see my father again for many years. Before I did, I would come to think of him much differently.

I worked that summer, slinging popcorn, candy, and pop at the old Paramount movie theatre on King's Square in Saint John, watching the movies on my breaks, trying to figure out what I would do when I graduated. I'd always thought I'd work with children in some capacity, picking up on my earlier experiences at the nursery at the Child Development Clinic in Winnipeg. Still, despite any clear sense of direction, I don't recall being particularly worried as I began grade twelve. After the two previous years of skipping classes and goofing off, I finally felt ready to study and my early term marks reflected that. In some respects I was growing up, leaving the turbulence of adolescence behind.

The timing of the crash made no sense. I was in a biology class taking a test, feeling confident about it, when the floor fell from below me. The sensation of dropping made me grab the edges of my desk. A few seconds later, I looked around with astonishment at the other students quietly bent over their test sheets, unconcerned. I realized the desk had not moved. The floor had not fallen from beneath me. Only I had experienced whatever tectonic shift had just occurred. My heart was knocking within my chest and I couldn't catch my breath. Rushes of adrenalin felt like cold fingers pulling at the base of my skull. I could feel sweat on my forehead, under my arms and breasts, at the small of my back. I had an almost irresistible urge to get up and run, anywhere, to escape the terror that was overwhelming me for no obvious reason.

Breathe, breathe slowly, I thought from within the cacophony of my panicked brain. *Something must be really wrong with me.* The room still felt precarious, as though the walls were undulating almost imperceptibly, the floor tilting. I looked around again, expecting people to somehow be aware of the crisis taking place in me, but no one looked my way. Even the teacher, facing me from his desk, had failed to notice anything out of the ordinary.

I sat, trying to control my breathing and my skipping heartbeat, until the bell finally, mercifully released me. I ran for my locker, grabbed my jacket, and rushed for the door. I didn't go back for weeks.

"Acute panic attacks," the doctor at the emergency room said the next day, after another episode. This time the floor hadn't dropped, it had swayed. I had staggered. I was with Paul at the mall where his mother ran a card store. I worked there part-time. When the tiled floor began to lurch, I grabbed his arm, frantic, certain I would fall.

"What are you doing?" he asked. His voice seemed far away, muffled. The lighting seemed crystalline, exaggerated, and I squinted my eyes, trying to block it out.

"Are you okay?" Paul was looking at me with alarm.

"No, something's wrong." My voice was shrill, my hands now shaking. I hated how afraid I sounded, but I had no control.

We closed the store and he took me first to his house, where I lay on the couch and his father remarked on how the pendant of my necklace was bouncing on my chest from the forceful pounding of my heart. Lying down had not calmed me.

"You'd better take her to emergency," he told Paul.

The doctor didn't seem impressed or particularly alarmed by my symptoms.

"Do you get regular exercise?" he asked.

"What?" The question seemed crazy. Had he misheard my alarming list of symptoms?

"You're having acute anxiety attacks," he said. "You should take up tennis or running. Stress relief," he advised cavalierly.

I didn't believe stress could trigger such dramatic sensations. I thought it must be a side effect of the magic mushrooms Paul and I had taken the previous weekend. I thought they must be making me crazy.

Paul took me home, where I told Mom what had happened that afternoon, and the day before in biology. We'd been fighting and I'd been avoiding her, but now I realized how much I still needed her, how reassured I felt by her calm presence, how I hated when she had to leave for work the next morning.

Over the following days, I found I was afraid to go out, terrified there might be another episode, sure that the next time I would pass out, or have a heart attack, or run into traffic. I sat in the tall-backed chair in the living room, staring out the window, gripping the armrests, fighting to hang on to some type of equilibrium, afraid my sanity might slip away at any moment. I couldn't eat, my stomach a rebelling knot when I tried. I started losing weight quickly.

Today, with the ongoing stress of electronically connected lifestyles, anxiety disorders seem common among teenagers. But when I began experiencing anxiety attacks, they were more unusual. Our family doctor referred me to a psychiatrist, who confirmed the diagnosis and prescribed Xanax. It helped enough that I eventually went back to school, but for months I feared a return of the lurching floors, pounding heart, and racing, doom-filled thoughts. I continued to see the psychiatrist from time to time for some months. He monitored the medication and taught me relaxation techniques, but he could offer no explanation of why the panic attacks had begun.

It seems obvious now that after our disappearances, and years of living in the miasma of some unspoken crisis and my mother's mysterious tears and distress, something had broken. Just because I didn't know the source or cause of the fraught and fearful atmosphere at home didn't mean I wasn't reacting to it. My pot smoking and drinking had been part rebellion against and part self-medication to treat the frustration and anxiety of trying to interpret and manage the unnamed threat. The panic attacks were simply a signal that the stress was taking its toll.

The relaxation exercises helped, and I did start to get more exercise. I forced myself to go into situations where I feared an attack, and became more assured when nothing happened. I managed to catch up on the schooling I'd missed and I graduated the next June, with no clear idea of what to do next.

Once again, Stan came to the rescue. He'd been talking with social workers at the local community services department. They'd identified a need for a special daycare for children who were abused or neglected. It was conceived as a last-ditch intervention for families at risk of having their children removed to foster care by the department. The hope was that putting them in a safe environment for weekdays might lessen the pressures at home that could trigger abuse. It would also ensure the children got a good meal every day, and some structure. Stan's church had agreed to set up the daycare in its second-floor gym, upstairs from the adult daycare that Mom ran, and I was one of three people hired to take care of the preschoolers.

Kenny and Kerry were the first to arrive, by themselves in a taxi. He was three, she five. Their dad was in prison for stabbing someone, Kenny told me. Their mom was still sleeping because she worked at a bar until three or four in the morning. Before she could write her name, Kerry was getting herself and her brother up and dressed for daycare each day and calling the taxi, using a chit that social services provided. They were always hungry when they arrived, like many of the kids, and would eat slice after slice of toast with peanut butter or cheese spread, and chunks of apples and oranges. Kerry was also responsible for supper when they went home at the end of the day. She would stop in at the corner store down the street from their apartment to choose a can of spaghetti or ravioli, and she would heat it on the stove at home. Her mother had already left for work by then, she said.

"Who takes care of you at night?" I asked, appalled.

"The neighbour. We leave our doors open. She checks us."

Kerry was smart and wise. Her large brown eyes beneath overgrown, uncombed bangs were knowing, sometimes defiant, and often sad. Kenny was charming and manipulative; he turned on his brightest smile to mitigate the discipline after he'd seized the best dump truck from a smaller boy, unconcerned that he'd knocked him down in the process. I had no trouble picturing a life of crime ahead of him. I still wonder what happened to them both.

There were other equally heartbreaking stories among the children at the daycare, and for a year it was enough to care for them, give them nutritious meals, hold them when they raged through a tantrum, and help them learn a few basic skills so they wouldn't be too far behind when they went to school: how to tie their shoes, print their names, say please and thank you. But at the end of every day they went back to the same poverty-stricken homes, endlessly loving and forgiving their neglectful, sometimes violent parents who seemed so woefully unequipped for the demands of parenthood. I felt ineffectual and frustrated.

I'd been taking a few university courses in the evenings, but the next year I left the daycare and enrolled full-time to study psychology, sociology, biology, English, history, philosophy, drama, and French over the following years. I loved how knowledge in one class could spill over and inform another seemingly unrelated discipline, and I was excited by the connections.

Mom had also been taking university classes part-time. In my second year she decided to go full-time. She'd discerned she had a calling to work in the church, not as a secretary or audiovisual clerk or daycare administrator as she'd done for so many years, but as an ordained minister. It was not a big surprise to me. I'd always known how important her faith was, how she felt sustained and strengthened by the Sunday worship services she rarely missed. And Mom loved learning and studying. She'd proven to be an apt scholar in the courses she'd done while she was working. There was also a looming hole in her life. The Searses were moving away, and this time we wouldn't follow them. Stan was transferring to a new church in Maitland, Nova Scotia. And her children were on the cusp of independent lives: Ted had left for university that fall, so I was the only one left at home. She, too, needed a new beginning.

But before she could do a theology degree she had to finish her bachelor of arts.

"How would you feel if I sold the house to go back to school?" she asked one night after dinner. "Would you be okay?"

She explained she'd have to move to Fredericton and would be going to the same university as Ted, just over an hour away. She would study and work part-time as a fill-in lay minister at a small church outside the city. After that, she would move to Halifax to go to the Atlantic School of Theology.

"My mother is leaving home," I joked with her as we packed up the house. We had lived in the little house on Duchess Street in Saint John for eight relatively uneventful years. It was the longest I'd ever lived anywhere.

By that time I was dating Terry, and working part-time at the Saint John *Telegraph-Journal*. I'd decided to be a reporter. I'd done a bit of freelancing at the CBC—the Canadian Broadcasting Corporation—but layoffs that spring meant there'd been no summer work there. I was lucky enough to have landed a summer job at the paper and they'd offered me shifts through the school year, working around my class schedule. Mom loved to hear about the characters in the newsroom and the stories I was assigned to. She listened intently, her face animated by her interest, her pride in a daughter doing work with such entrée to compelling people making news on interesting issues.

She liked to hear about the cases I covered as a court reporter, the people I wrote about for the features page, and my
description of the press room, where I would sometimes be sent
to pick up the first copies of the evening paper—I would pull
them from the conveyor leading from the giant undulating,
pounding machinery that printed, cut, and folded the sheets of
inky newsprint. I'd take them up to the newsroom, where the
editors would scan for typos and other errors.

She looked shaken the evening I described an investigative
piece I was working on, about a municipal councillor in a village
outside the city who, I'd been told, was accepting money from a
businessman reputed to be linked to organized crime.

"Be careful," she warned, suddenly very serious. I didn't tell
her the councillor had also warned me off. It had frightened me,
and I didn't want to scare her.

"So tell me about today," she'd ask each evening as we sat
down to supper, and we'd share stories from the day. Those
evenings marked a new phase in our relationship, a friendship
that grew into the spaces between us that had been taken up by
the concerns of parenting, the resistance of growing up. I felt
that she now saw me as an adult as well as a daughter and found
me worth knowing better. In return I began to see her as more
than the mother I had clashed with, who I'd seen as trying to
thwart me, limit me. Over the final months we lived together on
Duchess Street, we were once again gentle with each other, listening and affirming, reknitting the threads that had frayed
through my adolescence. She was grateful for my company, and
I was happy to once again be enjoying hers.

It was a good interlude, but life was changing again. I found a
co-op apartment and a roommate. On our last night on Duchess
Street, I came back for the final load of my belongings and

discovered Mom washing the floor. She'd been crying. Earlier that afternoon she'd had our old dog Pixie put to sleep, after the vet discovered tumours under her skin. I realized for her that day marked the end of family life, the daily connections and functions that had given her purpose. The kids, the house, the friends, the dog, the job: they were all falling away in one fell swoop.

I was overwhelmed with the understanding of how lonely and indistinct the months and years ahead must seem to her. I watched my mother dip the rag in the bucket of soapy water, wring it out, and scrub into the corner of the kitchen floor. She was a small, determined woman. I was filled with admiration for her dispro-portionate strength, and sorrow for all that she had endured.

SIXTEEN

IT SEEMED, FOR a time, that it was now up to me to create my life, to choose how it would be. I felt the weight and the excitement of that as I continued my studies, my work at the newspaper, and my relationship with Terry.

Mom had settled into a 150-year-old manse on the St. John River, outside Fredericton. There was a rowboat in the driveway, its white paint flaking.

"Why is there a boat in the yard?" she'd asked the man who met her with the key on the day she moved in.

"Flood season," replied the man, who was one of her new parishioners. "The river gets high in the spring. Might come over the banks."

We joked about Mom manning the oars, with the new cat that I'd given her for company keeping watch from the stern. She laughed, but she approached the spring with trepidation.

"Keep your life jacket handy!" I teased her.

That year she went to school during the week, wrote sermons on Saturdays, and on Sundays conducted worship services at the three small churches in the pastoral charge she worked for. As an unordained supply minister, she couldn't conduct weddings or baptisms, but she was allowed to do funerals and with the aging congregations she got some practice at that before the year was out. She was good at funerals; she had a natural ability to empathize with sorrow and loss.

I made the hour-and-a-half drive to visit her every few weeks, sometimes with Terry, sometimes on my own. It was odd to see her standing at the front of her little rural churches, leading the services. But she seemed at ease, in her element, her sermons an opportunity for her to expound on the social justice issues that she'd always been passionate about. One of the churches no longer had an organist, so she did double duty there, announcing the hymns from the pulpit and then leaping to the organ to play and lead the singing. She'd catch my eye mid-pivot and we'd each look away and try not to laugh.

Sometimes Ted and his friends would come from Fredericton for a Sunday dinner and we'd all be together again, briefly. Mom delighted in a full table and the lively conversation, and we appreciated her home-cooked meals.

"Mrs. D," one or the other of Ted's friends would always say, "you make the best pie."

"My Great-Aunt Mary's recipe," she'd reply.

That school year seemed a short reprieve before larger distances were to separate us all. In the summer that followed, Mom moved to Halifax for her theology studies and Ted decided to move back to Vancouver, to live with Dad and Thora. Mom tried to discourage him, but her arguments seemed weak, her worries groundless and vague. She must have longed to tell him the real reason for her anxiety.

"Don't worry, Mom," Ted said, hugging her. "I'll be fine. Dad is sober. Thora will be there." I sensed that none of this was reassuring.

We heard from Ted sporadically after he left—phone calls and occasional letters, this being the era before email and texting. He seemed to love being back in Vancouver. The relaxed easy living of the West Coast appealed to him. He was playing beach volleyball, selling electronic equipment, and had bought a sports car. Despite her anxiety, Mom said little, at least not to me, but there was a reluctance in her responses to his news that signalled her unhappiness.

The Searses were now living in Maitland, a small village on the Bay of Fundy side of Nova Scotia. It was to be Stan's final church before he retired. They planned to go back to the West Coast eventually, to be closer to their surviving son. It seemed strange that we no longer got together for dinners at Christmas, Easter, or Thanksgiving, and there were no more camping trips. Sybil stayed in touch with letters and birthday cards. When I graduated from university, she came back for the ceremony and the celebration. And once when I went to Halifax to see Mom, I detoured to Maitland to visit her and Stan. That was the last time I heard him preach, in the little clapboard church, and afterwards I had lunch with them before heading home to Saint John.

I had one letter from Stan, but he and Sybil now seemed like friends that I would remember fondly who no longer played an important role in our lives. I figured that as we all moved in different directions, the connection would fade.

The shock I felt seeing Stan walk into the motel room that night in Sussex sprung from that belief. His presence was the first signal that my understanding of our lives and the dynamics that drove them was incomplete. Ted and I were right, had always been right. Our family was strange, and I was about to find out why.

WHEN ALL HAD been revealed, I wished it to be unsaid. As unsatisfying as my previous ignorance had been, it was better than this story, and easier to live with than my struggle to weigh that truth against the possibility that . . . that what? That Stan and my mother were both insane, although that clearly wasn't the case. And I could think of no possible purpose for creating this narrative of horror and fear. I could only fall back on my trust in them that had always been justified.

Nothing was the same when I left that motel. Even after the initial waves of terror began to flatten and recede, I found I could not settle back into life as usual. The stories of attempted hits and poisonings, failed kidnappings, and narrowly averted dangers made the world feel like a fearful and threatening place. I thought I had in fact been just like Mr. Magoo, blithely walking through life in oblivious ignorance. I developed a fear of being poisoned. I worked out a strategy for eating out, preferring fast-food restaurants because I thought that would provide the least opportunity for anyone to interfere, to get into the kitchen and slip something into my food between the time I arrived and the time I was given my food, or to bribe or coerce someone else to do it. That was melodramatic, catastrophic thinking, but if there really was a threat, I needed to heed the warnings that my life could be at risk. When I walked or drove somewhere I was no longer unmindful of my surroundings. I was on alert, scanning for people or cars that might be following me, shadows with some dark intent. Even at home I worried, because my bedroom window didn't open and I would have no escape route if someone broke in. I imagined hoisting my bedside table to break the window and wondered if I could do it cleanly and quickly enough.

I could feel myself sliding into dysfunction, fuelled by fear and paranoia. My anxieties were amplified in the echo chamber of my mind. Had I been able to talk to Terry or any of my friends, there might have been some relief, a dilution of the dark viscosity of my thoughts. But I chose to heed the warnings that, for my own safety and the safety of everyone around me, I should stay quiet. Loose lips sink ships.

My mother's worry about how I was dealing with what I'd been told was matched by her relief at no longer having to lie to me. I didn't see her frequently once she'd moved to Halifax, but when I did visit, I could tell she was grateful she no longer had to carry the knowledge alone when Stan was inside. We talked about incidents from the past, and I drew new significance from events that had just seemed odd. She nodded as I made connections and drew new conclusions. The threats hanging over us coloured everything and there was great comfort in being with someone else who understood that. But then I would go back to the imposed silence of my own life.

I've wondered what would have happened, how it might have been different, if I'd told Terry. Maybe I underestimated him. Maybe he would have risen to the challenge, been able to comfort and reassure me, been willing to protect me if needed. But I didn't tell him and we increasingly grew apart, the secret a fog between us that we couldn't disperse.

Stan came out to see Mom when he could, flying in "the Bird"—the government-funded aircraft of the Weird World—if it was coming our way. Occasionally he caught a riskier commercial flight. If I could get away from work, I would join them for a day or two.

One night as we sat eating a takeout dinner in a motel room—I don't remember where—Stan began to receive a message. I could tell when it happened because he would grow still and preoccupied, focusing on the code tapping in the receiver that was hidden in his wallet and vibrating through his back pocket.

"Butt call alert," I joked, aware that the message could herald something not at all funny.

Mom handed him a little notepad and a pen and he began writing random letters and numbers. It was always difficult to wait for the message to be transmitted and for Stan to decode it. It could be something harrowing. Occasionally, it was just an observation or even a joke. The guys liked to tease him, Stan said.

On this night the message was about Terry.

"He's taken your car to a used-car dealer on Rothesay Avenue," Stan said. I could picture the car lots that lined that street. "He's getting them to value it. The guys want to know if you knew he was doing this."

I shook my head. Terry wanted to buy a van for his painting business. He'd floated the idea that I trade in my car, the beautiful little Prelude I'd bought myself after I'd graduated from university. He framed such a trade as an investment in our future. We argued about it. I thought the matter was decided. Now I had access to intelligence that indicated Terry hadn't given up. The car was mine, registered in my name. Terry could shop it around all he wanted but he couldn't sell it. Still, I was shaken by his sneakiness, and by this secret window on his activities in my absence.

That may have been the factor that finally tipped the scales and steered me to my decision. I could not be so isolated, attempting to have relationships with people I could not share the most relevant details of my life with. I could not live in continual fear, looking at everyone around me with suspicion. I thought the revelation that we were targeted by the Mafia had destroyed my ability to live a normal life. I dreaded being left alone with that knowledge once Mom disappeared inside.

This fear, of being abandoned with such dire information, made me feel profoundly alone. It had preoccupied me for months, eating at my confidence.

Finally, it seemed the only solution. I would go inside too. I would join Stan and Mom. Maybe Ted would come too, once he knew. It was both a relief and a defeat, putting my new-found independence into someone else's hands and consigning my future to an invisible world in which my activities, my acquaintances, and my opportunities would be limited. It felt like jumping off a cliff into the unknown and hoping for a soft landing.

But I thought of how it would be to live without fear, to no longer look over my shoulder. I decided I needed that more than I needed some undefined freedom. I knew it would be a final decision, no turning back, and I tried and failed to think of any draw or pull strong enough to make me remain outside. There were friendships, the hope of a career, dreams of travel, the wish for a partner and maybe children someday, but it was all amorphous and so much less real than the daily sense of dread.

"We will have work for you," Stan promised, after I told them. I could tell he and Mom were relieved I would be with them inside, and safe. They had a vision of their lives together inside. Stan said Sybil was happy with her life outside on the West Coast, so once Mom went inside they could finally, really be partners. And now it wouldn't mean being separated from me. But I was not excited. I was resigned.

Stan had an idea, he told me—one he'd have to talk to the other leaders about. He was trying to give me tools to imagine a new life.

"What would you think about writing a history of the Weird World? It's something we've talked about, something we need. It could be an important document if we need to convince government to continue our funding. We always worry about budget cuts."

"You want a history of this secret world no one's allowed to talk about?" I asked, incredulous.

"It would only be for the Privy Council, military leaders . . . but it could be vital one day," he answered. "It would mean you'd have to travel to all the facilities, interview a lot of people, capture their stories."

He knew I dreamed of travelling and that would be one of the most difficult things to give up, along with my work reporting. It was the consolation prize, an offering meant to blunt the losses. So it was decided. I would move to Halifax, to be closer to Mom while we waited for the all-clear to go inside. That would allow our security coverage to double up and make us safer.

I could not tell Terry, or anyone, but I began laying the groundwork for my move. It was critical I get Terry's co-operation to sell the house. His name was on the mortgage too, and I couldn't allow him to hold up my plans. He'd been talking about going out west again, about all the lucrative job opportunities in beautiful, remote places in British Columbia. He knew I missed B.C. so I suggested a plan to him. A false plan.

"Maybe we should sell the house. You could go ahead and get established, and I'll go to Halifax and get my education degree so I could teach, and join you later."

"What about reporting? You love your job." He was proud of my work.

"I could always come back to it. But there wouldn't be reporting jobs in remote B.C. or that kind of place. Besides, it's a one-year degree," I argued. "Then we could go anywhere."

He was intrigued by the idea of a new adventure, and it didn't take long for him to agree.

"When the house sells, we can buy you a van and you can take some of the furniture with you," I suggested. Like me, Terry loved a road trip.

I felt sick at the deception and had to live with that for the couple of months it took to sell the house and wrap up my life in Saint John. I stayed busy at work and away from home as much as possible. It was excruciating, trying to pretend we were launching a new phase of our lives together when in fact I was preparing to walk away. I still cared about Terry; I mourned the exhilaration of the connection we'd shared, the times we'd spent dreaming of a future together. But his inability to discern my deceit and intuit the coming end confirmed for me that it was the right decision. We were no longer attuned. Besides, I comforted myself, if he knew my real story, he'd probably be relieved to be rid of me.

When I gave my notice at the paper, my bosses thought I was crazy.

"This is a great job, Pauline. You have prospects here. Are you sure?"

No, I wasn't sure, but I couldn't tell them so. They wrote generous letters of recommendation for me, and the reporters and editors in the newsroom presented me with gifts and good wishes on my last day. They couldn't understand why I'd leave such a prized reporting job without another job nailed down, and from their point of view it did seem frivolous and irresponsible.

I left Saint John with my car packed to the roof with belongings, my cats howling in the big wicker laundry basket in the back, and a bizarre sense of unreality. Movers would bring my furniture the next week. I'd gone to Halifax a few weekends earlier and rented a cheap apartment, not far from Mom's. I'd had an interview with a television station that was interested in hiring me as a news producer. They'd told me to call once I arrived in town.

I arrived in Halifax in early July, hopeful that job would carry me through until we were cleared to go inside, however long that took. It would be an interesting job, probably hard to leave when the time came, and I felt bad that they'd invest in training me for what might be a short tenure. I needn't have worried. When I got to Halifax and called the man who'd interviewed me, I was told he'd been fired and no one there had any record of my coming. I decided it wasn't wise to be aggressive, so I restated my interest and continued to look for work.

The local newspaper gave me an interview and asked if I'd be interested in working in the paper's bureau in Yarmouth, a small town more than three hours away. I explained that I had to be in Halifax for family reasons, but there was no Halifax job. I made the rounds at other media outlets, but there was nothing available.

I took a job waitressing in a motel restaurant to pay the rent. The tips were poor, but I met a man staying in the motel who was looking for someone to drive a truck delivering heavy equipment around the province. It was temporary, but the money was good, so I did that for a couple of months. I liked being on the road, driving the truck. When that job ended, I still couldn't find a reporting job so I went to work part-time at a fabric store and started a small design and dressmaking business on the side. I found a partner who also worked at the fabric store and we rented a studio and made prom and wedding dresses, drapes, and on one occasion a dozen kilts for a women's lacrosse team. It was hard to make a living at this, but I was doing some freelance writing as well and managed to make ends meet. Some nights I would come back to my tiny apartment with its outdated shag rug and try to remember what it had felt like to have a career, a fiancé, a house, a future. It seemed as though I'd stumbled into someone else's life.

One night as I was getting ready to go to bed there was a terrible ruckus in the hallway outside my third-floor apartment. It began near my door. I could hear someone crashing against the wall, and grunts as at least two people struggled. The wall shook with the violence of it. The fighting—I was sure that's what it was—moved farther down the hallway. I wanted to open my door and look, but I was too afraid. I called Mom and told her what was going on.

"Just keep your door locked and stay back from it." She was frightened too.

"Should I call the police?"

It was always a question because of Stan's stories of cases in which police on local forces had been found to be corrupt, working with organized crime. Calling them wasn't an obvious choice. While Mom was contemplating that option, the noise suddenly stopped. I realized I was trembling.

"I think it's over, whatever it was," I told her.

"I was going to tell you to use your radio," she said. I thought of the small transistor radio Stan had given me, that had been adapted so I could call for help—but only if I thought I was at serious risk.

"If you use it to call for help, the guys will come, and they'll have to reveal themselves, and that could put them in danger," Stan had warned me.

Mom and I agreed I would use it if there was any more commotion in the hallway, near my door. I lay in bed unable to sleep.

The intensity of the threats against us, or at least my perception of danger, seemed to be accelerating. A few weeks earlier, my car had been stolen and not found for three days. When it turned up, abandoned in a grocery-store parking lot, it had been badly damaged. It needed a new front end, a new clutch, and a rebuilt engine.

"Wow, someone was really determined to drive the piss out of it," the guy at the service counter of the repair shop commented.

I'd talked to Stan on the phone after the car was found. He'd told me our guys had picked up the two men who'd stolen it. They'd confessed it was meant as a threat, a means of destabilizing me and making me feel vulnerable.

"But why?" I asked. "What's the point?"

"It's psychological warfare," he said. "The more unsteady you are, the more likely you are to be easily recruited, turned. They have plans for you. That's part of what we're trying to protect you from."

A few days after the fighting in my hallway, Stan called Mom. He was inside, but had ventured out to a pay phone to tell her about the man who'd been killed outside my door. He said what I'd heard was someone coming after me who was intercepted by my security coverage, who'd shot the intruder.

"I didn't hear a gunshot." The words felt unreal, and Mom's more so.

"He must have had a silencer," Mom said.

The next day I searched the hallway for any sign of a shooting—blood, a bullet hole—but there was nothing. I continued down the hall, forcing myself not to run from the scene of horror I imagined, even if I couldn't see it, and out to my newly repaired car. I stalled it as I backed out of the parking spot. My legs were jerky from tension and wouldn't operate the clutch smoothly. As I lurched and jerked my way out of the lot, I felt myself teetering on the precipice of a dark hole. I could feel the dreaded bubble of anxiety in my chest. I worried I was going to crack, go back to those terrible days of anxiety in grade twelve.

"I need medication," I told Stan the next time we talked, when he'd arrived for a short visit. "I have to go and see someone."

"You can't talk to anyone about this, about what's causing your stress," he said quietly. He reached out to touch my hand. "I'm sorry."

But there was help. Within a week I received a package in the mail. A bottle of pills I recognized as the anti-anxiety drug Anafranil, and a long letter from a man who introduced himself as the psychiatrist at PH. It started:

Dear Miss P,

Few young people have to face the realities you are facing. (A) WD [my father's initials]. (B) Weird World that so far is sort of hazy if real, and at times seemingly unreal. (C) Leaving the known world for a new life in an unknown and untried world. Scary? Yes, for anyone who is not an idiot. So don't be too hard on yourself.

He said the pills he'd sent would last for a while but he couldn't reliably send medication by mail, and I would have to see a doctor to get a prescription.

You can't tell your doctor the truth, so it is hard for him to help you. To a degree it defeats the purpose for which you go to him. Tell him pressures of no permanent employment are a good deal of the cause of anxiety. That is at

least part of the truth. Once in here we will soon have you
freed from the need for medication of any kind.

The pills were enough to dampen the adrenalin cascade and
hyper-arousal that kept me from sleeping and flooded me with
foreboding. They helped me continue to run my business while
we waited for word that it would be safe to go.

On Stan's next visit, we once again left the city and headed
west on the highway toward New Brunswick. It was early fall
and the leaves were just beginning to turn colour—golden
first, the reds to follow later. We were driving along a remote
stretch of Cumberland County, an area that would in years to
come be part of the route for a new toll highway. But on that
day there was only a two-lane route and trees as far as the eye
could see.

"If you look over there to the left, up that hill, that's where
one of the homes is," Stan said out of the blue from the back seat.
"PP, Place of Peace," he added. Our eyes followed his directions
but there was nothing to see except forest. "They know we're
driving past," he continued. I turned and saw he was taking
notes. He was receiving a message, not from our coverage but
from the staff at the nearby hidden institution, he said.

"Pull over," he told Mom, who was driving. She complied and
we sat idling by the side of the road while Stan continued to
scratch code on his notebook.

"They want to know if we'd be willing to drive a little closer
so some of them could see you."

"Why?" I thought it sounded creepy. "Who are they?"

Stan said mostly they were people I wouldn't know, but there
was one exception. My half-brother Tom was there. He'd been
brought there to work on an electronics project.

"He'd like to see his little sister," Stan smiled. I tried to imagine Tom somewhere in the woods not far away. Tom the brash party guy, now hidden away and hungry for the sight of his sister. I looked at Mom. She raised her eyebrows in question.

"Okay."

Stan directed Mom back onto the highway and a few kilometres down the road he told her to turn from the asphalt onto a dirt lane. We drove through thick forest a few more kilometres up a hill.

"You can stop here," Stan said as the road started to flatten. "They're just over there, watching through the trees."

We looked over but could see nothing. And yet it did feel as though we were being watched. The power of suggestion, or maybe some underutilized sensory ability? I scrutinized the brush and branches looking for even a glimpse of clothing or colour.

"How would you feel about taking a little walk up the road for a couple of minutes?" Stan asked. "They'd like to see you better."

"I'd like to see them too!" Being so close to these people, to one of the secret communities—to visible proof of their existence—was tantalizing and frustrating.

"You long to see into their world and they long to see out," Stan said. "But they can't be visible to you, in case anyone else is watching, even all the way out here. It's too dangerous."

He said we could just walk a hundred metres up the road and then come back.

"Don't wave. Just act as though you're stretching your legs after a long drive. And if you see anyone, anything, don't react."

I agreed and we got out of the car, Mom and I. We walked up the road. The sensation of being closely watched made me want to run, to duck back into the car. I could tell we were moving awkwardly, woodenly, up this gravel catwalk.

"Can you see anything?" I whispered to Mom. I could see her scanning the woods as eagerly as I, but she shook her head.

A few minutes later we were back in the car. I was quiet with disappointment, thinking that every time there was a possibility of encountering some concrete evidence of the Weird World, it never materialized. Always I was built up and let down.

"They say thanks," Stan said from the back. "Pauline, Tom says you've grown into a beautiful young woman. He says he can't wait to meet you again, once you're inside."

Whenever that is, I thought.

SEVENTEEN

I STILL HAVE THE carpet sample. It's a small square, about the size of my palm, in a rich blue, like the ocean on a sunny day. Stan chose it for me and brought it to me from inside, for my approval. This was to be the carpet in the living room of my new home. My home on the inside.

After I'd made my decision to go into protection, Stan told me a small cabin would be built for me at PH, Place of Hope, not far from the house being built for him and Mom. He drew me a sketch of the plan, joking about his lack of drawing skills. It was a simple rectangular building with one bedroom and a small deck out front that would look out at the mountains, and from which he said I would be able to hear the stream that ran nearby.

Stan continued to deliver letters to me from people inside whenever he came out to visit. There were letters for Mom too. Dozens of them. Most of the writers were commiserating over the delays to our arrival inside. They said a party was being planned to celebrate our arrival.

As the fall went on, Stan began to convey hopeful messages from the intelligence team. There had been a tip that led to a raid somewhere in California where documents had been confiscated that named Ted and me. These were resulting in more leads to be followed and more arrests, as well as helping to unravel the tangle of underworld ties that was preventing us from disappearing. It seemed, he said, the threats would soon be neutralized.

"I think you should buy yourselves some party dresses," Stan said happily on one visit. He said a rack of dresses and suits had been brought to PH on the train so those anxious to greet us would also have something fancy to wear for the welcoming party. He described how the promise of a celebration was so meaningful in that place where too often the news was grim.

As my first Christmas in Halifax approached, Mom and I decided we would go and visit Ted, with a stopover in Hamilton to visit her brother, Murray, and his family. I have a photograph from that stopover. It was a day or two after Christmas and in it I'm wearing a bright blue blouse given to me that day by Murray, his wife, Grace, and their three daughters, my cousins Cathy, Jenny, and Alison. We are all in the photo in front of their mantel. Someone had set the auto-timer and our faces are lit up with the hilarity of getting into position before the ten-second countdown ends and the camera flashes. But my eyes are red; it's clear I've been crying. I cringe at this memory.

Mom had begged Stan to be able to tell her brother that this was likely the last time she would see him. He said he'd talked to the leaders inside and they'd given permission. She could say she was going into protective custody, but could give no further details. Would that do? Yes. She was relieved—that would do.

That afternoon at Murray's we all sat around their living room.

"We have something we need to tell you," Mom began. I could see she was struggling with what to say. "I need you to promise you won't talk about this with anyone, no one."

They exchanged puzzled glances, and then nodded.

"Okay," Murray said, speaking for his family. I could see the skepticism in his expression. "We won't."

"We've come because we won't be able to see you any more after this," Mom said. I was suddenly filled with the sadness of it, of Mom once again being separated from her family. I was also embarrassed by the cloak-and-dagger routine, knowing that it sounded melodramatic, and that after disappearing twice before and emerging months and thousands of kilometres away without any reason or explanation, we had little credibility. I began to cry, and I could see how my tears alarmed them all.

"Oh Ruth, we'll have more visits," began Grace, attempting to be soothing.

"No, Grace, we won't be able to visit you again."

That was when Murray interjected. "What do you mean? What are you talking about?"

"We're going into a type of protective custody. I can't tell you any details. Just that we aren't safe right now and we will be when we get there. I don't know exactly when that will happen, but we're waiting to go now."

It was not an announcement anyone could have anticipated or imagined. There was a stunned silence, and then, cautiously, some questions.

"I'm sorry, I just can't tell you any more," Mom said. I had progressed to hiccupping sobs that only intensified with my attempts to suppress them. I felt ridiculous. We were creating a scene. *They must think we're crazy*, I thought.

If so, they were too kind, too concerned, to say so. Grace served us a large holiday dinner that night and we all behaved as though nothing strange had happened. My cousins and I laughed appreciatively as our parents told family stories and jokes. Occasionally I noticed one of them looking at me thoughtfully, speculatively. I could only smile back ruefully. *I know*, I thought, *we are very odd.*

After an awkward and emotional goodbye we continued on to Vancouver the next day. I couldn't help imagining their conversation after we'd gone; they would be speculating and probably questioning our sanity.

Ted met us at the Vancouver airport. He was excited to see us, happy to be escorting us in his sporty little Celica to the motel where we were staying. He negotiated the frenetic Vancouver traffic smoothly and ably. We would not tell Ted anything on this trip. It was meant to be a chance to enjoy some time with him, because this was possibly the last time together as a family when he was not burdened with the knowledge that we were planning to disappear. The plan was that once we got the all-clear to go inside, we would come back to tell Ted, on our way to PH. Despite the bittersweet purpose of the trip we had fun together, as we always did with Ted. There is a photo of the three of us in the motel room, red-faced from laughing. I think for Mom and me there was a desperation in our giddiness, a need to make the most of this time with each other.

One afternoon, while Ted was at work, Mom and I went shopping and chose our party dresses. I went with blue—no surprise—with a fitted bodice and a flowing skirt. But Mom's was none of the muted greens, beiges, or greys she usually chose. It was a fuchsia-pink moiré taffeta, a colour for a celebration, she said. She was excited, imagining what she thought of as a homecoming, a new and meaningful life, freed from the struggles and dangers of being outside. She allowed herself a bit of anticipation but it was soon tempered by her sadness at the idea of leaving Ted at the end of the week, and more permanently in the weeks or months to come. If we hugged him a little longer or more tightly as he left us at the airport to head home, he didn't seem to notice.

Flying back from one coast to the other, I thought about the uncertainty of life, how it is such conceit to believe we can plan our lives. Doing so is a challenge to the universe to make mockery of our schemes.

ON STAN'S NEXT visit he said the undercover staff was still making progress in freeing us up to go. Several more people had been picked up and interrogated, producing a cache of documents and new information. There was one progress report that, while appalling, seemed to partly answer many questions.

"It turns out," Stan reported, "this is part of a structure that your father set up years ago. He was putting plans in place for you and Ted, and Tom and Linda, to run particular aspects of his syndicate. You were only small children at the time, but he was orchestrating your future in crime."

Part of the intelligence included his fallback plans for what would happen if we didn't co-operate, ways and means of implicating us and roping us in, forcing us to tow the line. If all that failed, if we disappeared or were for any reason not controllable, there were contingencies for ensuring the business of the syndicate continued in other hands without our interference. There were differing interpretations of what that might mean, Stan said, all of them horrifying to contemplate.

"In one scenario you were to be kept drugged and restrained," he told me.

I now think back to my reaction to such things at the time in terms of the frog in the pot. According to that aphorism, a frog tossed into boiling water will jump out. If it's put in a pot of cold water that slowly but continuously gets hotter, it won't react and will slowly allow itself to boil. I had become desensitized by the steady drip of the unthinkable, my emotional responses diminished. That was how I managed the information that my father had plotted such cruel scenarios to keep Ted and me in line and further his crime and profit. I nodded as if I were taking it all in, but I couldn't have been. It would have been too much to internalize. Much of what I should have been feeling simply didn't register, not deeply.

Stan told me how he hated telling me such things, wished he could just be my papa and not the guy who always brought bad news and nightmare stories. I think he tried hard to offer compensation.

"You're finally going to get that horse," he said at some point during those months of waiting. He brought me a blurry Polaroid picture of a horse grazing near a fence—a deep chestnut gelding with a dark mane and tail. The background was a wash of indistinct greens, grass melting into shrubs and trees. *Ha! The promise of another horse for another move,* I thought. I remembered my bitter disappointment when the horse that was the enticement for the move to Saint John had not materialized; once we arrived and saw the reality of the suburban neighbourhood and not just the fuzzy black-and-white photo torn from a newspaper real estate advertisement, I realized it had never really been a possibility. Something in me resisted the lure of this new fuzzy photograph, although I was touched by Stan's delight in this gift to me, a welcome home, an offering to give me hope.

"He's there now, waiting for you."

He wanted to make this move enticing, and he'd often tell me of others who'd gone inside and come to believe there was nowhere else they'd rather be. The horse, the history project, the little house, all were meant to ease my way to the Weird World.

"The way your house is designed, you could add a bedroom or two in the future," Stan said, smiling, his blue eyes twinkling. "You might meet some fine young guy once you get there."

"Oh, you mean one of the gangsters in the cells?"

He laughed. "No, I mean one of our guys. Someone in administration, or on the medical staff, or the intelligence team. You never know."

The idea held no appeal. I didn't want a romance with some freak living in a shadow world. A freak just like I would soon be, I realized.

In hindsight, I think that made meeting Kevin seem shiny and compelling. Friends we had in common introduced us at a dinner party, and soon we were spending a lot of time together. He was interesting, earnest, reliable.

The budding relationship was nurtured in rarefied air and grew in the heat of extreme circumstances, with the context of a ticking clock making every moment significant.

As I got to know Kevin, the colours seemed brighter, sensations amplified, feelings heightened by the expectation of their impermanence. I knew that our relationship was doomed, that there could be no future with a man who lived in the outside world, which I was poised to leave. But there was sweetness in that. It was perhaps an unconscious attempt to hold on and stay in the real world.

Kevin was curious about the world, and liked to travel. I joked with a friend that he was a Renaissance man: sailor, snorkeller, traveller, curler, woodworking craftsman, entrepreneur. He had a great day job and a little side business, and he was taking evening classes at the university. He loved jazz, had a connoisseur's delight in stand-up comedy, and could even cook a decent meal, which he did for me in his cramped apartment.

The first time I cooked for him at my place, we sat talking for hours after the meal. He told me about his travels, his family, how he'd left home young and gone west, as so many young Maritimers did in those years. He talked about his job and his interest in investing. He seemed optimistic about the future and, in contrast to the madness of my own life, a bastion of steadiness.

Stan was in town with Mom that week, and the next day I went over for lunch and told them about the date.

"But he did talk a lot about money, investing," I recalled, picking over what felt like the one negative from the evening, testing it on them.

"He's probably trying to impress you," Stan said. "He wants you to take him seriously."

"He sounds nice," Mom added. "When do I get to meet him?"

I was surprised, given our circumstances, that they weren't discouraging me from seeing more of Kevin. I was relieved, because I'd been lonely living in suspended animation, having left Terry so many months earlier and moved away from my closest friends.

In the months that followed, Kevin would drop by my studio during his lunch hours, or if he happened to be going by. I would hear his footsteps on the stairs up to our workroom, where the floor would be scattered with fabrics in various stages of being cut, pinned, and sewn. We'd go for a coffee or a walk, make plans for a hike, a sail, or a drive on the weekend.

It came to feel inevitable in the growing intimacy of our relationship that I would have to tell him something, prepare him for an eventual parting. On the night I revealed my story to him I'd intended to tell him only that I couldn't make any kind of commitment, that there were things going on in my life that meant I would be leaving, maybe soon. At first I tried to give the impression I might move away for work. Of course, my vagueness created more mystery and led to more questions.

We'd been walking in one of the small parks in downtown Halifax, and found a bench under the trees, the glare from nearby street lights softened by the leaves overhead.

I ended up telling him everything. We sat for a long time. He was shaken by my story, incredulous, worried. I was shaking as I told it, aware that I had just brought him into a world from which he might, should, bolt. It was as though I was watching myself with disbelief as the words were coming out of my mouth, and to a man I had known for only a few months. I hadn't told Terry or any of my friends and yet I was telling Kevin. Maybe it was timing; maybe the longer I held the story inside, the more I felt I might burst with it and this was the relief valve.

Kevin never questioned the truth of my story and he didn't shy away from it, even when I warned him that knowing it might put him in danger. He sat, holding my hand, and listened, occasionally interrupting with a question, but mostly just listening.

When I was done, I felt deflated, quiet with the stillness that fills your body and mind after the exertion of a long run or an exhausting workout. I half expected someone to appear from the shadows and drag me away. Stan had warned me of the dangers of talking, even saying that if I became a security problem, I could be taken without warning, for my safety and that of Mom and the people protecting us. I'd sworn secrecy, and now I'd violated that. Even as I nervously scanned the park around us, I realized it felt good, like exhaling after holding your breath too long.

Did Kevin tell me that night that he would go inside with me, or did he wait, think about it, and tell me the next day? It's strange that I can't remember. But whenever it happened, he was unequivocal: when I went, he would go with me if I wanted him. He'd lived away from his family for a long time, he said. He could leave them again. I was relieved at the idea of not facing the future alone. I was grateful to be with someone who would make this sacrifice to be with me. These feelings overwhelmed any doubts I might have had about forging such a link when the path ahead was so uncertain, about committing myself to someone I really didn't know very well. But that is the path we started down together that night under the trees, and we set our feet to it with determination. When we decided to get married, I worried about telling Mom and Stan, but they weren't surprised, only concerned. The next time Stan was in town, the four of us sat down and together officially told Kevin the story he already knew. I didn't let on to them how much of it I had already told him, and he managed to appear suitably taken aback by the details and the conditions.

"You won't be able to tell your family what you're getting into," Stan warned him. He and Mom were worried about how Kevin would handle the need for secrecy. Of course the intelligence unit had checked Kevin out, Stan told me. They had to be sure the Mafia wasn't using and positioning him to get close to me. The report on him came back clean. He would be welcomed inside, the message had come back from the administrators there. They were already planning for how they could put his specialized telecommunications skills to work, Stan said.

We were married in June, and Stan took the remarkable risk of coming out to be at our wedding and give me away. Of course I didn't—couldn't—invite my real father.

Now there were three of us waiting to go inside, living life on hold, hoping for our new lives to begin, to rescue us from the sick anticipation of leaving everything we knew behind. But new complications continued to interfere with that. Stan told us that several people had been picked up around us. Our security people were worried there was a leak, that somehow our plans had been leaked to the O. Under interrogation, the thugs admitted they'd been sent to deliver warnings—my grandfather Cliff or other family members would pay if Mom or I were to disappear. We were stuck. We couldn't risk triggering a disaster, we agreed. The undercover agents and intelligence team were following leads and links as quickly as they could, Stan tried to reassure us, but no one could say how long it would take.

The uncertainty was becoming unbearable. I contemplated a stopgap future, never fully committed to the time and place in which I was living, always poised to move on to a new, safer life, but always conflicted. I was desperate to leave the fear and drama behind, but I tried not to think of the permanence of the move, the inability to escape if I changed my mind once I got there. Sometimes I was secretly relieved when we received word of new delays—"not yet, soon we hope."

I didn't know what to hope for, but I knew I was losing faith.

EIGHTEEN

M Y BROTHER WAS a small boy, but in his teens he had a dramatic growth spurt.

"He's shooting up," my mother said.

Suddenly he was giraffe-like, long legs and arms, his gangly limbs and neck-craning height discordant with his still-childish face, but that's when the girls began to take notice of him. Somehow his feet anticipated the new height, his body knowing that larger feet would be needed to balance the budding stature. I was struck by their size one evening as we watched television together in the family room in our pyjamas and sock feet. I said nothing at the time, but the next time he annoyed me I cruelly told him to flap those big feet and fly away. Siblings have a guided missile-like instinct for the soft places of insecurity. Ted, on the other hand, was gracious with his knowledge of my own weaknesses and faults and never retaliated.

As an adult, Ted grew to six-foot-four. But in some respects he would always be my little brother and I would always be the protective, sometimes domineering older sister. I worried about him as Kevin, Mom, and I waited to go inside. He was living in Vancouver in happy ignorance of the dangers swirling around us all. Drawing from our occasional phone calls and a rare letter or two, I pictured him in his world, working in a home electronics store, playing semi-pro beach volleyball at Kitsilano Beach, having drinks and mimosa brunches with friends, bombing around the city in his sporty little Celica. I envied his carefree freedom even as I sometimes clenched with fear for his safety. I couldn't stop thinking about how awful it would be for him to be left behind when we disappeared.

Stan told us that Ted was essentially surrounded, that not only was he living at Dad's, or at least in the condo with whichever double was playing Dad at the time, but he had been strategically befriended by Mafia minions who were keeping track of him, working to win his trust, and possibly trying to draw him in to illegal money-making schemes that would implicate him and allow them to control him.

"He's not doing anything illegal," Stan was quick to reassure us. "It's more subtle than that. A slow seduction."

I bit my tongue, gritted my teeth when Ted talked about these friends, handsome socially able young men whom I thought of as opportunistic high flyers. They lived as though the world was their oyster; there were trips to Mexico, skiing excursions, and always lots of partying. But the veneer of their pretty world covered something much darker, we were told.

The worry and the months dragged on, with no all-clear for us to go inside. Losing faith that it would ever happen, I once again started looking for work as a reporter. A new television station called MITV, which would become a Global affiliate, was opening in Halifax, I read in the paper. I called the news director, Bruce Graham, who until recently had been a popular anchor with a rival TV station. He agreed to see me, even though I was a print reporter with no television experience.

"I'll work for you for a week for free," I told him, hoping I could show him in that time that I could make the transition to broadcasting. It worked, and soon I was once again doing what I loved. I gave up the dressmaking studio and threw myself into TV reporting, learning to do stand-ups for the camera and to write for the pictures. I began to specialize in court reporting, as I had done at one point at *The Telegraph-Journal*, and covered murder cases as well as the trial of abortion doctor Henry Morgentaler in his fight with the Nova Scotia government to continue offering the procedure at his Halifax clinic. I filled in as an anchor and even spent a couple of weeks presenting weather forecasts. I produced my first television documentary, and longed to do more.

I'd just been promoted to assignment editor when Stan let us know the intelligence people thought they'd made a significant arrest—a breakthrough, he called it, one that might finally clear the way for us to go. It was time, he said, to tell Ted. When the kingpin who'd been arrested was interrogated, he'd let slip information suggesting the O had some kind of a plan that focused on Ted. The details weren't clear, but the idea was concerning, Stan said. It seemed the Mob was closing in around my brother. It was time he had the information he needed to help protect himself, and to prepare himself for our pending disappearance.

We went to Vancouver for what we expected to be our last chance to see Ted, to tell him the terrible secret, warn him of the dangers, and offer him the opportunity to come inside with us.

I remembered the terror I'd felt that night in the Sussex motel room. I dreaded inflicting that on Ted.

He met us at the airport in Vancouver. It was the first time I'd met Elaine, the woman he'd been seeing for a while. Their relationship seemed serious and I quickly saw what had attracted him. In contrast to his height, she was petite, with a pretty face and a sensuous dark riot of long, wavy hair. Intelligence and warmth were apparent in her greeting and her conversation as we waited for our bags.

Ted drove us to the motel that Stan had instructed us to check in to, on Kingsway in a commercial area east of the downtown. We all spent the evening there, catching up and getting to know Elaine. We laughed a lot, as we always did with Ted, and then we made plans to see him the next day. A short time after they had driven off, Stan arrived. He would be with us to tell Ted the grim story that would change his life. Stan hugged us, and handed me a key for the adjoining room.

"Courtesy of the government," he said. I smiled weakly. I'd lost count of how many motel rooms the government had rented for us, all the times when we were on the run. Invariably they were housekeeping units—clean, practical, with outdated furnishings. Never a chain hotel or anything fancy. Always these anonymous, utilitarian backdrops. Suddenly I was filled with rage, and sick of it all. Sick of the drama of our lives, sick of constantly being on alert for the next crisis, and sick of these interchangeably shabby rooms. Why couldn't the government spring for a Hilton on the occasion of ruining my brother's life?

"I'm going to hit the sack," I said, knowing Mom and Stan would be glad to have time alone together.

The next day, after Ted finished work, he came back to the motel room where we were all nervously waiting for him. Just as I had been at the Sussex motel, he was astonished to see Stan, and looked back and forth from Mom to me as if asking what this was all about. We didn't tell him immediately. He must have been wondering where Sybil was. We ordered Chinese food and sat around the little table. Ted and Stan did most of the talking, catching up. Mom was quiet, occasionally interjecting or commenting. I sat back, wishing the moment was just as it appeared: an old friend and family enjoying a reunion as we passed through town.

"We have something we need to tell you, Ted," Stan began. I don't remember exactly how the conversation went from there. Ted probably made a joke, trying to counteract our sudden seriousness. I think he grew up thinking it was his role to counter any tension, keep things light and amicable. The details of the conversation are gone, but I can still see his reaction as the story was revealed to him and he began to understand the implications, the effect this had had on our lives, and the impact it would continue to have. He leaned forward, his elbows on his knees, and stared at the floor. His forehead furrowed, and he began to chew at his lower lip, running his upper teeth across it, over and over. Occasionally he shook his head and looked to me as if for confirmation that this was really happening, as if hoping I might suddenly jump up and say it was all a joke or a mistake. At some point he stood up and started pacing, unable to withstand the physical inertia in the roar of his racing thoughts and emotions. It was horrible to watch as the weight of the news settled on him, as his shoulders rounded and his head dropped, as if in submission to the gravity of the situation.

We were there for hours and in the end Stan asked Ted's permission for a tracking device to be put on his car. Stan gave

Ted the same kind of pocket radio he'd given me and showed him how to position the buttons to activate an emergency call. He also gave him a phone number.

"Memorize it, and only use it if you think your life is in danger."

Ted was stricken, pale, and quiet as he pulled on his jacket. He hugged us as he left, promising to come back the next day. Then—he told me years later—he drove to see Elaine, seeking comfort perhaps, maybe guidance or reassurance. Despite the warning not to divulge what he'd been told, he confided to her the broad strokes of what he'd learned.

"He was so upset, and embarrassed," Elaine recalled. "I was so worried about him."

We were worried too, but a few days later we left him alone with this terrible knowledge, unsure of when or if we would see him again.

Later, when Ted and Elaine became engaged, we were still waiting for the all-clear to go inside, the hopeful arrest having led to only more loose threads. Stan and Mom went back to Vancouver to bring Elaine into the picture. They didn't know Ted had already revealed part of the story. They said in fairness she had to know what she was getting into. Once again they stayed at the motel on Kingsway.

Elaine remembers the night she learned the details of the Weird World and the O. She, Ted, Mom, and Stan had been watching a hockey game on the motel-room TV. It was game one of the 1990 Stanley Cup Final. The Edmonton Oilers and the Boston Bruins were tied at two early in the third overtime when the power went out. There was a twenty-five-minute delay. And that's when she heard the details Ted hadn't told her.

The next day Ted and Elaine went back to the motel. It was a chance to ask questions before Stan and Mom left. Later in the afternoon they went to a nearby restaurant, but Stan decided to stay behind.

The threesome returned an hour or so later to find the door ajar, the room tossed. Some of the furniture had been knocked over. It looked as though there'd been a fight. Mom rushed in, alarmed, and found Stan lying on the floor beside the bed, dazed, with a bad cut on his arm. For Ted and Elaine, it was a dramatic illustration of risk, the danger that could flare without warning.

THE DAY MY brother got married was a tinder-dry scorcher in early August, in the once-sleepy B.C. town of Kelowna, in the Okanagan Valley. The air seemed to shimmer over the road as we drove—Mom, Kevin, and I—to the little church where Ted and Elaine exchanged their vows. We, the family and friends, sweated and swiped damp foreheads, in our dresses and suits, as they made their promises. The pews became an undulant sea of waving wedding programs, as we feebly tried to move the stifling air in some facsimile of a cooling breeze. At twenty-four, Ted looked achingly young and proud. Elaine was beautiful in her brilliantly white gown and flowing dark hair, and in the way she looked up at Ted, more than a foot taller than she. It was meant to be a joyful beginning for them, but our mother could think only of the gathering threats around them that could prevent any future happiness.

Naturally, Ted invited our dad, whom I'd seen only once in the previous decade. Stan and Mom hadn't told Ted that our father was part of the Mafia, thinking that part of the story was too much to burden him with so soon. Dad flew in from Vancouver with my half-brother, Tom. Ted had also invited Mom's siblings, Murray and Penny. Stan noted to Mom and me—as if we needed any reminding—that this meant we were surrounded by doubles, but Ted didn't know. The revelations in Vancouver hadn't included any talk about the doubles. Stan thought it would be too much for Ted, living in the midst of them with that knowledge. But Mom and I steeled ourselves to their presence at the wedding and reception. The idea that these people who looked just like the real Warren, Tom, and Penny were imposters, surgically altered or made up with prosthetics and makeup, was chilling. Mom was jittery, barely able to greet them with stiff civility. She cried during the ceremony, even as she went to the front of the church to do one of the readings. Perhaps people mistook her tears for a sign of overwhelming happiness. I did not.

"Sensitive!" I heard Tom whisper loudly to Dad. They were sitting right behind us in the small church, on the groom's side. I winced, knowing Mom and many others sitting nearby had heard this too.

As the new couple left the church, heading off for pictures by the lake, Ted stopped to hug Mom. He'd been troubled by her emotional response. "It's okay, Muvver," he jollied, using his childhood moniker for our mom.

We were to follow, but Mom wanted to wash her face first. She dabbed powder below her swollen eyes and added a new swipe of lipstick to her lips, hoping to mask her sorrow.

"I hate that they're here pretending to support Ted and Elaine when God knows what they're really plotting," she whispered. She was angry, outraged at the intrusion of the fake Warren, Tom, and Penny. She was also mourning because Ted's wedding day had been tainted by those she knew would use and even destroy him if they deemed it necessary or expedient.

At the lake we all posed for wedding pictures. The bride and groom. The bride and groom with her parents. The bride and groom with his parents.

It was strange to see our parents in such proximity and it was clear even Dad felt the strangeness. "Come on now, Mom and Dad," the photographer chirped, admonishing them for the awkward distance they inserted between themselves, their wooden smiles. He was oblivious to all the years of animosity, resentment, and fear that made the idea of a happy family photograph ridiculously implausible. I squirmed as I watched the photographer attempt to create a scene of closeness.

At the reception and dinner, held in a nearby barn that had been renovated and gentrified as a rental space for large gatherings, I greeted Dad, Tom, and Penny, feeling false and afraid. I knew I seemed cold and distant, and could do nothing about it. I was terrified of raising their suspicions that I was onto them, that I knew they were pretenders, doubles. It was important to behave as normally as possible, Stan had coached us over the phone before we left for the wedding.

"It's mind-bending," my mother whispered to me. Like me, she couldn't stop staring at the small details of their faces and bodies that we each remembered as being distinctive. I was fascinated by how the man calling himself my father looked just as I remembered my dad, perhaps slightly greyer, paunchier. His mannerisms were the same; even the small yellow nevus, an overgrowth of cells on the cornea of his bright-blue right eye, was perfectly replicated. "Contact lenses," Stan would later guess. It was that eye that shook me the most; and his hands, the long fingers and deep nail beds just as I recalled them. *What if he really is my dad?* I asked myself, feeling a terrible and treacherous doubt. My stomach was contracting and I couldn't look any of them in the eye. All I could do was watch them intensely when I thought they wouldn't notice. Their familiar appearance sowed doubt. What if I had cut myself off from my father based on some bizarre fantasy?

Mom was even more shaken after repeated surreptitious looks at her sister. She fixated on Penny's toes, peeking out of her sandals. She said Penny had always had distinctive toes.

"I don't understand how they could make them look the same." She sounded panicky. "Even if she had plastic surgery, how could they copy her bone structure?" I had no answer for her, and wondered if she was facing the same bigger questions that were percolating in my mind, whether she ever questioned the reality of the Mafia threats, the collusion of family members. It seemed that asking her out loud would be too dangerous; that an admission of my own doubts might completely undo the situation, undo her. She left the reception early, as soon as the speeches and the first dances were over. Kevin and I stayed longer. We were a small contingent, Ted's family and friends, among the battalion of Elaine's extended family. It felt important to be there with him. And as disturbing as it was, I was drawn by my curiosity. I wanted more time to examine these supposed imposters. I was fascinated by their banality.

I was leaning against a giant wooden beam watching the dancers when the father imposter approached. I could feel my heartbeat at my throat as I tried to smile naturally. He commented on the meal, complimented Elaine's appearance, smiled at me, and said I was looking well.

"I was hoping to get to know your new husband a bit while we're all here," he said, gesturing across the room toward Kevin. "And I have something for you. Can we all have lunch tomorrow?"

I hesitated, knowing he was noticing my reticence, wondering what he made of it. He smiled encouragingly. I couldn't think of any reasonable reason why a daughter would say no, at least a daughter who didn't think her father was a double or a Mafia kingpin gunning for her, or maybe both, so I said yes. We agreed to meet in the dining room of his hotel the next day.

I slept only fitfully that night. It's just lunch, in a public place, I tried to tell myself. But what if it was a set-up? The food could be poisoned, the drinks drugged. I lay in the motel room envisioning being rendered insensible and hauled off to some awful fate. I plotted excuses for Kevin and me to get away from the table if we sensed anything strange. I castigated myself for these melodramatic imaginings but then remembered the stories I'd been told about the horrifying things Dad and Tom had been involved in, before they were taken. Would their doubles be any less threatening? I thought about the letters the real Tom had written me from inside, and about Stan's descriptions of the real Warren in a prison cell in the Weird World, broken and yet raging and unrepentant, destroyed by his own evil.

We walked into the hotel restaurant the next day at the appointed time. Dad and Tom were seated at a booth. They stood as we approached, hugged me, and shook Kevin's hand. We made small talk about the wedding, I asked about people I'd known in Vancouver; he asked about my work. I tried to be careful in my answers, having been cautioned by Mom not to give away any information that could be used against us.

"Like what?" I'd asked.

"Your routine, your movements, your plans for the rest of your trip." Kevin and I were going to spend some time in British Columbia after the wedding.

When the food came I forced myself to eat some of it. I could feel my cheeks burning. I pictured my mottled neck, the rush of blood to the surface of my skin giving away my nervousness.

I mentally scanned myself for any possible symptoms or signs that would indicate something had been slipped into our food or drinks. I had no idea what that might feel like. I told myself it would be different than the anxiety I was feeling. Somehow we got through the meal. I have no memory of the rest of the conversation, until the meal ended.

"Let's go up to my room," Dad said, speaking directly to me, smiling pleasantly. "I have something for you."

I reacted as if he'd put a gun to my back. My adrenalin spiked, my heart pounded, and I desperately fought to keep my voice steady. *It's happening*, I thought. *He's really going to try to kidnap me or hurt me.* I looked at Kevin, but I couldn't tell what he was thinking.

There was a long pause before my stuttered reply.

"I'll just wait here and visit with Tom if you don't mind bringing it down."

My father, or the man disguised to look like him, gazed at me, his expression unreadable, for what felt like a long time before he reverted back to his usual jovial self.

"Sure, I'll meet you in the lobby in a minute," he said smoothly. "Don't go anywhere." He headed for the elevators and we walked toward the lobby. Tom seemed to be smiling knowingly. I wondered how obvious my fear was to him. I tried to slow my breath and gather my thoughts, reaching for something to say to fill the yawning silence that seemed to betray me, to hiss provocatively about my suspicion, my distrust.

When my father returned he was holding the handle of an expensive-looking airline carry-on bag, white with ribbed seams.

"It's some of your Grandmother Hope's china," he said, handing the bag to me. When I was a teenager visiting him in the summers he'd often cited the inheritance list: "Tom as the eldest son gets the Kenderdine painting, the gun collection, Grandpa's swords, and the war medals. Ted gets my Indian-head painting and the English seaside watercolour, the diamond pinkie ring, and the two Tudor watches—mine and my father's."

I don't remember which of the spoils Linda was to have. We daughters seemed to be afterthoughts when it came to dispersing the family treasures. Still, I was to have the Royal Crown Derby, my Grandmother Dakin's massive china collection—a service for sixteen, complete with serving dishes, coffee and teapots, a milk jug, egg cups, and mustard and candy dishes. It seemed overwhelming. I couldn't imagine where I would keep it all. When I'd visited him, Dad had used the dishes every day, and I did love their delicate cobalt-blue Chinese figures.

As I took the white carry-on from him I remembered Ted describing Dad, living alone in his bachelor condo after Thora had left him, serving his frozen dinners on the delicate gold-rimmed china.

"I'll be sending the rest a bit at a time," he said as I opened the bag to look in. All I could see was bubble wrap surrounding the pieces of china. "No point in waiting till I'm gone for you to enjoy it. I don't need all those settings."

I thanked him, for the china and for the lunch, and said we'd better get back to our motel to check out. I was vague about where we were going from there. "We're going to drive through the mountains."

"Take care, dear," he said as he hugged me, just as my father would have. Dad never said "I love you"; "take care" had always been the substituted expression of caring for every goodbye.

Later that afternoon as we drove through the mountains, Kevin pulled the rental car over at a picnic park. I got out, retrieved the white bag from the trunk, and brought it to a picnic table where I opened it. I took out the bubble-wrap-enclosed pieces and unwrapped each of them. There were several pieces of china, nothing more. Silently I examined the interior and exterior pockets of the bag, running my hand along the seams and into the corners. Looking for listening devices? Planted drugs that could be used to set us up? This was how I now thought. Part of me felt aloof, as if I were watching my careful examination of the bag on the picnic table from a distance, watching myself cautiously peeling back the layers of plastic, and gingerly removing the antique plates and bowls, turning them over in my hands, looking for and not finding anything unusual. That part of me understood how preposterous the scene was, how paranoid the behaviour and the fear.

But when I'd rewrapped the plastic around the dishes, I didn't put them back in the carry-on. Instead I took them to the trunk of the car, opened my suitcase, and tucked them among my clothes. I went back to the picnic table, retrieved the bag, and took it over to a large green garbage can, stuffing it in through the hinged opening in the lid. You couldn't be too careful. I knew what Stan would say, that it might contain a hidden tracking device that would lead the bad guys right to us.

As we pulled back onto the highway the distant, doubting part of me was regretting the waste of such an expensive, well-made bag, speculating that someone would come along and rescue it from the bin and wonder who would throw something like that away and why. A small flickering, demanding awareness was pushing to the surface of my thoughts. I found myself contemplating once again how, if it was all a ruse, if we weren't really being targeted by the Mafia, that would have to mean that the two people I most trusted in my life were actively betraying me for some unimaginable purpose. It would mean my mother had been alienated from her family and torn us from our father based on a lie. It was unthinkable. I could not, would not, believe anyone who loved me would deliberately inflict such damage. Implacable, I pushed the disloyal thoughts away, turned up the car stereo, and gazed at the jagged peaks of the immovable, enduring mountains I had missed so much.

NINETEEN

IT'S MY FIRST night back at the trailer after a harsh, endless winter. My daughters, Avery and Laura, came out with me last weekend, just for the day.

"What I really want for Mother's Day is for you two to spend the afternoon with me and help me open the trailer and get it cleaned up," I told them. They even agreed to stay until after sunset.

Now, with the mouse shit swept up, the counters wiped, and the sheets and towels washed, I am once again writing in this peaceful place. The blue bay lies before me and the early morning bird calls provide accompaniment. A fishing boat putters just offshore; its captain, out checking his lobster traps, motors in small circles around the bobbing buoys that mark them. He comes alongside each one, pulls up the pot, empties his catch, and throws the trap back.

The cyclists are back too, silently whizzing past on the road below in groups of brightly coloured neoprene with matching

helmets, pedalling the ever-popular scenic loop of the Aspotogan
Peninsula. There are few cars on the road and I can pick out
the tourists and day trippers. They always slow as they round the
corner to the west and are confronted by the ocean spread out
before them, with the bleached wood of the picturesque but
tumbledown wharf in the small cove just below me. Many pull
over to gaze, or to get out and take a picture, trying to preserve
this perfect scene. I pull my eyes away, back to the screen in
front of me.

At some point during those years of running and waiting to
go inside, I gave up. I decided there would never be an all-clear
that would allow us to disappear; there would always be some
new complication to prevent our escape. I would never see my
cabin by the stream or my horse. And, increasingly, I began to
allow myself to explore the possibility that none of it was real.
Always, when I felt doubt or questioned details in Stan's stories,
I'd shoved those feelings away, unwilling to allow mistrust to
upend my life. If the Weird World and the threats that had propelled us across the country were not real—if they were part of
some demented ruse—that would mean much of our lives had
been wasted, many relationships lost in the midst of much
unnecessary terror. It would mean I couldn't trust my mother or
the man I loved as a father. I was more afraid of this than I was
of being chased by the Mob.

Once when we were on the run, staying for a few days in a
cottage somewhere in remote rural Nova Scotia, I witnessed
these feelings at work in my mother. It was both disturbing and
a relief. Something Stan had just said didn't jive with what
he'd told her previously. Part of the story didn't line up. I don't
remember the detail. It doesn't matter now. She jumped to her
feet from the chair where she'd been sitting beside him.

"But you said . . ." Her voice was shrill and full of condemnation. I could tell she felt the same fear I did, that if Stan's stories weren't real, it would mean we had built our lives on a sandy foundation of lies that would crumble into meaninglessness.

Mom didn't back away from this fear. She demanded truth. She pushed him relentlessly to explain, which he began to do. Suddenly there were tears on his cheek.

"What?" My mother stopped her interrogation, alarmed. "What is it?"

Stan shook his head, wiping his cheeks.

"Tell me." Her voice was softer now. She was unable to stay angry with the man she loved so completely when he was in some kind of pain. She knelt by him, placing a hand on his shoulder.

"Michael," he finally choked out. Michael, his lost son who'd drowned in a bathtub. My mother could imagine nothing more catastrophic than the death of a child. She was disarmed by her own empathy and turned herself over to comforting Stan. Eventually, he began to speak.

"The guys confirmed it a couple of days ago," he said, his eyes down, his mouth hard. "It was the O. It was not his epilepsy. They killed him, found him in the bath and held him under, while his baby slept beside him." He said he'd always had suspicions but the undercover team hadn't found the proof until days before.

New tears dribbled down across the scar on his cheek. He had survived so much—such injuries and loss. I felt tears in my own eyes, but my sympathy was muddied by nagging doubt. What about the explanation for the inconsistency? Was Mom going to let it go? It would be cruel to push this sad man, she must have concluded as she hugged him, comforting him with consoling whispers.

———

WITHIN A FEW months of beginning their life together, Ted and Elaine called to say she was pregnant. I tried to imagine my brother as a father, how his life would change. There was a new protectiveness about him, expressed in small and large concerns for Elaine's well-being. The prospect of fatherhood was wondrous to him, but also intimidating. It would be for any young man, but it was particularly so for Ted, who'd been told he'd been targeted by people who meant his family harm. He didn't talk about it at the time, but he's since told me of his constant worry about Elaine and the baby that was coming. A worry that seemed to be confirmed one night as he and Elaine, four months pregnant, drove home from her grandmother's home where they'd had dinner.

At some point Ted realized the same car had been following closely behind for many blocks. He sped up, changed lanes, but the car behind remained firmly on his tail. He sped up again. So did the car behind him. It was following aggressively now, lurching close to Ted's rear bumper and then backing off, only to surge forward again. Ted's adrenalin pumped as he tried to fight off thoughts of hit men and kidnappers, and fear pushed his foot to the gas pedal. He found himself speeding through downtown Vancouver, his pregnant and wide-eyed wife beside him clutching the door handle. Ahead, a brightly lit gas station loomed at the corner of an intersection. Ted knew he had to get somewhere with other people around. He pulled the steering wheel abruptly and his car squealed across the station lot, stopping under the neon glow of the canopy over the gas pumps. As startled gas customers looked on he threw the gearshift into park, and without even shutting off the engine, he sprinted toward the following car that was now stopped, idling at a red light at the corner. Its rear windows were darkened, but Ted could see the shapes of multiple heads through the passenger window and windshield as he ran onto the road toward them at full speed. He didn't slow as he approached the car, and launched himself across the hood toward the driver's side.

"Who are you? What do you want?" he screamed as he grabbed for the door handle, intending to drag the driver from his seat. It wouldn't open. It was locked. But as he looked through the window, he was arrested by the faces inside: a carload of wide-mouthed teenagers horrified by his violent rage. In a stunning flash of understanding, he realized they'd been joy-riding, thinking the driver in front was sharing their reckless pleasure, egging them on.

The light turned and the boys peeled off, likely relieved to watch as the angry man receded in the rear-view. Ted stood watching them disappear, his heart still racing and chest heaving as he tried to catch his breath, muscles twitching with tension.

Someday Ted and I would laugh about this until we cried.

THERE WERE OTHER incidents—strange happenings that kept Ted and Elaine on edge. They were living in the lower apartment of a house when Stan called to warn them, telling them to be sure to lock their doors and windows. In careful language, signalling his worry the phone line might be bugged, he said he'd had word that something was brewing and someone might be coming after them.

On one of the following nights Ted heard a noise at the back of the house. He thought someone was breaking in. In light of Stan's warning, he decided the situation justified the use of the radio Stan had given him to call for help. He set the dials in the way he'd been shown and, feeling ridiculous, spoke into the back of the device. He explained the situation and then waited for the cavalry to come. Nothing happened. More sounds came from the back of the house. Still no help arrived. Eventually Ted decided to take matters into his own hands. He found his baseball bat and slammed out the side door, yelling and swinging.

"There was nothing," he said later. Maybe someone had been there and ran away. Maybe it was a raccoon or a cat rattling around in the garbage cans. "But at times you thought you were going to have to fight for your life," he recalls now.

Later, when he asked why no one had responded to his radio call for help, Stan took the device away for inspection. Word came back it had malfunctioned. It might have gotten wet.

Another night, driving through the darkness of Stanley Park's old-growth forest, Ted and Elaine again thought they were being followed. No matter which turn they took, whether they drove slow or fast, the dark sedan remained determinedly behind them. Ted didn't have the radio, which he no longer trusted anyway, but he had the secret phone number Stan had given him as a backup. These being the days before cellphones, he drove to a brightly lit pay phone on a busy street and dialled as the sedan drove slowly by. The number was out of service. By the time he got back in his car, the sedan had disappeared.

There were investigations and explanations for these failures. The radio malfunction. The emergency phone line had mistakenly been cut off. But for Ted it was too late for excuses. He was done with the Weird World. His worry had shifted to Mom and how she was being manipulated.

On the other side of the country, I was also struggling. My own feelings of suspicion wrestled with my loyalty and love for Mom and Stan. An argument was perennially raging in my head. *It has to be real*, I thought. How could Stan, a minister now living on a small pension, afford to be flying back and forth across the country so frequently? How could he afford to pay for all the motel rooms and cottages that we so often slipped away to and hid out in? What about the times he'd been injured? I enumerated the supporting evidence: the medication that had arrived in the mail in an unmarked package; the times I'd thought I'd spotted my undercover security; the presents that had mysteriously arrived on our doorstep at Christmastime when I was a child; the terrifying fight I'd heard in the basement at Stan and Sybil's house in Winnipeg; the ruckus outside my apartment after I moved to Halifax. I remembered Mom telling me about being chased in her car by men with guns, when we still lived in Vancouver. She said there were other things she'd seen, witnessed. Other things she wouldn't talk about.

If these incidents weren't real, if they were part of a hoax, Stan could not have pulled them off by himself. He would have needed help. He would have to have hired or persuaded people—actors—to support the story, to stage the fights, the chases. How could he have done that, afforded that, explained that?

And there were the letters, all the hundreds of pages of correspondence from people inside that I had received and replied to. Over the years Mom had received many more letters, from dozens of people. It wasn't possible for Stan to have written them all, to have made up the cast of characters, their distinct stories and personalities, each with their own style of handwriting, and to have kept them all straight. No one would have the time to do that, never mind the will. Even if someone did . . . why? Why would anyone go to such extremes to create and maintain such a crazy story?

I knew that my mother believed it all and that she would never choose to deceive her children; for her, truth and trust were fundamental values. She continued to believe even though she had a clear understanding of how insane it all sounded. My mother was not a credulous person. She was a critical thinker who responded to many situations and people with skepticism, particularly where money, power, or arrogance were involved. I thought her utter faith in Stan should count for something in my own thinking. But, increasingly, it did not.

Kevin was also growing more skeptical and we no longer talked about the little cottage at PH and a new life inside. Instead, we talked about how to determine the truth or falseness of the story; what it would mean if it really wasn't real, how that would affect my family; whether if we expressed our disbelief, Mom and Stan would just disappear and we would never see them again. I could reach no clear decisions, so I maintained a facade of normalcy as I tried to sort it all out in my head and my heart. We moved ahead with our lives as if the future would be whatever we chose it to be, making investments in our current place and time. We bought a house, we made couple-friends, I planted a garden.

One weekend we were waiting for Kevin's mother and brother to visit from New Brunswick when we got the message from Stan via Mom that we needed to run. It was a Friday, early evening, when she called.

"You're to come down here," she said. She had recently moved to Port Mouton, a tiny fishing village on Nova Scotia's south shore, where she was the minister for three rural churches.

"We need to all be together, for strength in numbers," she said cryptically, always careful about what she said on the phone, especially at times when there was a heightened threat. Each of us continued to have an agent covering us, ensuring our safety. But Stan had told her that whatever was coming looked like more than they could handle individually.

"We'll see you soon then," I said, noting how sulky I sounded and felt about being pulled away from weekend plans. Unbidden then, the thought: maybe Stan was worried Mom was lonely and was orchestrating this so she'd have company for the weekend. It was a mutinous musing I wasn't ready to voice out loud.

"My family will be here in an hour!" Kevin was angry, upset. "What am I supposed to tell them?" Soon he came up with his own answer.

"I'm not going," he announced, daring me to challenge him. It was the moment he decided he no longer believed, or at least the first time he was willing to act on his disbelief. For him, doubt was gone. I still couldn't make that leap, with my closest relationships at stake. I felt compelled to go. I went by myself, a lonely drive during which I dreaded my arrival and the conversation that would follow.

Predictably Mom was shocked, then frightened, and, finally, angry that our protection would be split up and weakened because of Kevin's refusal to come, and that he was rejecting the narrative, the story that defined our lives, after having been trusted with it.

"What did he say?" she asked again once we were sitting in her living room. She was wondering if this was a definitive decision, whether he might change his mind and his car would pull into her driveway at any minute. And if not, she worried about what it would mean for everyone's safety going forward. I wondered too, half-waiting through that night for the sound of his engine in the driveway, but it didn't come.

From that day on, my mother was coolly polite and cautious around Kevin, regarding him with suspicion, I thought. We didn't talk about it much, not Mom and I, not Kevin and I. I felt trapped in the silence between them. In another treacherous moment I, the budding apostate, wondered how long it would be before Stan or Mom told me the Mafia had already grabbed Kevin and the man I lived with was the double they'd replaced him with.

From then on, I saw less of Stan. Occasionally, when he was in town, Kevin and I would join him and Mom for a meal, ignoring the unspoken schism and the new awkwardness between us all, enduring the stilted conversations that were now essentially meaningless chatter about the weather, something in the news, or developments at work or with the renovations Kevin and I were doing to our house. Kevin had become an outsider and I, his wife, was treated with caution. Perhaps Stan and Mom were more careful about what they said to me in part to limit my sense of being caught in the middle, but I had the sense of becoming "other," no longer a part of the trusted inside circle. I knew they still loved me, and I still loved them. But there was now a chasm between us, a moat of mistrust, and we stood on opposite sides, looking across at each other with feelings of uncertainty and loss.

THE MOMENT I could no longer pretend came some months later. Mom had moved to a new pastoral charge and was the minister at a big old church in Tatamagouche and two smaller ones in nearby villages, on Nova Scotia's north shore. Stan was visiting her, and they were on one of their road trips. It seemed to be for pleasure; if they were on the run, they didn't tell me so. They'd come to the city and I'd joined them for a meal in their motel room. It was after dinner and the television was on, so I wasn't following the conversation, but a change in the tone of Mom's voice alerted me. It was another instance in which something Stan had said didn't add up for her. Her voice was angry, urgent, demanding explanation. I watched quietly, not wanting to interrupt, anxious to hear his response and see what would happen next.

Then it happened again. Stan hung his head, his voice became ragged, and somehow he had shifted the conversation to Michael's death. Once again Mom, overcome by compassion for this unimaginable loss of a child, allowed his sorrow to sweep aside her mistrust.

Suddenly I saw the pattern. Michael was the perfect diversion when the conversation got dangerous. Stan knew Mom couldn't cause him more pain with her misgivings in the face of such grief. He knew and he was relying on it.

Why can't you see he's manipulating you, I wanted to scream. But I sat quietly, stunned by what I took to be evidence of a terrible betrayal.

That night, as I lay in my bed, Kevin sleeping beside me, I pondered a new stillness in me. The noise of the debate and conflicting thoughts had quieted. A bitter calm and clarity had replaced the churning doubt.

Stan, whom I had loved like a father, was my family's betrayer. He had seduced us with caring and gentleness, earned our trust with his wisdom, steadiness, and charisma. But all along he'd been deceiving us, drawing us into his secret world of madness. I couldn't conceive why. But I knew that now I had to prove it. I had to find a way to rescue my mother from his dangerous duplicity.

TWENTY

TESSA, AT TWO, had remarkable blue-green eyes topped by a head of long, thick light-brown hair that seemed as though it should belong on someone much older. My brother's daughter lived in photographs for me until the summer she turned two. That August, Kevin and I went to visit my brother and his family in Kelowna. They'd left Vancouver and gone back to the Okanagan town where Elaine's mother lived.

The night before we flew west, I dreamed Tessa was sitting on my lap facing me and we were rocking as we looked intently into each other's faces. I decided it was a reflection of how much I wanted to know this child.

We spent the time in Kelowna boating, waterskiing, and swimming in the lake that was just down the lane, enjoying the heat of the desert town I remembered it as a place where we'd vacationed and camped as kids. On a couple of days that Ted and Elaine had to work, I took Tessa to the beach, or for walks with her old dog, Gilligan. One evening Tessa stayed with Elaine's mother while Ted, Elaine, Kevin, and I went for dinner at a Greek restaurant.

We were well into a bottle of wine when the conversation turned to Stan and Mom and the secret life we were all trying to forget, to move on from and live as though none of it had ever happened. But the scale of the lie was undeniable, the impact on our four lives immeasurable. In hindsight, in this candle-lit space with the warmth of our reunion and the wine leavening the moment, it began to seem ridiculous, hilarious even. We began to recall scenes from this unlikely past, mocking the absurdity of Stan's story.

"Remember the horn? The warning signal?" Ted said. His face was lit up with memory and the excitement of exorcising it in this way. "We were driving in the mountains. I was in the camper with Stan and Sybil, and the horn started honking. He wasn't touching it. Just driving along, horn honking, Stan acting like nothing was happening." We howled at the image.

"When they came to Vancouver to tell me all this shit, he reminded me about that day and told me it had been a warning signal from the undercover agents."

We all laughed gustily at the notion. Undercover agents fiddling with the horn, ha ha!

"What do you think it was really?" I asked, ready now for the satisfaction of an explanation rooted in reality.

"It must have been a wire shorting out. Or maybe he rigged it," Ted guessed.

"How about the time we had to wash our feet in the bathtub with an antidote because someone put powdered poison on the rug?" It was my turn, my offering to the panoply of the bizarre we were laying out before us.

"Or the time we were on the run and hiked up Mount Seymour and hid in some old cabin to escape the hit men?" Gales of whooping laughter. That was the trip on which I slid on the snow into a tree and sprained my leg. I'd had to keep going; no emergency room for me. Too dangerous to leave our hideout. Less funny.

"What about Stan—code name Lt-GGF—flying in on 'the Bird,' the spy plane?" Snorting derision. "Yeah, the Weird World's private jet, seized from organized crime and pressed into service to save us from the O." More laughter, our eyes glittering and mouths wide with the relief of it, putting this terrible secret in its proper place.

We regaled and entertained each other with the unlikely, the impossible, the ludicrous, the illogical, dismantling a lifetime of belief and trust in Stan and Mom, ridiculing our own susceptibility, our stupidity. How could we have been caught up in this? How could Mom have allowed this to happen to us?

That sobered us, as we contemplated our mother still entrapped in the story, faithful and determined in her belief.

"How are we going to extricate her?" Sometimes I wanted to forget it all and continue the brittle pretense Mom and I had built over the past year—acting as though everything was normal, fine, yet feeling it was anything but. We carefully avoided talking about what was often uppermost in my mind: she'd been deceived, deluded, victimized by the man she considered her saviour. She must abandon this craziness, cut ties with Stan. But after all the years they'd been together, maintaining their secret relationship over vast distances and endless obstacles (including Stan's marriage), I doubted she would ever turn her back on him.

"Psychologically, I wonder what it would do to her to stop believing," I mused. Ted understood immediately. Having invested decades of her life in the story, having traumatically uprooted her family twice, having severed relationships with her father, sister, brother, and countless friends, how could she ever allow herself to acknowledge it was all needless, based on lies she had allowed herself to believe.

"It might unhinge her," we agreed. Still.

"I went to the RCMP," Ted said, after a pause.

"What? When?" I was shocked that he'd done it, and shocked I was only now learning of it.

It was just after Tessa was born, he said. He'd gone to the Kelowna detachment and asked to speak to someone in charge. Even now, when Ted recalls that day, he shakes his head with . . . embarrassment, shame, wonder? I imagine him trying to convey this story to a uniformed officer, not wanting for his family to seem crazy, but needing to put it to rest.

"I told him the story and asked him if there was any way it could be real. The cop was blown away; he said, 'Are you kidding me?' But he had no suggestions. He just said it wasn't possible."

Not possible to hide entire communities like PH, or create and run an undercover justice system dealing with organized crime. Of course not, although sometimes truth is stranger than fiction. We admitted that even now something could trigger the fear, a momentary flash of uncertainty. Could it really be true? What if it really was true? What if we rejected this and it turned out to be real? I sometimes imagined being grabbed or attacked or cornered by a hit man and in the final moment of my life, realizing I'd been wrong—Stan had not lied, he'd just been trying to protect us and I had rejected his help, broken his heart, and put myself in danger. I thought about how it would feel to know that my disbelief might have caused my imminent death, or that of someone around me.

We knew it could not be true, but as Ted said, "You believed it because how could your mother do this to you, because you knew she loved you. There was no question she loved us more than anything in the world," he said. "So unless it was true, how could she do this? She wasn't stupid."

The question remained: how to get Mom unentangled, deprogrammed—how to prove to her that she didn't need to live in fear for herself or her children? We didn't come up with any answers that night at dinner, but we did come away feeling a little less alone, united by our circumstances and by our concern for Mom.

It also became clear during that trip that Ted and Elaine were struggling as a couple. They talked to me about it one night, sitting on the back deck. They were both in pain. I felt Ted was grasping for some way to save their marriage. I think Elaine was undone by the drama, anxiety, and fear that had dogged their time together. It must have been difficult to remember the uncomplicated time when they fell in love, before Stan drew them into the world of mobsters. It must have been hard to foresee a time when a life together would not be haunted by the fallout from all that. In the end they separated, after a couple more years trying to hold it together, of wanting to preserve Tessa's family.

My marriage was suffering too. Mostly we didn't fight, but there were cold silences, resentments that were stacking up in unspoken remonstration. Our relationship waxed and waned, and Kevin seemed as determined as I was to stick with it, although increasingly there were periods when we felt like disconnected strangers living in the same house. Kevin would sometimes surprise me with his sporadic efforts to please me, support me. But there were ugly times too, when he would be lost in rage and I retreated, shaken by the depth of his anger.

On one of my birthdays he gave me some cement stepping stones with stained glass embedded in them, for the garden. Someone he knew had made them. I was delighted.

"The cement isn't completely set," he warned, looking pleased by my reaction to their beauty. "Don't step on them."

I took them out to the garden to look for places to put them. As I was testing them out in different spots, one of them cracked.

"Oh no!" I was upset, but as Kevin came over to look at the split in the cement I was already trying to think of how to fix it.

"Maybe we can use some mortar mix to glue it," I suggested.

He looked at me. The muscles in his face moved as if to smile, but it was a twisted, mocking result, and his eyes were hard. He lifted his arm and waved it dismissively at me, as if signalling he was done with me, finished with my stupidity, my clumsiness. I watched, stricken by his display of disgust, as he walked away, up the deck stairs and through the back door into the kitchen. A few minutes later, I followed him in. He was at the sink, rinsing some dishes.

"I didn't mean to break it," I began. He snorted.

"We can fix it, if we just . . ."

"You always do that, Pauline." No longer outwardly angry, he was now all long-suffering frustration and disappointment, exercising an exaggerated patience, as with a small but disappointing child. He meant that I minimized problems, made light of adversities, that I framed every fix and posited every solution as simple and not requiring any great amount of time or effort. It drove him crazy. And it was true. That's how I coped. I tried to make challenges seem smaller, more manageable. In my head, I cut them down to a size I could handle, my own exercise in denial of what might otherwise crush me. And for me, it worked. It allowed me to work away at something, telling myself it wasn't a big thing, until it was actually a smaller thing. That went for all kinds of tasks, all kinds of feelings. It even worked to keep me in a marriage swollen with dysfunction, one day at a time.

———

I DON'T REMEMBER if Kevin and I talked about it much when I finally came up with the plan. I hoped I would prove once and for all, to Mom and to myself as well, that the Weird World and the Mafia threats were the construction of a sick mind.

I decided to set a trap, conduct a sting. I thought carefully about what I could do to make the results clear and undeniable. I waited for a time when I knew Stan was visiting Mom, when I could get an immediate response from him, and then I put my plan into action. I staged a break-in at our house, pulling the cabinet with the television and other electronics out from the wall, opening drawers and cupboard doors, leaving the front door ajar. I don't know why I bothered physically setting the scene. No one would see it. Perhaps it was how I worked myself up to committing what felt like a treacherous act, my own lie, intended to deceive and entrap. I was turning the tables.

I felt the momentousness of my action and was aware that this could forever change, or even end, my relationship with Stan, maybe even with my mother. As a result my heart was beating hard, my breath catching in my throat as if I really had come upon a break-in, when I dialled Mom's number.

"Mom?" I started.

Immediately, she knew something was wrong. "What is it?" She was always primed for disaster and I could hear in her voice she was bracing to hear the worst. That was the inheritance of decades spent on the run, being told your life and your children's are always at risk.

What's wrong? I thought. *I'm calling you to lie to you in hopes of undermining your entire world view, convince you to leave the man you love, and make you see him as the betrayer I believe him to be. If I am successful your world will shatter, you will hate yourself for being deceived and for inflicting the resulting chaos on your children.* And yet I felt it had to be done.

"Someone has broken into the house," I said shakily. I described the scene and said I couldn't see anything missing.

"Should I call the police?"

"Are you sure there's no one still there?"

"Yes."

"Let me talk to our friend and I'll call you right back."

I knew that Stan, "our friend," would process the information and send a coded message to his intelligence people, who would question my undercover man who was supposedly sitting in a car down the street or around the corner from my house, and wait for a coded response tapped out and received in his butt receiver. Sure. I imagined him at Mom's table in Tatamagouche, deciphering the code with letters and strokes into his notebook, and her watching and anxiously waiting for the reply.

It came quickly. I looked at my phone as it rang, feeling unprepared for what I might hear, even as I desperately wanted to know the results of my test. This was the moment of truth I'd craved and now that the phone was ringing I had to force myself to answer it. It was Mom. She said she couldn't talk on the phone, and that I should come to her place that evening. "Don't delay."

Two hours later I pulled into her driveway. It was dark and I could see the light around the edges of the curtains in her kitchen window. I sat for a minute dreading what was to come. I didn't want to face them, didn't know how I'd react to whatever they had to say. I felt sick and tried to settle myself before opening the car door and walking to the house.

Mom hugged me as I came in. Stan was at the kitchen table and smiled at me while shaking his head, commiserating with me and the fright I'd had, the stress he knew I must be feeling. *You have no idea.*

"So, what's happening?" I asked. I was incapable of small talk. I wanted this over with.

"It was two guys who broke in," Stan began. I watched his mouth moving and wondered if he or Mom could see any signs of the cataclysmic shifting happening within me in reaction to those words, the confirmation of Stan's deception. I'd thought I'd feel relieved to know for sure. I'd thought the worst thing would have been if he'd said no, there was no Mafia involvement in the break-in, we know nothing about it, you'd better call the police. Then I would have been faced with uncertainty, a failed test with no definitive results. But now I had my answer and I wasn't feeling relief. I was feeling horror, and white-hot anger. And profound sadness. And even though it was the expected outcome, utter disbelief.

None of it was real. He was making it up. This was the proof, the evidence that I could not deny, that I must act on. I was now deaf to him as he spoke, my attention focused inward to scenes and memories unfurling in rapid progression. All the moves and disappearances; all the running; all the sick, terrifying stories; all the upheaval; all the isolation. It was all because of a lie. A fucking lie. All made up. All the layered creation of the brilliant, twisted imagination of this man whom I'd chosen to love and trust as a father. I was shattered, a flurry of innumerable jagged little pieces coming apart.

I realized he'd stopped talking and was looking at me.

"What?" I mumbled, feeling disoriented, pulling myself back to the present. He looked over at my mother with concern. She looked worried too.

"Can you repeat that?" I asked, and he did.

He said mobsters had been picked up in my neighbourhood shortly after I'd discovered and called about the break-in. Photographs of me had been found in the back of their car—they'd been watching me. Once this would have frightened me. Now I wondered at Stan's ability to make up these creepy details designed to terrorize me.

"Why? What did they want?" I asked, not looking at him, my eyes on the floor.

He said they were looking for all the china my father had been sending me over the years. After that first carry-on bag presented around the time of Ted's wedding, other pieces had followed, mailed in Styrofoam peanuts. The individual pieces were bubble-wrapped and accompanied by notes instructing me to enjoy them, not to stick them away in a cupboard.

"Why the china?"

He said information and the names of Mafia contacts had been written in invisible ink on the backs of the plates. Their instructions had been to use ultraviolet light to reveal and copy the information. He said sensitive information was often hidden with innocent people for later retrieval, so that implicating evidence couldn't be tied to kingpins like my dad if their homes were raided. *How could I ever have believed this crap*, I wondered silently.

"Our guys are in your house now, cleaning up the china. There won't be any writing left on it by the time you get home tomorrow."

I nodded. Right.

I suddenly saw that the beautiful Mikado-patterned china represented a connection to my father and as such Stan perceived it as a threat. It belonged to a part of my mother's life before she'd loved Stan. That made the delicate plates and bowls and cups a target, not for mobsters but for this man before me who had portrayed my father to me as a depraved mobster, a monster without paternal feelings. My staged break-in was just another opportunity for Stan to paint my dad in yet darker shades, to further alienate me from him, and once again underline for my mother how right she'd been to leave him.

I looked up at Stan and then Mom. Should I confront them, reveal that I had tricked them and they had failed my test, accuse Stan of betrayal? I saw only love and concern in their expressions. I couldn't think.

"Do you want something, a cup of tea?" My mother could see I was upset and wanted to do something to help.

I rejected the offer and said I needed to get some sleep. I took my bag up the stairs to the spare room, which I knew Mom would have prepared for me. Below me I could hear the indistinct murmur of their voices. I knew they would be conferring, discussing my abrupt behaviour and what it meant, trying to decide whether I was okay.

I slept little that night, turning and shifting restlessly. I'd been spit out the other side of the narrative that had propelled our lives since I was a small child and from this new perspective I was appalled by how ludicrous it all seemed. I twisted in my bed, wrestling with my anger at my mother and my own shame that for so long I had believed.

I thought back to the night in the Sussex motel room, more than five years earlier, and how the story Stan and Mom told me had lifted a curtain to reveal both a horrifying new reality and an explanation for the oddities of our lives. It was an account that—at the time—seemed to answer so many questions and make some of the missing puzzle pieces fall into place.

Once again, I thought, *reality has shifted and the puzzle is awry.*

TWENTY-ONE

I N T H E W E E K S that followed, I couldn't stop remembering and picking through scenarios from childhood and the Mafia-related explanations Stan had later provided. The time he said he'd been darted at the campground in Algonquin Provincial Park and sat around the campfire looking dazed and confused—he must have been acting. I tried to figure out how he could have staged the attack in the basement when we lived in Winnipeg, and the crashing, fighting sounds I'd heard when the Italian mobsters had supposedly come after us. We'd all been together upstairs—he wasn't making the noise. He must have hired or somehow convinced others to do that. The time the men with guns chased him and Mom, they must have been confederates, hired for the job. The horseback shooting—all made up. He'd probably just fallen off the horse and used that as an excuse to claim he'd been shot, because his injuries and his hospitalization were very real.

I still wonder about the time my car was stolen shortly after I'd moved to Halifax and the horrible fight outside my apartment door. Were those circumstances that Stan co-opted to bolster his deception—happily taking advantage of situations that would reinforce my belief, ascribing them to Mafia bad guys—or could he have set them up somehow?

I couldn't imagine how Stan had found people willing to be involved in his ruse, or how he could have afforded to pay them. After all, he'd been paying for all the motel rooms in which we'd hidden out, and his flights back and forth across the country every few weeks or months. I didn't understand how he'd funded all of this on a minister's salary and, later, pension. As far as I knew, he hadn't come from or inherited money. Hadn't he called himself the Grand Manan dulse picker—joking about his humble beginnings? None of it made any sense, and I would spend years trying to figure it out.

After leaving Mom's, I said nothing to her about my sting, the artifice that had provided the evidence I needed to be sure, to convince myself and soon her, that Stan was deceiving us. I went home the following morning, relieved to escape their searching looks. They knew I was acting strangely, that I was distracted and distant. I hoped they'd attribute it to my being upset about the supposed break-in. I couldn't accuse them directly; I wasn't ready.

I tried to imagine Mom being complicit with Stan, helping him weave the stories about the Weird World, the O, the doubles. But I knew it wasn't possible. "If we haven't got trust, we haven't got anything," I could hear her say, using a maxim she'd often repeated to Ted and me when we were growing up. Whatever her weaknesses or faults, she was incapable of lying. She'd been honest even when it had cost her. I believed the ruse was solely

Stan's construction. She was his accomplice only in that she believed and completely trusted him, crediting him with saving her life, rescuing her from the torment of her depression and abuse, and supporting her as she struggled to leave her marriage. For decades Stan had been her source of strength and love. She could not credit the idea he would deceive her.

And what about Sybil, I wondered. Did Stan actually live with her when he was supposedly inside? Were they still together? Stan and Mom had told me she was aware of the Mafia story and accepted it, was a willing partner in our disappearances. But if Stan was actually with her in Gibson's when he "came out" to visit us, where did she think he was going? I also thought about their son John, whom Stan described as successful in the produce business. John had been told and rejected the story, to Stan's sorrow. What did he know or think about all of this?

The following week, before Stan was scheduled to fly back west, he and Mom came to Halifax, planning to spend the night at a motel and have dinner with Kevin and me. I knew I was now unable to pretend there was nothing wrong, and I was tense when we arrived at the motel. Mom had prepared some food in the small housekeeping kitchen, and somehow we got through the meal. I struggled to look Stan or Mom in the eye, to talk casually about work, to ask about their week.

After we finished eating, I suggested that Mom and I go and pick up some ice cream for dessert. I needed to get her alone and as we walked across the parking lot to the car, I steeled myself for what I had to do. The store wasn't far and we drove in silence. After I'd parked, I turned to her. She was looking at me intently, a questioning eyebrow raised. I thought how the dramatic moments in my life so often happened in cars or motel rooms. I remembered the crescent moon over the Sussex skyline. It seemed a lifetime ago.

I thought of the note Mom had handed me when I got into her car at the gas station, instructing me to take off my jewellery in preparation for the drive to the Blue Bird Motel. Here we were again in a car, but this time I was the one about to shatter her world.

"I have to tell you something," I began. "You're going to be upset." She nodded calmly and I began. I told her how I'd set up the break-in, faked it to test Stan. I said I had proof now that it was all a hoax. "It's not real. He's crazy or something."

She looked at me with horror. "What have you done?" She shook her head, momentarily at a loss, and I wanted to hug her, imagining her pain as she tried to process this information. But when she finally looked up at me, I realized her anger and fear were not directed at Stan.

"You are making a serious mistake," she told me. I could see the silent appeal in her expression: *don't abandon me, don't become one of them*. She was afraid I would become a disbeliever who would put her, Stan, and the people who protected them at risk. I realized she saw my actions as potentially endangering me, and she was panicked.

"Pauline, there will be an explanation for this. You can't think we would betray you like this!"

"Not you, him."

We sat in the car for a long time, arguing. I reminded her of the times Stan had appeared to trip up in his stories, times she had called him on inconsistencies. I pointed out how he'd distracted her from her questioning by bringing up Michael's death.

"He used that, he used your love, he made you feel ashamed for questioning him by playing the grieving father card!"

She refused to acknowledge those times. She was stalwart in her defence of Stan, her faith in the Weird World, and her fear of the O.

"There's been too much. Things you don't even know about."

Eventually, I gave up and we returned to the motel. I understood I would now have to directly accuse Stan without the support of my mother.

I can't remember the words I used. His reply was that something must have gone wrong, that perhaps there'd been some kind of betrayal within the ranks of the Weird World that could explain the flawed response to my test. He said he'd have to investigate. He warned me of the danger I could be in, how I still needed the protection of my coverage, the guys who had so many times put their lives in jeopardy to successfully prevent harm from coming to me.

It was no less than I expected, but I was unprepared for his evolving response as I continued to shake my head. No, I would no longer be convinced. I was done.

He looked at me with profound sadness that affected me more than all his arguments. He, my papa, felt I was now lost to him. I had irrevocably removed myself from the circle, but never—his deep and sorrowful gaze told me—never from his heart.

I was disarmed by this sadness, and felt my own welling to the surface, overwhelming the anger and betrayal. I was losing another father. One who had been gentle and loving, supportive, my advocate. He'd celebrated my wins, been stalwartly present in the difficult moments, had known when to tease and have fun, when to listen, when to offer advice.

Kevin and I rose to leave, and Stan followed us to the door. He hugged me.

"You'll always be my girl," he said softly. He was crying as he let me go and turned away. I was crying as we left.

It felt like the most final of goodbyes. It felt like the end of an era.

———

I SAW STAN one more time. We met at a restaurant at Peggy's Cove, overlooking the moonscape of giant undulating granite rock on the edge of the Atlantic Ocean that attracts tourists from around the world. He was visiting Mom and asked if he could buy me a lobster. It had been our annual ritual and I thought of the other times we'd sat in this restaurant, looking out over the unchanging primordial landscape and the churning ocean.

Mom had told me he'd been sick earlier that year. For weeks she didn't hear from him. There was no one to call, to see if he was okay. She imagined the worst. He'd been shot, or poisoned, or grabbed. He was being held by the O, perhaps tortured for information. At the time, she didn't tell me any of this, perhaps feeling she could no longer rely on the support of an unbeliever. She bore it all alone until finally one evening he called, from a pay phone in a hospital lobby. He'd had an aortic aneurysm, been rushed to the hospital for emergency surgery, barely survived. I can't imagine her relief.

As we waited for our lobsters, I picked up the flimsy plastic bib with the orange-red outline of a lobster emblazoned across the front and started tying it around my neck. While I was doing so, Stan showed me the scar on his chest where surgeons had opened him to repair the burst blood vessel. It was a miracle he hadn't bled to death. "I was heading out the exit," he joked, "but they pulled me back."

It was a sad reunion, the silent grey static of unspoken questions, condemnation, and regrets buzzing invisibly between us, around the measured words of our stilted conversation. My sadness and confusion had overpowered my anger toward him. I didn't know how to be with him anymore. Our easiness with each other had gone.

We settled for being gentle with each other, sharing our unspoken anguish at the falling-out, but still irrevocably separated by our different versions of reality and truth.

We hugged as I left. He looked older and I realized he must be in his mid-seventies now. He had never seemed old or tired before. As we parted, I had the feeling I would never see him again.

TWENTY-TWO

I'M SITTING IN a coffee shop, laptop on the table before me. Laura is at volleyball practice; I'm killing time until she's done and I can pick her up. That's when the first one walks through the door: a Mountie in full uniform, with the blaze of gold stripe down his leg, the black Kevlar vest underneath his jacket, the gun on his hip. Soon two more follow. I'm engrossed in my work and it's not until the next pair comes in, also in full uniform, that I realize I have that old feeling of anxious alertness. They're here only for coffee, I realize, releasing my breath.

It can still make me tense up, put me on the watch for danger for a few moments, before I remember. It was never real, I tell myself. There is no threat, there never was. But sometimes I still have unbidden moments when I wonder, *What if I'm wrong? What if it was all real?* That's ridiculous, of course.

Those moments, the mental double takes of questioning reality, don't happen much anymore. But in the days following my break with the Weird World, the realization that the same car had been behind me for too long could emotionally capsize me. Were they following me? Or seeing the shadow of someone lingering in a doorway, if the person happened to be looking at me. Were they intending some harm? The familiar adrenalin-fed drumbeat would start and I would have to talk myself down, reminding myself of the reasons I had determined we were not, had never been, on a Mafia hit list. The fix, the antidote, was to focus on my work, and there were other rewards in doing so.

". . . And police are saying little about possible motives. Pauline Dakin, CBC News, Halifax."

That had been my first live sign-off for the national radio network. I was covering what looked very much like the murder of a high school student. Her body had been found in an alcove by the school. It was now covered by a small tent-like structure the police had placed around it, to preserve evidence and, I assumed, prevent the television cameras from getting too much of a lens-full. I'd been camped out with a gaggle of other reporters for hours, waiting for police to tell us something we could file to our respective newsrooms. After a short scrum, during which the commanding officer on the scene offered few details beyond what we'd already gleaned, I'd roughed out a script. I found a quiet spot around the corner of the school, at the edge of the broken pavement of the parking lot, and did live hits into *Canada at Five* and *The World at Six*, the flagship evening newscasts.

I'd been working with CBC Halifax, mostly local reporting, for just over a year. I filled in as a chase producer with the local morning and afternoon shows and worked shifts in the newsroom when they needed me. It was all short-contract work, but I felt that I'd found the place I was meant to be: the public broadcaster, where I didn't feel pressure to torque my stories for ratings or worry about offending advertisers; where the audience was assumed to be intelligent and engaged; where journalism was about telling true stories and unveiling useful information.

The work was engrossing and stimulating enough to distract me from thinking about the wreckage of the life I'd turned my back on. When I was unoccupied, I felt the effects of my destructive accusation, the heavy emptiness of having cut myself off from Mom and Stan. In doing so I'd also closed the door on their utopian Weird World and its unworldly values: forgiveness, reconciliation, and grace. That world and the community in the mountains, Place of Hope, were supposed to have been my destination and my home. Now I had to reset my idea of what the future might look like.

Gradually but determinedly I loosened my attachments to the imaginary blue-carpeted cabin by the stream and the horse in the paddock nearby. They existed only in Stan's imagination. Who wanted carpet anyway? I stopped myself from imagining that place and put away the letters I'd received from the people who inhabited that pretend, shadowy world; I told myself firmly they didn't exist, no matter how intimate my correspondence with them might have been. Stan had to have written all those letters, I now realized. The supposed authors were creations of a deluded mind, drawing intricate and complex characters to further lure Mom and me into the Weird World. How many hours he must have spent imagining and writing those letters, figuring out distinct styles of handwriting for each character, which I carefully checked and compared. It was remarkable and disturbing. In the case of my half-sister, Linda, he had captured her left-handed back-slanted script. She had only ever written me a couple of letters, when I was a teenager. He must have somehow seen them in order to emulate her broad, loopy letters.

I thought about my godfather, Roy, who'd written letters to me when I was a child and then been reintroduced to me as an adult through letters delivered by Stan, who described Roy as a now-trusted prisoner of the Weird World. Roy's notes from inside had taken me back to the warm, fun man I remembered. I marvelled at Stan's ability to recreate that, to fool me.

There had also been a letter, ostensibly from my unrepentant father, written from his prison cell. Telling me he could never be a father to me. It's interesting to read these letters now, to imagine Stan writing them—aiming to transmit surreptitious messages through the words of others—and to think about his need to reinforce the separation between my dad and me.

The letters are now piles of paper towering on my dining-room table. When I pick through them, I can see how they worked to bind my mother to Stan and his vision. One that's from an old First Nations man, an officer in PH who signs off with his jesting undercover name "Chief Turtle Neck," commiserates with her difficulties. It would have been written when we were running away from Winnipeg:

> Perhaps [there are] still some storms and uncertain days when again the mists of toil and struggle will threaten to hide the sun. Yet in the storm and mist I see you moving onward, at times perhaps slowly and with confidence not too strong. But always going on, stepping, if hesitantly at times, in the footprints of the Child of Bethlehem.

My mother would have loved the lyrical language, the wisdom, the references to her faith, and his reflection on the beauty of nature. He wrote that he'd been thinking about her, praying for her, as he sat by a campfire at PH beside a little brook:

*As I sat there a fairly new moon rose over the mountains
and its rays reflected off the frozen snow in rare beauty.
Somehow that beauty told me that you, my friend, were
going to be all right. That the Great Spirit and His Son
would abide in your lodge and heart and daily from sun
up to sun down you will see and know His hand upon your
life, as gentle as the touch of a fox's paw and solid as the
mountain peaks which abide forever.*

How could the author of such sentences intend to deceive
and harm?

It's clear from other letters that Mom's correspondence with
those insiders must often have been messages of hope and
reassurance for people she believed suffered from loneliness or
guilt, because so many of the replies now on my table thank her
for her support, her wisdom.

"This will only be a note to tell you this is the most beautiful
morning of my life. Yes, yes—a really new clean life!" wrote a
man she'd once known as a friend and business associate of my
father's. One of those who'd supposedly been implicated, picked
up, and incarcerated in the Weird World. He was writing to tell
Mom he'd found redemption, and said:

*Your prayers, letters, and caring plus some of the beautiful
people here and their witness did it. The chap here in
charge gave the prayer this morning. As he prayed in his
soft voice I felt a . . . what? Change in me from head to toe.
He just seemed to be talking intimately with One who was
real, close though unseen, and I think mentally I said I
want that intimacy with the infinite, and He came to me.
I know now what you mean by new life and love.*

It's hard to imagine such beauty and beneficence being the product of a sick mind. Books, television, and movies condition us to think of psychosis as expressing itself through acts of violence; through dark, disturbing behaviour; and through wild-eyed madness—not through a quest for nirvana. There had been unnerving manifestations: the organ-harvesting ship, the times Stan described discoveries of warehouses or buildings full of women and children being sold or used as sex slaves, or raids that liberated young drug-addicted Mafia soldiers. And they were incarcerated, yes, but Stan always described them as saved from a life of brutality and evil. Always these horrific scenes were in aid of positioning Stan and his made-up anti-Mafia agency as rescuers, the bringers of love and light. In Stan's case his psychosis was expressed in aspirations to do God's work in an imaginary world, but all the while he was creating chaos in the real one.

The religious aspect of Stan's stories appealed to my mother, who'd been raised in the church in a time before society began to view religion with skepticism and suspicion. For her it was a reassuring element of the fabrication. For others it might have been a warning, a clue.

I thought of the people that I'd been taken away or turned away from, having been told they were gangsters, or worse: Linda; my half-brother, Tom; Dad; Aunt Penny; and others from our Vancouver life. I'd been told they were doubles. I thought of all the people that Stan and Mom had convinced me were involved in plots against us and that had ultimately been captured and imprisoned at PH or one of the other prisons in the Weird World. And then the letters from inside, in which people begged my forgiveness and told me they could now have more real and meaningful relationships with me than when I'd known them outside because they'd changed, had found new lives.

Now I had to forget who they were in their letters and deal with the real people, here in the real world. How to repair those relationships, I wondered. And if it was possible, was it desirable? After all, I had begun to think that the surest way for anyone to have been fingered by Stan and accused of being involved in organized crime was to have somehow hurt or made life difficult for my mother. The link seemed so obvious once I saw it. Those Mom perceived as disappointing or disloyal, those who had caused her pain, had somehow all become entwined in the O. Perhaps it was Stan's distorted attempt to take them out of my mother's way, to undermine or negate them and the pain they had caused her. *Look, your ex-husband, step-children, sister are not really those people. The real ones have been co-opted by an evil force or taken away. They will re-emerge, as phoenixes from the flames, as new, clean people who will send you letters asking for your forgiveness, seeking your love and wisdom.* Maybe Stan thought that transferring the responsibility for the pain to a nefarious force would remove some of the sting for my mother. Maybe he was trying to heal her broken relationships by refashioning them through reconstituted characters who lived for her through the letters. Maybe it was a twisted gift of love and protection, damn the consequences.

I sometimes wondered if I would drive myself crazy trying to figure out Stan's motivation. I performed cognitive contortions to understand why he would have done this to us. Eventually I made an appointment with a psychiatrist and told him the story, hoping he would have some insight. He was fascinated and his questions made me wonder if he was thinking of writing us all up as a case study. But a case study of what affliction, what diagnosis?

His theory was that this was a case of *folie à deux*, a shared psychosis in which a delusional belief is transmitted from a stronger personality to a weaker one. There are some interesting cases in psychiatric literature, of siblings or spouses who share fantastical beliefs. In some respect, the diagnosis fit Stan and Mom. The idea of a dominant person imposing a delusion onto a secondary person who otherwise would not have become deluded—that felt right. Cases often involve beliefs that the sufferers are being persecuted. That fit too. But another classic symptom, that the two sufferers typically live in close proximity and are socially or physically isolated, having little interaction with others . . . that didn't fit at all. Stan and Mom had seen each other only intermittently after he'd retired to B.C. and Mom had moved to Halifax to do her theology degree. They both had always been engaged in community and church work. And Mom made close friends at school and in the churches she served. They were not isolated. *Folie à deux* also didn't provide a primary diagnosis for Stan's delusion.

Still, there was a hopeful element to it. The psychiatrist told me that Mom's belief would fade away if she were permanently separated from Stan. I couldn't imagine any such separation other than his death but he was nineteen years older than her.

In the months that followed I did see my mother, but there was a terrible formality to our infrequent encounters. A brittleness that encompassed both our anger and our fear of losing each other.

"I was wondering if you'd like to come for Christmas dinner?"

"That would be very nice, thank you," she replied stiffly. She never assumed she would be invited and that both annoyed me and made me grateful. I wanted her to confidently take it for granted that we would spend holidays together as other families did. But still I was relieved that she didn't.

We were often combative, each desperate to convert each other to what we knew to be true. Initially we had long arguments. She tried to convince me of the truth of Stan's story. I tried to convince her it was a sham. Eventually we agreed to disagree, but it was an uneasy truce. In its wake, I instead argued with her about other things, silly things, later realizing I'd been trying to show her how wrong she was about small issues, hoping she would capitulate on these less important things and then somehow internalize and generalize her wrongness and realize she'd been duped in this bigger thing. I wanted her to acknowledge that she'd been deceived and had allowed the resulting fracturing of our family and our lives. I was often cold to her. Yet despite the pain, she must have felt her love for me would not be shaken and we continued to go through the motions, getting together for awkward and painful dinners and weekend visits. I held her at bay emotionally, rebuffing any closeness, requiring of her the one thing she could not offer up to me: her faith in Stan and the Weird World. And so the standoff continued. We held tight to the fraying threads of our relationship, each longing for the closeness we'd once felt, and unable to get beyond the impasse.

At some point I realized that Stan had probably told her that Kevin was a double, the real Kevin having been picked up and replaced. How perfect an explanation for why I had abandoned my belief in the Weird World, I thought. How much easier for her to believe I had been influenced by my husband, who had been turned, recruited by the O. Whether the Kevin double was "one of ours" or put in place by the Mob likely changed over time in the ongoing war between good and evil. That would explain my mother's coldness toward Kevin.

That chill put another strain on my marriage, but didn't prevent me from becoming pregnant in late 1995. Kevin and I intensified our efforts to repair the growing strain between us and went to a marriage counsellor. That helped for a while, and the anticipation of our baby brought détente.

My pregnancy also brought a thaw in my relationship with my mother. She was excited about another grandchild and we both made more of an effort to spend time together. I thought how strange it was that Stan would never know this baby. Mom and I no longer spoke of him as a matter of course, but I did relate this thought to her. Her reaction was strange and she didn't say anything about telling him I was going to have a baby. I realized she was trying not to cry.

"What's wrong?

"I haven't heard from Stan in weeks," she said. I could hear the anxiety in her voice. I knew she was worrying that something had happened to him, and wondering who would let her know. She had no way to find out if he was okay. She believed he and Sybil were no longer together, so she wouldn't call Sybil.

At other times when he'd been out of touch for a while, there had always been an explanation, his aneurysm most recently. But earlier absences had been explained as being a result of some undercover operation that had required his silence or the result of his inability to get to a phone that had been checked for bugs. Once he said he'd been kidnapped by a Mafia gang and it had taken weeks for his security agents to find and free him. Another time he'd been injured in an attack, but that time there'd been a letter, delivered by regular mail, from someone calling himself "R McC."

"He is OK or will be," he wrote. "He can't talk but sends his love."

Once there was even a call, Mom said, from someone who didn't identify themself but simply said "Lt-GGF" had been injured, would survive, and would call when he was well enough.

I shook my head at the initials of Stan's inside name, Lieutenant-General George Fraser. Such aggrandizement.

"He has nine lives," Mom once said to me. "All his scars . . . He has a remarkable capacity to heal from terrible injuries, to survive." I think that was part of his mystique for her, the sense that he was meant to survive because he had important work to do, God's work. I thought of the scar down his cheek and neck from his childhood collision with the barbed-wire fence.

This time there was no call, no explanation about some undercover operation. No word, for what must have seemed like a lifetime to Mom.

A couple of weeks after she'd told me about his silence there was, finally, a letter. It was from Sybil. I got one too. It said Stan had died a few weeks earlier. I thought it strange that Sybil hadn't called or written sooner, given how close we had all once been. She wrote that his end was quick, a stroke. She called it his release from an aging and tired body.

I waited to feel something. Loss and sadness, or maybe relief and triumph. I felt nothing, except worry for my mother and the purely cognitive understanding that his death would trigger a tectonic shift, a fundamental reorienting of my mother's life.

This is what I had come to wish for, Stan's death. But the hollow sound of my mother's voice on the phone when I called her, after getting the letter, frightened me. Based on what the psychiatrist had told me, Stan's death should mean Mom would relinquish the fantasy of the Weird World. Yet it was such a loss that I worried about her ability to continue.

I wondered what she felt about the letter coming from Sybil, whom Stan had supposedly not been living with. When I asked her she said Stan had had a double who lived with Sybil, to keep up appearances and protect her. Incredible as it seems, he told my mother that Sybil knew this was a double. Another layer of twisted deceit.

Mom did carry on, as she always had in the face of hardship. But in the weeks that followed I could see she was struggling, exhausted, and without her usual animation. From our phone conversations, I could tell she was dragging herself though her days, no longer with any goal or destination in sight.

The loss of Stan also severed her connection with the Weird World and a life that was at least as real to her as the one she lived in every day. She would receive no more letters, no more intelligence about the machinations of the Mafia and the life-saving responses of our undercover agents. She would never move to her refuge, would need to abandon the dream of the little house in the valley between the mountains. She would never live in full partnership with the man she had loved and been loved by for a quarter of a century. Her dreams and her sense of direction had died along with Stan.

TWENTY-THREE

WARREN DAKIN WAS a soldier. He was a businessman. He was a father, with four children from two families. He was a husband, three times. He was also a storyteller, although he had a limited repertoire of tales that he told over and over again.

One of them was about how his mother always told him not to eat the crabapples from the tree in their backyard or he'd get a stomach ache. One day she was hosting a luncheon for some ladies when young Warren, perhaps four or five, wandered in to say hello to them. He noticed one was pregnant, her belly distended.

"I know what you've been doing!" he said with a smile. The ladies gasped, shocked.

"You've been eating the crabapples from our tree!" Relieved laughter.

Dad enjoyed his own stories about growing up, going to war, starting out in business. His favourite story about me was that, like him, I loved steak.

"You were just a little thing and you ate the whole twelve ounces!"

But most of his stories were not about his kids. I was never sure what he thought or felt about the years Ted and I were missing from his life. We never talked about it.

When I decided to re-establish contact with him, I realized how little I knew him. How little he knew me. I hoped to remedy that when Kevin and I flew to Vancouver to visit him.

Dad was between condos, living temporarily in the lower suite of my half-brother Tom's house in North Vancouver. It was the same suite where Tom's mother had lived until she died of brain cancer. Tom and his second wife and their two little boys lived in the main house, and Dad stayed with them while Kevin and I took over his suite.

Just as I don't know how he felt about our disappearances, I don't know what he thought about my reappearance, my seemingly out-of-the-blue desire to re-establish contact. He seemed simply happy to see us, the first time since Ted's wedding.

"So bring me up to date, tell me what you're up to." He was smiling expectantly. There was no underlying sense of hurt or condemnation, no attempt to make me feel guilty for the years of distance I had put between us.

I don't know whether this was my dad's innate avoidance of difficult or emotional subjects or a generosity in not pressing me or demanding an explanation. But even if he'd wanted to talk about it, to know what had gone wrong between us, I don't believe I would have told him about Stan and the Mafia story. Telling him I'd been told he was a Mob kingpin plotting to harm Ted and me seemed too big a hurt, too monstrous an insult to inflict on him at that stage of his life. Even then he was suffering the effects of the emphysema that would eventually kill him.

What was done was done, I thought, and there was nothing to be gained by telling him why I'd stayed away.

As I recalled from my visits as a teenager, he began making plans as soon as we arrived. We would see some old family friends, and go out to dinner at some favourite restaurants. It was a short visit, he noted, only a few days before we took the ferry to Vancouver Island to see my Aunt Penny (another reconnection), and then continued on to Tofino, where we'd booked some time at an inn on the ocean. We would make the most of the time we had, Dad said.

The first morning, Dad was taking us out for breakfast. He drove. I was in the passenger seat, Kevin in the back. We had just pulled away from the driveway when there was a loud clicking noise as the locks in the car doors engaged, all controlled by a button on the driver's side. I'd never seen automatic locks like these. My adrenalin surged. We were locked in, trapped, and there was no way to escape from the car. My heart was thudding, my mind racing. Was it all true after all? Was my father actually a mobster, taking us somewhere and ensuring we wouldn't be able to jump out when it became apparent our destination was not a restaurant, but likely some warehouse or hideout? I gripped my hands in my lap and tried to appear calm. My mind was racing through escape strategies. I looked over my shoulder to see how Kevin was reacting, but I couldn't read his expression. I glanced sideways at my father. He interrupted whatever he was in the middle of saying to smile at me. I smiled back weakly.

As we drove along familiar streets, my father continued to talk, relating updates and stories about people I'd known when I was younger, remarking on the record number of games at his regular haunt, the Capilano Golf Club, thanks to the great weather.

And then we arrived at the restaurant. He pulled into a parking spot, shifted the gear into park, and turned off the engine. The locks disengaged, popping up to free us.

"Here we are!" Dad sang out. "I'm thinking Eggs Benny. How about you?"

I am an idiot, I thought, *to once again get caught up in the madness of the narrative I've so recently escaped.* But of course breaking free of that world, that mindset, would require more than a cognitive choice to stop believing. It would take time to disentangle my subconscious reactions from a lifetime of secrets and running, and overcome the demonizing of my father. That was the first of many visits to see my dad over the years that followed. It was a long time before I conquered the unease I'd felt that first day or so when we were together.

WHEN I WAS seven months pregnant with my first baby, Mom called me at work in Halifax one morning to arrange a lunch. Since Stan's death we'd both been making a bigger effort to see each other and stay in touch. I had the sense my pregnancy was the brightest spot in her life these days and we talked about colours for a baby room and chose a pattern for a baby sweater and cap she planned to knit.

I was covering a murder trial at the courthouse downtown and we met at the Bluenose II restaurant during the noontime recess. Amid the cutlery rattle and the conversation buzz of lunching business people and the early tourists in for a lobster roll, she told me she'd been diagnosed with breast cancer.

The ambience of the room receded. I was aware of nothing but the intensity of my mother's gaze, her eyes locked on mine as if searching, asking for something, I wasn't sure what. We grasped hands across the table. I felt immobilized, silenced by shock and yet at the same time not completely surprised. I realized that on some level I'd been waiting for this since I was fifteen—the age Mom had been when her mother had died of breast cancer. It was like recognizing a sinister face in a crowd, one that I'd been half-watching for and hoping never to see.

I went with her to her next appointment with the surgeon who would remove her breast. She was an older woman who seemed no-nonsense and competent, if not particularly warm.

We left the surgeon's office, retrieved the car from a parking lot, and drove back to my house, having been instructed about preparations for the surgery. Mom sat in the passenger seat, silent.

"Are you okay?"

"I'm glad Stan will never have to know about this," she said. She was still thinking of him, still banking her thoughts off the backboard of what Stan would think, how Stan would feel. I didn't reply.

The mastectomy took place within a couple of weeks. I'd always thought of Mom as strong, stoic even. But I could tell as we sat in the waiting room that morning, watching for the nurse who would come to take her behind the swinging doors, that she was afraid. She wore a green hospital gown and disposable slippers. Her face was ashen and her hands restless, clenched in her lap, then grasping the arms of the chair, then smoothing the wrinkles of the gown across her lap. When the nurse came, I put my arms around Mom and told her I'd be there when she came out.

When she was released from hospital, she spent six weeks recovering at our house. My usually determined mother seemed traumatized, and she shrank from the drain she was supposed to empty each day. Its tube snaked beneath her shirt and under the bandages where her breast had been, collecting the fluid that seeped from the wound. The oncologist said the margins were clear, they'd got all the cancer, and chemotherapy wouldn't be necessary. She could take tamoxifen, a drug that had shown promise in preventing cancer recurrence, but it probably wasn't necessary.

Mom didn't seem as relieved as I'd expected her to be—as relieved as I was—but she was glad to be avoiding chemo and said no to the tamoxifen, which had its own scary list of side effects. Physically, she began to heal, but it was a long time before her energy returned.

It was around that time that she bought the little house in Malagash, across Tatamagouche Bay from her churches on the north shore of Nova Scotia. It was an old white storey-and-a-half that looked out across the water. She hung bird feeders near the windows and watched the hummingbirds and chick-adees flit from an overgrown rose bush to the feeders and back. She strung a clothesline and hung laundry to flap in the salty breezes. She planted a garden along the side of the house, and when Ted came to visit during her first summer there, we planted trees for both of her granddaughters—a vote of confidence in the future. She was attempting to put down roots and make a home in this peaceful retreat with the beautiful mauve skies over the bay in the evenings, and the bats that would swoop to her chimney as the light faded.

AVERY WAS BORN in July that year. I immediately understood the stories I'd heard about parents running into burning buildings or single-handedly lifting cars to save their children. I felt a rush of vulnerability as I realized I would do both those things; I would unquestioningly put my own life in jeopardy to prevent anything from harming this little blond squalling thing who, when she was quiet, looked at me so intently with her big blue eyes. It was as though we knew each other deeply from the moment she arrived, and she brought us all a great gift: she united us all again in our love for her, in our delight in this bright, busy being. Kevin and I found new accord, and for Mom and me it was as though Avery was a safe conduit through which to express not just our love for her, but our love for each other, which had been smothered in anger and resentment on my part, by fear and worry on hers.

By then Mom was back at work for her three churches. She tried to get to Halifax for visits every couple of weeks, and I would take Avery to her for overnights once in a while. We didn't speak of Stan or the Weird World. Neither of us wanted to jeopardize the harmony between us. I hoped that as time went by she would let go of her belief and fear, as the psychiatrist had said she would once she was separated from Stan. Whatever she was really thinking, she had chosen to behave as though life consisted only of what was before and around us. She worked six-day weeks, often long days visiting people in her congregation who were sick or old. She prepared for weddings, funerals, or baptisms, attended meetings, conducted Sunday services. She volunteered on the local community health board and continued to see her friends. She seemed tired, deeply weary, but she was putting one foot in front of the other. I hoped with Stan and his drama out of her life, she could find a new equilibrium, some peace.

I was seven months pregnant with my second baby when Mom discovered another cancerous lump in her remaining breast. This time she was less stricken by the news. She knew what had to be done and she set herself to it.

"I'll have the mastectomy and then I'll be even!" We joked that I couldn't get pregnant anymore because Mom had no more breasts to lose.

Again she recovered from the surgery at our house. But this time the recovery was much slower. It was as though her conviction to move forward had been removed along with the cancerous tissue. As my belly grew, she seemed to shrink into herself and spent long hours in the upstairs bedroom. Her post-operative pain was worse, her appetite negligible, her energy alarmingly low. Eventually she went back to Malagash, but she couldn't go back to work.

"You can't do that demanding kind of job anymore," the oncologist advised. I thought Mom would bristle at the suggestion her activities be limited, her work life cut short, but she just nodded. She seemed relieved. And she accepted a referral to a psychiatrist for suspected depression.

"It's fairly common," the doctor said. "You've been through a lot."

You have no idea, I thought.

LAURA WAS BORN in November, as the days became shorter, the sun a more distant visitor. She was a warm, bright light in a dark time for Mom, for all of us. Mom would sit for hours with Laura curled into her shoulder. It was the closest she came to happy in those months. When she was awake, Laura was endlessly content to lie on Mom's lap, her eyes locked on her grandmother's face. Mom made faces for her, sticking her tongue out, then in, and Laura would try to copy her. I know now how this must have stimulated her brain development, forging and strengthening cognitive paths within her tiny brain lobes. I was relieved to see Mom engaged, and Laura responding.

When Mom turned sixty, we had a small surprise party for her. Laura was almost four months old and happy to be passed among the dozen guests who were all anxious to hold this beautiful, serene child. We all marvelled as she willingly turned her imperturbable gaze to each new admirer, charming them all. I could see how they only reluctantly let her go to the next person waiting with outstretched arms. Laura had a calm sweetness about her that was both engaging and comforting, and we all drank it up, grateful.

Other than her visits to the city, Mom retreated to her little house on the Northumberland shore, trying to recover her energy and find a sense of purpose. Most days she could summon the strength to walk down the driveway, across the road, and along the beach. When we visited, she would take the girls, Avery's hand in hers and the other holding Laura on her hip. They sat on the beach and explored the wonders of hermit crabs and seaweed, and the grit of sand between their toes. Sometimes, if it was a good day, they'd walk down the road to the wharf and look at the fishing boats. Mostly, though, Mom spent months sitting in her big chair by the picture window, looking out over the bay and watching the birds at the feeder. Her doctor adjusted her medication, which helped a bit with her energy but had no impact on her sorrow. We still didn't talk about Stan, but I could see how she missed him, and missed both the drama and the purpose he'd brought to her life. She was mourning many losses that year.

It was during one of my visits to Malagash with the girls, in the evening after I'd put them to bed, that she told me about the dreams. She'd begun having dreams so powerful that they stayed with through her waking hours. They were dreams that she thought offered the possibility of healing and hopefulness. They seemed to be pointing her in a new direction. I realized that other than when she was interacting with her granddaughters, it was the first time in many months I'd seen her energized and enthused.

She began to do research about dreams. At the time there was no internet service in her rural area, so she started at the library. She borrowed and bought books about the science and spirituality of dreams and dreaming. On a visit to see Ted, who by then was living in Edmonton, he showed her how to do online searches and she spent hours clicking and reading. She discovered the website for The Haden Institute in North Carolina, a spiritual training centre with a focus on dream leadership and Jungian studies. The faculty was mostly clergy who used what they called dream work, or dream analysis and coaching, to help people deal with old traumas and decipher new understanding or directions for their lives. She was excited by this.

"Dreams and visions have been a source of spiritual knowledge and understanding for millennia," she told me. "All those strange dream images are messages in metaphors, in archetypal images." She compared them to parables. "They're not literal. But when I work with a dream, it can help me, help anyone, find deeper meaning and awareness."

She made notes about her dreams, and sought their meaning and messages. She called it listening for the Divine. All her listening and reading had helped her interpret what she called her "big dreams" and their messages of healing that had reanimated her life. Now she decided it was her calling to learn to help others interpret their dreams.

For two years she studied with The Haden Institute, travelling back and forth from North Carolina. She was engrossed and, as she learned, her depression lifted, and she was once again filled with her characteristic eagerness for challenge and meaning in her life. She had found her next path and would become a dream coach and counsellor. It would never be a financial success because she never turned people away if they couldn't afford to pay, but the rewards were deeply satisfying for her nonetheless.

I was also about to embark on a different path. After more than a decade together, Kevin and I were ready to acknowledge our marriage was over. We'd had some happy times, but there was a fundamental disconnect we couldn't overcome, despite our best efforts. The rollercoaster of going inside, not going inside, coming to terms with the deception . . . these all took their toll on our relationship. But there were other problems too. Family life, with the scripts and ideas we had in our minds of what it should be, seemed to emphasize the absence of deep connection.

We agreed to separate amicably. The most heart-rending part of the process was telling Laura and Avery, who were by then two-and-a-half and five respectively.

The four of us sat at the kitchen table. Avery shook her head. "No, no, no," she said as tears rolled down her cheeks. Laura watched us silently, her eyes big. She wasn't old enough to understand but she was absorbing our sadness, her sister's sorrow.

Kevin moved just around the corner and continued to see the girls regularly and be involved in their lives. There were changes for all of us. Mom was busy with dream work. I began specializing in health and medical reporting for CBC national news. The girls started school and became busy with piano lessons, gymnastics, and swimming. They got a dog at their father's house, where they spent a few nights a week.

Mom continued to visit and eventually decided to move to Halifax, to be closer to us and to have a larger market for her dream-coaching business. She would have us all over for dinner once a week. I'd pick up Avery and Laura from their after-school babysitter and we'd go to her apartment nearby. She'd choose from all our favourite meals—meat loaf, roasted chicken, and home-made stews and soups—and I was grateful for one less meal to worry about. When I had to be away for work, she would sometimes bring the girls to pick me up at the airport, giving me the pleasure of coming down the escalator to pick their excited faces out of the crowd, and having them run to me for hugs and kisses. She'd drop us at home and I'd find that she'd bought and left fresh milk and bread for us, knowing I wouldn't get to the grocery store until the next day. She did what she loved to do and what she did so well: she cared for us, showing us how much we mattered to her, how much she loved us.

When the girls' long-time babysitter retired, Mom began picking them up from school and bringing them home, spending hours with them at the playground across the street. We looked like a normal family in those days, and I thought we were finally moving on from the madness that had ruled our lives for so long.

During those years I continued to see my dad, either with the girls or on my own. If I happened to be in Vancouver for work, I'd stay a few extra days. One fall, before Kevin moved out, Dad came to visit us. It was the first time he'd travelled to see me since that terrible visit in Winnipeg when I was eleven. I took him and the girls to see Prince Edward Island. He loved the tidy houses, the green rolling hills.

"If I was young again I might just move here," he said as we drove through the bucolic countryside. We talked about his experiences during the war, and he told me about starting his postwar life with an investment company in Regina and then Vancouver. I asked him what he remembered from the years when Ted and I were small, when we still lived together as a family. We had never talked about his drinking or the years we were apart. I realized he'd done the best he could, loved me as much as he was able. He couldn't say he loved me, but he did say he was proud of me, and of my children.

"What good girls they are," he admired as we sat in a restaurant together. "So well-behaved." It was high praise from a man for whom children had always posed a bit of a puzzle: they were messy, noisy, and required entertaining. He was gingerly happy to be around his grandchildren, but for limited periods of time. As an old man, increasingly limited by his emphysema he was gentler, and I sensed that he regretted the time he'd missed with both his families, Tom and Linda first, and then Ted and me.

In the end, despite this and his long stretches of sobriety, he couldn't stay away from the booze. He was hospitalized after Tom found him in his condo during a bender. Linda flew up from Oklahoma to be with him as he suffered through the painful disorientation of withdrawal and the terrible psychosis and tremors of the DT's, delirium tremens. When that had passed, he didn't bounce back as he had always done before. Too much damage had been done, his emphysema exacerbated by the drinking. Linda held the phone to him as he tried to speak to me from his hospital bed. I was at a conference in Toronto and trying to decide whether to leave and head for Vancouver. He'd pulled through so many of these episodes before, I couldn't believe he wouldn't again. I spoke slowly to him through the phone line.

"Dad, I hope you're comfortable. I love you."

His response was a mumbling I couldn't understand. Linda came back on the line.

"What did he say?" I asked her.

"He said he loves you." If that's what he really said, it was the first time and I was grateful.

Late the next night, as I lay in bed in my Toronto hotel room, Linda called to say he was gone. It seemed unreal. I called Ted, who agreed to meet me in Vancouver. I booked a flight for the next morning and spent the rest of the night walking through Toronto neighbourhoods, hoping I could relieve the flood of feelings if I just kept moving. I was sad and full of regret. Mostly what I mourned was the lost years, and the finality of death that prevented me from ever truly knowing my father.

I wondered how my mother would react. She had spent most of her adult life feeling terrorized by Warren, running from him. Ted and I called her from his condo, in the midst of cleaning it out, along with Tom and Linda.

"I'm so sorry," she said. "Are you both okay?"

I said we were, told her we'd be there sorting things out for a few days.

"I know you don't want to hear this but be careful," she said. "You're in the middle of a shark pool and you can't trust the people around you there."

I shook my head. Warren was dead, but for Mom that didn't change anything, didn't mean the fear was over. For her, Stan's stories and the Weird World had not receded at all and this world was still a threatening place.

TWENTY-FOUR

IN OCTOBER 2009, I was in a hotel room in Paris when I got the call. I was dressing for the gala dinner of an international HIV vaccine conference when the phone rang. I was there through a fellowship with the Washington-based National Press Foundation that involved several days of training and lectures from virologists and vaccine experts, and then reporting on the news of the conference for the CBC. When I picked up the phone, I expected one of the other international reporters in the program to be on the line, checking whether I was ready to go.

It was my mother. She was calling from the hospital emergency room back home.

"I have Corrie and Donna with me," she said. In the past few years Mom had become a Quaker and increasingly involved with the peace movement, protesting against wars and Western involvement in the Middle East. Corrie and Donna were Quakers who'd become close friends.

"What's wrong?" I asked. I knew she'd been having some digestive problems just before I left, and we'd exchanged a few emails while I'd been gone in which she'd complained of severe stomach cramps that weren't going away. In her last email she said she thought she might have the flu.

"Pauline, honey..." She took a deep breath. Her voice seemed small and far away. I imagined her sitting on a gurney in the busy emergency room, her friends around her. I waited for her to continue.

"They've found a tumour. It's in my abdomen and they think it's ovarian cancer. They say it's advanced and I should get my affairs in order quickly."

She began to tell me other details, but I couldn't hear anything beyond the rushing of the blood in my ears. A crushing dread blotted out everything else, making it impossible to take in her words. She put Donna on the phone but I couldn't focus on what she was saying. Mom came back on the line.

"I can't understand. I can't hear you. I'm coming home. I'll be there as soon as I can."

She told me she'd be at Corrie's house until I got there.

"I love you, Pauline."

"I love you, Mom."

I've always said I'm a good person to have around in an emergency. I don't react to crisis in the moment; I keep my cool and the emotional response comes later, sometimes much later. But not that night. I began rushing around the room randomly throwing things into my suitcase. I was frantic and panicky. I stopped and tried to calm myself when I realized I had to book a flight. *I should call Air Canada*, I thought. But I couldn't think of how to find the number, couldn't slow myself long enough to think through what I was doing. Forgetting about my existing reservation, which I could have changed, I called to book a new flight—the first one leaving.

"The next one leaves in two-and-a-half hours," the agent told me. "It goes through London, but you won't be able to make that one. The next after that is tomorrow morning."

I couldn't wait that long. "I have to make it. My mom is dying." As I said it I was struck by the harshness of those words and flooded with the need to be with her. I began to cry. "Please."

She booked the flight and I called the hotel desk, cancelling the rest of my reservation and asking them to call me a cab. The man at the desk was alarmed when he saw me emerge from the elevator with my suitcase in hand and tears coursing down my cheeks. I couldn't stop them.

"The taxis are busy," he said. "It will be some time."

I begged him to call back and tell them it was an emergency. He looked concerned and asked me what was wrong. I couldn't say it again.

"Please, I have to go home. It's an emergency."

He called back and I went to wait outside. It was raining lightly. The desk man came out several times to check on me. "I'll call again," he said after about ten minutes, looking awkward but obviously wanting to help.

By the time the cab arrived, I wasn't sure I could make the flight. I sat in the back seat, soundless tears still streaming down my face. I had never felt so sad, so lost and alone. The driver kept glancing back at me in his rear-view mirror.

"Something is wrong?" he asked.

"My mother's in the hospital," was all I could manage. He nodded and drove faster. I made the flight, barely, and then spent six nightmarish hours waiting in London for my connection to Halifax.

I arrived the next morning and picked Mom up from Corrie's. I was astonished at how much her appearance had changed in the short time I'd been gone. She was in pain; the Tylenol 3s the hospital had provided weren't doing the job. And she was afraid, not of death I think, but of what she might have to endure on the way there.

I brought her home and set up the downstairs family room for her. I had built this addition to my house a couple of years earlier, with French doors looking out to the back garden and skylights providing lots of light, and I'd painted it a pale green that I suddenly realized was one of my mother's favourite colours. I'd thought I was building it as extra space for my kids, now thirteen and almost eleven, to have their friends over. Maybe I'd actually built it for my mother.

Soon after the diagnosis, Ted and Tessa came from Edmonton, where they were now living. That was the week I caught the H1N1 or swine flu virus, which had been detected for the first time in Mexico earlier in the year. As a health reporter I'd covered the international outbreaks, reporting on the symptoms, deaths, and the World Health Organization's declaration of a pandemic. I knew sick people could be especially vulnerable, so Ted took Mom back to her apartment and stayed with her there, hoping she wouldn't catch it. The girls went to stay with their father. When I was well again, Ted came and wiped down every surface in my house with a strong disinfectant before he brought Mom back.

The new oncologist quickly scheduled surgery. She met me in the hallway of the surgical floor after it was over. Her expression was solemn as she took the surgical mask from her face and told me what she'd found. She was matter-of-fact.

"Her abdomen is frozen with tumours," she said, describing how she'd been able to remove an ovary but that was all. The tumours had filled her abdominal cavity, curling around her organs, creeping into the surrounding tissue, pushing into her bowel. Yes, they'd been growing for a while. No, there was nothing more to be done surgically.

The biopsy showed that the new cancer was metastases of her first breast cancer, the result of some malignant cell or cells having escaped the surgeon's scalpel thirteen years earlier and travelled in her bloodstream, hiding and biding their time, waiting to bloom in the tender flesh of her belly. Her case was transferred to a breast cancer specialist, Dr. Daniel Rayson—a knowledgeable and gentle man I had interviewed as an expert voice for my CBC stories many times. He sat beside her, held her hand, and spoke softly. She visibly relaxed. He said there was a chance that a newer drug, a so-called targeted therapy called Herceptin, could buy her some time, maybe some years. They would try it. In the meantime, he promised her pain would be controlled. She smiled at him and I could see she had completely entrusted herself to him and was relieved to be handing the situation over to someone so quietly competent, so empathic.

In the following months it became apparent that hers was not a cancer that was receptive to the expensive anti-cancer drug. Her symptoms continued to worsen. She had no appetite and even if she managed to take a few bites, struggled to keep food down. The opioid painkillers managed the pain but they made her sleepy, and unable to concentrate.

My girls and I watched helplessly as she wasted; it was as if she was slowly but relentlessly disappearing before our eyes. I made foods I hoped would tempt her, but she had lost all desire for things that she would once have found irresistible. The son of a friend gave me some marijuana, hoping it would give her back some appetite, and she agreed to try it. A good friend and neighbour came and smoked it with us. A psychologist, he'd had cancer years earlier and used pot to reduce pain and increase appetite. That made Mom feel safer in her first encounter with the drug. I opened the windows and shook my head as I watched her take the joint and pull from it. I could never have imagined having this experience with my mother at my kitchen table.

"Will you smoke with me?" she asked me.

"Do you want me to?"

She nodded and I took a puff.

"Have you smoked this before?" she asked.

"Yes," I answered simply, and she nodded. I remembered hiding a little bag of pot in my bedside drawer as a teenager, knowing my mother wouldn't find it because she would never invade my privacy.

We continued to sit around the table after the joint was finished. Mom and our neighbour had a meandering philosophical conversation while we waited to see what effect the drug would have.

"I think I just saw a doughnut go by!" Mom raised her hand to describe the imaginary circle of the suddenly desirable doughnut. We all laughed and the neighbour rushed out to buy doughnuts. When he returned shortly with a dozen, Mom chose a chocolate-covered one and ate it all. She had a few bites of a honey-glazed one next. It was the most she'd eaten in weeks, and we rejoiced. For a couple of weeks the bit of pot she puffed before mealtimes seemed to help, but too soon even that effect faded, and the wasting resumed.

It is remarkable how, when all is bleak, there can be signs of grace. For me it was sleep. I'd suffered from insomnia on and off as an adult, but now in the midst of such a terrible time, I slept long undisturbed stretches, like a teenager again—precious dreamless hours of escape. I would feel myself becoming sleepy right after supper and, with effort, was able to stay awake long enough to get the girls and then Mom settled for the night. By now we had a hospital bed in the living room, even the two steps up from the family room being too much for her to manage. I would help her to the bathroom, get the pillows arranged around her in a way that relieved pressure against the most painful spots on her body, and bring her medication to her.

"Are you okay if I go to bed now?" I asked.

"Yes, you must be exhausted."

Many nights the final thing she said to me before I headed upstairs to my bed was thank you.

"I'm so grateful. I don't know what else I would have done, where else I would have gone."

"Of course, Mom." I hugged her. She never took anything for granted, not even my love. *She should be able to take that for granted,* I thought. And then I would climb the stairs to my room, lose myself to ten or eleven hours of unbroken sleep, and wake the next morning in the same position as when I'd fallen into bed.

I will always be grateful to the palliative-care nurse who told me when it was time to leave work to be with Mom full-time. That gave us time. I'd been working, trying to avoid any travel, and continuing the usual activities with the girls. As a result, my limited time with Mom had been busy—attending to her care and meals; sorting her medication; taking her to appointments, or often to the emergency room when some complication would arise in the middle of the night. She'd had blood clots in her lungs, not uncommon in cancer patients. As her death approached, Mom and I both knew that this was our last chance to heal our relationship. I was aware I needed to fully and finally forgive her for the ways her decisions had affected us all. I wasn't there yet, but we were gentle with each other, we talked about her life, and she recalled family times together when Ted and I were small. We hadn't talked about Stan until one evening Mom broke our unspoken pact of silence. She knew the end was near—only a couple of weeks away, as it turned out—and she wanted, needed, to give me one last warning.

"I know you don't want to hear this," she began in a preamble that immediately raised my hackles, as I realized the gist of what was coming. "Please, be careful. Don't trust the old Vancouver crowd, the people who were around your father. Please."

We were in the kitchen and I turned away to wipe the counter so she wouldn't see the flare of my anger. Even now, with her death imminent, she would not let this fantasy go. But when I turned to her and saw her earnest, pleading expression, I realized how much of her life, her heart, and her mind had been invested in the story. She couldn't stop believing, given all that it had cost and what she had put her family through for its sake. Still, I could not acquiesce and promise to protect myself from something that didn't exist.

"I don't need to be any more careful than anyone else," I said, hoping my voice was neutral and not betraying my impatience. But instead of continuing the argument, she sighed heavily.

"Oh, Pauline, if you think I'm crazy for believing, how you must have hated me." Her eyes were moist and I felt tears welling too.

"No, I never hated you, Mom. I have always loved you. But I have been very angry."

She nodded. It was as close as we could come to apologizing for the pain we had caused each other, the best we could do to make our peace.

———

MOM HAD PLANNED to die at home, but it became clear we couldn't make her comfortable. The day the ambulance came to take her to the palliative care unit at the hospital her eyes, huge in her skeletal face, were locked on mine as the paramedics lifted her onto a gurney and rolled her out the door. I tried to smile as I walked alongside, promising to follow in my car soon, but barely made it back in the house before the wrenching sobs began.

It was the moment that undid me, that tore away whatever scraps of denial about my mother's coming death I had managed to wrap around myself despite the pills, the hospital appointments, and her rapidly diminishing form. I thought of all her comings and goings from my door, the times she'd taken the girls to the park and brought them back tired and happy. Arriving with armfuls of contributions for a meal, or flowers from her garden. Coming late every Christmas Eve when the girls were young, after conducting her church service in Tatamagouche and then driving on lonely highways to be with us for Christmas morning. I thought of how her arrivals had enriched our lives, even during the times I'd been angry and unappreciative. I thought of how she would not come in my door again.

OVER THE NEXT days at the hospital, Mom's friends came to sit with her, to say goodbye. Ted was there, sleeping on the couch in the visitor's room. On the Saturday before Mom died, Avery and Laura each spent some time alone with her in her room. It would be their last visit.

That night the moon was full, raining white light and casting shadows below the trees and between the buildings nearby. I moved Mom's hospital bed around so she could see its brightness out the window. Was it something magical about the moonlight, or was it—as they say—that just as a light bulb burns brightest before it fizzles out, dying people will sometimes have a surge of new life and energy in their final days or hours? Either way, after weeks of declining energy and more hours spent sleeping, Mom was suddenly fully awake and invigorated. She asked me to raise the back of her bed and sat up, looking alert. When an orderly brought in sheets for the cot I would sleep on that night, she joked with him that we were having a sleepover.

Ruth was back and I was intoxicated by her presence. It was like being with the true essence of the woman who had raised me. She seemed to radiate her natural enthusiasm and desire to be deeply engaged, fully caught up in the intimacy of our conversation. I sat in the chair beside her bed and we talked for hours, deep into the night. We both knew it was a temporary state and revelled in it together. We wrote her memorial service that night, talked about the readings, reflected on the adults her three granddaughters would one day be. She tried to prepare me for the impact of her death, telling me about her grief when her mother died.

"It's like waves," she said, holding my hand. "You'll think you can't bear it and then that wave will recede and you'll catch your breath. You'll be okay. It will get easier."

We were together as we hadn't been for years. It was her last gift to me.

For the next four days, she was only semi-conscious. She died in the early dawn of Canada Day, July 1, 2010. Ted and I were both there, as she'd predicted we would be, holding her hands. When she was gone, we gathered her belongings and walked out of the hospital and into the sunrise, numb and disoriented.

As I tried to digest this ending, I realized the story of Ruth and Stan was over too. It was a story she believed in until her last breath. I wondered if he'd been waiting for her, if they were finally together in some other realm without gangsters, where they could simply love.

TWENTY-FIVE

"WHAT IS YOUR mother's birthday?"

The automated voice at the credit-card company's call centre is asking a most routine question, for security purposes, it intones.

And the realization washes over me, along with a mix of shame and incredulity.

The answer is today, February 27th. How did the significance escape me when I woke up this morning? All week I have been aware of this day's approach. It has been steadily advancing toward me, a square on a calendar bearing down, loaded.

Despite this, it has taken an automaton to remind me this morning.

My mother would have been seventy-five today.

In the years since her death, I've found she was right. Grief has a tidal action, sweeping in as a dark swirling assault, threatening to pull your feet out from under you, and then receding. As I cleaned out her apartment in the weeks after she was gone, I talked to her, and sometimes raged, sometimes wept. There were discoveries as I cleaned out drawers and sorted what to donate, what to throw out, what to keep. Photographs and journals, and in a corner of the porch, a plastic grocery bag full of letters that she'd probably meant to burn. I sat on the floor and read them. Once again I was drawn into the remarkable stories of the Weird World and the finely crafted characters that peopled it and took on life through the letters. They wrote for advice, for comfort or to comfort. They told heartbreaking stories of how they'd become caught up in organized crime, picked up in a sweep, imprisoned, and then saved; over and over, compelling narratives of redemption, grace, and beauty emerging from evil and ugliness. I could see how this would have been irresistible to my mother, these miraculous happy endings that found the sufferers living contented, illuminated lives. Stan would have understood my mother's longing for reconciliation and spiritual elevation. I pictured him in his office typing and handwriting letter after letter, pausing to contemplate the most effective narrative arc for each missive, to recall the details, the turns of phrase, script, style of each particular character he'd created, fleshed out in ink and paper. Did he have a Rolodex of all the people he'd made up, complete with notes about their individual stories and quirks, and samples of "their" writing? Or did they all live in his head fully formed? I think the latter. I think he was brilliant, and that allowed him to maintain the complexity and subtlety of his stories, great constellations of lives and worlds at play in his impressive but corrupted mind.

After years of trying to forget, trying to put it all behind me, I once again became preoccupied with possible explanations for what had happened to us. Psychiatric pathology aside, I decided that Stan, a moral man, could not simply fall in love with another

294 \\\ PAULINE DAKIN

woman and betray his marriage. On some level he needed a compelling reason to be with our mother and, consciously or subconsciously, he constructed the wild tale that was the excuse that threw them together, that necessitated moving around the country in lockstep, sometimes on the run and hiding together. What better environment could he have designed to encourage intimacy than running for your life together, trusting only each other when danger lurked around every corner and anyone could be a double?

My mother's experiences also preoccupied me. She'd divulged the uglier memories from her early life reluctantly, recounting them only at my prodding, mostly on road trips as we drove with eyes facing forward, our thoughts focused on the past. I sifted through the stories she'd told me, the entries in her journals, the recordings she made at my request when we realized she was dying. I realized how the abuse and emotional betrayal at the hands of first her father and then her husband had left her vulnerable to the gentleness, the charisma of a man like Stan. When we first started going to his church she'd recorded his sermons, which she would listen to later for inspiration and sustenance, drawing strength and wisdom from them. She'd admired his mind, his faith, his humility. "I'm just an old dulse picker from Grand Manan," he'd drawl, making fun of his humble beginnings. But he was so much more and she couldn't help but be drawn to this man who encompassed such muscular spirituality alongside an irreverent sense of fun; a crusader for justice who also spoke with a soft, compassionate voice of the brokenness of the world, and worked so hard to repair it. I thought about Mom's need for purpose and meaning in her life, her longing for intellectual and spiritual engagement, her excitement at being part of something larger. She also had a strong sense of adventure. This was the woman who chose the life of a flight attendant in the early days of commercial flight. And I recognized some fundamental restlessness in her . . . the same restlessness that made her fidget and drove her father to eject her from his truck when she was small. All of these traits were fed and satisfied by Stan and his story of danger, intrigue, and reconciliation.

It made sense that they would come together, but still I had so many questions, and no way to get answers. Perhaps, I thought, I would never really know why our lives took such a strange turn.

I vacillated between a desire to put it all behind me and a compulsion to understand. I continued, periodically, to search the literature on psychosis, schizophrenia, paranoia, *folie à deux*, but none of the descriptions or case studies I read ever quite fit.

Until one day, one did. Maybe some upgrade in a search engine brought me the citation that had eluded me for so long. Or perhaps it was the first time my search terms included the word *delusional*.

It was an abstract of an article in the *Journal of Clinical Psychiatry* that talked about a condition called delusional disorder, describing it as rare and distinguishing it from other disorders that involve paranoia.

I felt growing excitement as I read more.

"Delusional disorder is an uncommon condition characterized by the presence of one or more non-bizarre delusions and the relative absence of associated psychopathology. The delusions concern experiences that can conceivably occur in real life."[1] Yes! Stan's delusion wasn't about disembodied voices, it didn't require him to wear tinfoil caps to fend off the signals from space beings. It was non-bizarre, possible, no matter how improbable.

---

1   Delusional disorder: The recognition and management of paranoia. Manschreck, Theo C. *Journal of Clinical Psychiatry*, Vol 57 (3, Suppl), 1996, 32–38.

It continued: "Generally normal appearance/behaviour; and the exclusion of other disorders. Patients are usually unaware of the psychiatric nature of the condition. Onset age is usually middle or late adulthood."

A later onset would have allowed Stan to become established in life, build his accomplishments and credentials. There were no signs of any other psychological problems; he was high-functioning, held responsible positions, could think and reason better than most, and he was respected and involved in the community. These were the traits that had always ruled out other diagnoses, that were incompatible with better-known psychiatric conditions such as schizophrenia.

Once I had the term, the name, the diagnosis, I searched obsessively. It turned out even Wikipedia was aware of delusional disorder:

> Delusional disorder is a mental illness in which the patient present with delusions, but with no accompanying prominent hallucinations, thought disorder, mood disorder, or significant flattening affect. Delusions are a specific symptom of psychosis... Non-bizarre delusions are fixed false beliefs that involve situations that could potentially occur in real life, such as being followed or poisoned.[2]

Followed or poisoned! I wished I could show this to my mother, point and say, "See, he was sick. It's not real!"

And the thing that differentiated this from so many other psychiatric conditions: "Apart from their delusions, people with delusional disorder may continue to socialize and function in a

---

2   https://en.wikipedia.org/wiki/Delusional_disorder. Accessed on 02-12-16.

normal manner and their behavior does not generally seem odd or bizarre."

I felt the rightness of this, the answers shifting into place, the plausibility of this explanation for Stan's beliefs and behaviours. But I needed to be sure. I wanted confirmation, from someone with expertise and an unbiased distance from the situation.

One of the great privileges of being a reporter is the entree it provides, the access to important thinkers or influential people and the licence to ask them questions. As a health reporter, I was accustomed to contacting the authors of studies and papers in medical and scientific journals all over the world. So I emailed the author of "Delusional Disorder: The Recognition and Management of Paranoia."

Dr. Theo Manschreck is a senior psychiatrist at Massachusetts General Hospital, a senior researcher with the Commonwealth Research Center, Clinical Neuroscience and Psychopharmacology research unit, which is associated with Beth Israel Deaconess Medical Center and Harvard Medical School. He's area medical director in the Massachusetts Department of Mental Health, and on the faculty of the University of Massachusetts Medical School. He's been associate editor of the journal *Current Psychiatry*, has published widely, and is cited by hundreds of other researchers. He's an authority on schizophrenia and has authored many papers on that topic, but is also one of the few researchers to become interested in and publish on delusional disorder. And he agreed to take my phone call.

He told me his interest was rooted in curiosity about paranoid behaviour, trying to understand its causes and mechanism. I told him I also had a particular interest.

"I'm writing about someone who I think had delusional disorder," I began. "Actually, it was someone my family came into contact with when I was young. And I've just learned of this condition." I told him about Stan and Mom, the running, the secret anti-Mafia organization.

"I'm hoping you can tell me more about delusional disorder and confirm whether I've got the diagnosis right."

"There are far more mysteries to this than understanding," he said, but began by filling in some of the history. It was once simply called paranoia. In the early 1900s, German psychiatrist Emil Kraepelin described the condition as being separate from schizophrenia or other psychoses. Kraepelin was a giant in the field and widely considered the founder of a modern and scientific understanding of major mental illness.

"Delusional disorder is very, very uncommon and that's a good deal of the reason why there is such limited information about it," Dr. Manschreck told me. "As a ballpark figure, I think of the commonality of this condition compared to schizophrenia as being 1/200th of it, and schizophrenia being a roughly 1-percent prevalence, generally. So it's uncommon, but I think it may be less rare than we think. The difficulty is people who have it don't see themselves as ill, so many cases have never presented to a medical evaluation and certainly not to a psychiatrist. I mean, they're actively opposed to the idea that this is a mental illness, so they come to our attention by causing trouble, getting into difficulty. In an outburst in a courtroom or if they have the somatic type [a delusion that they have a physical illness or a problem in their body] they go to surgeons or dermatologists."

He said that despite his long experience, he'd treated only a few people with delusional disorder—encounters he described as intense.

I was more convinced than ever that Stan had suffered from this disorder, but I was still troubled by the bizarre experiences that would have required the involvement of others: the time early on in Vancouver when he and Mom were chased in the car by men with guns; the time in Winnipeg the "Italian mobsters" broke into the Searses' house and we could all hear the violent fight in the basement; the tussle outside my apartment door after I'd first moved to Halifax, when someone supposedly died. Delusional disorder didn't fully explain those memories.

"Would someone with delusional disorder consciously manipulate the situation, say, hire or recruit helpers to make it seem more real?" I asked Dr. Manschreck.

"In other words to demonstrate the validity of the idea, to convince others?" He thought for a moment. "Well, the idea of bringing converts to your view, there's a subtype of delusional disorder called grandiose, with which that type of behaviour is associated."

I would later learn more about that subtype, but Dr. Manschreck seemed fascinated by the elaborateness of Stan's delusional world.

"The complexity of it. There is pretty good evidence that the complexity of the delusion may be a pretty good correlate of intelligence and capacity for creative thinking and consistency. And also the fact he was able to keep this under wraps from most people is itself an accomplishment; it's pretty interesting."

Then he had a question for me. "Have you felt particularly affected by this whole experience in your life? Because you were sort of caught up in it, basically it was part of your life."

I paused, realizing I was much more comfortable as the reporter gathering information than as the collateral damage of a major psychiatric disorder. Yes, I told him, it had greatly affected me, affected my choices and my relationships, and put a barrier between those I could never tell and myself. Always, even before I was told what was behind my family's bizarre behaviour, it had made me feel "other" and I discerned some fundamental yet unexplainable difference in myself because of it.

And now, as I sought understanding, I realized I felt shame for having been caught up in it, for believing. And guilt for the way others were impacted: Dad, Tom and Linda, my ex-husband, Ted, and all the friends growing up who must have wondered where I'd disappeared to without saying goodbye.

"I went along with it because I couldn't understand how someone who was such a good person, so good to me and so reliable in every other way, could be deliberately deceiving me."

"And your brother?"

"Yes, it affected him too. He has a good life, a loving partner, a responsible job, many friends. But I think he's realized in the last few years how much more he might have accomplished, how life might have been different, without the interruption and chaos."

"Uh-huh." Dr. Manschreck sounded like the archetypal psychiatrist, thoughtful and encouraging, and I couldn't help smiling.

"Yes," he continued. "If you have that sense of fear or being put upon and the conspiratorial forces being so ubiquitous in your life, and that potentially, you know, every city has some-body associated with this, you could imagine that you could never really feel away from it." Now he paused and then: "Wow."

The condition has undergone little quality research, he told me. Too few patients are identified to recruit the numbers needed for the gold standard in research—randomized con-trolled trials. The literature mostly contains studies with small sample sizes or case reports that rely on clinical descriptions alone. The resulting lack of data means that diagnosis is compli-cated and knowledge of the causes and processes of the disease is anything but clear.

"Things are slow to change. The bottom line is it remains elusive as a topic."

Dr. Manschreck said psychiatrists long believed delusional disorder was untreatable, but there was a psychiatrist—a man with perhaps the largest amount of clinical experience with people afflicted with the condition—who'd had some influential success using a drug that blocks dopamine receptors in the brain, a dopamine antagonist called pimozide.

"He's somebody in your country, a Canadian, at Dalhousie University."

"Dalhousie! That's in my city!" It seemed a remarkable coincidence that a pre-eminent, internationally known authority on this little-studied condition that had so affected my family lived a short drive from my home.

"His name is Alistair Munro and his understanding of this condition is first-rate."

The next step was clear. I called a contact with the university and discovered Dr. Munro was now retired and professor emeritus with Dalhousie University's department of psychiatry. My contact forwarded an email address for him and I sent my query, crossing my fingers he was still alive and well and willing to talk to me.

ALISTAIR MUNRO WAS exactly as he'd described himself in his return email.

"I am tall," he'd written. "Not in the first flush of youth and have white hair. If you see any handsome men around, they aren't me!"

I was delighted by his response and his self-deprecating humour. I'd written back to say that handsome was overrated, and I was looking forward to talking to him. Such an understatement. I felt as though I'd been waiting for decades for this conversation.

He arrived, dressed in professorial jacket and slacks, at the café in a food court in downtown Halifax where we'd agreed to meet. His wife and granddaughter were with him.

"They just wanted to say hello," he said, before they went off shopping. It turned out they knew who I was and wanted to meet me because they listened to the CBC documentary show I hosted on Sunday mornings. *How strange*, I thought, *the unexpected connections and conjunctions.*

Dr. Munro, as I'd learned from my conversation with Dr. Manschreck, had literally written the book on delusional disorder. In *Delusional Disorder: Paranoia and Related Illnesses* he wrote:

> To many mental health professionals, delusional disorder remains a shadowy concept and it is quite possible for a psychiatrist to have a busy practice and either not see, or not recognize, cases of the illness. This arises from a combination of a lack of knowledge about it and of relative rarity in the psychiatrist's office of patients with the disorder.[3]

His interest was piqued decades earlier when he'd worked in Liverpool, England. He'd encountered a patient who believed, was convinced, he gave off a bad smell. Over the years and especially after he'd moved to Toronto, Munro found more patients with so-called non-bizarre delusions, many of them who'd initially

---

3   Munro, Alistair, *Delusional Disorder: Paranoia and Related Illnesses*, Cambridge University Press, 1999 p.1. Accessed on 02-12-16 at http://catdir.loc.gov/catdir/samples/cam032/98017210.pdf.

consulted dermatologists or other doctors about physical symptoms central to their delusions . . . a somatic subtype of the disorder. He started writing about somatic cases in the 1970s. At the time he called it monosymptomatic hypochondriacal psychosis (MHP). But it became clear as he encountered more patients that it was one of a number of subtypes of delusional disorder.

He described the other subtypes to me as we drank our coffee. Erotomanic subtype is the belief that someone, perhaps a celebrity or public figure, is in love with you. It explains the obsessive fans who are occasionally arrested outside the home of some Hollywood star or other and claim the celebrity was secretly in love with them or sending them messages.

People with jealous subtype believe, lacking any evidence, that a sex partner is unfaithful.

With grandiose type, the patients believe they have great but unrecognized power, insight, identity, secret knowledge, or outstanding skill. Stan, I thought, with his exclusive pipeline to information about the Weird World, and his high position in it, fit the description.

Persecutory type involves the belief that the sufferer is being cheated, spied on, drugged, followed, plotted against, or otherwise harmed by a person or a group of people. *Oh yeah*, I thought. *That's the one.*

But Dr. Munro explained there is a mixed type that combines the traits of more than one subtype. This is what I now believe to be Stan's diagnosis: primary persecutory type delusional disorder, with secondary grandiose type. Munro confirmed this sounded right. *These are names that define the condition, that slot it neatly into clearly labelled drawers of dysfunction*, I thought, *but they cannot contain the magnitude of the impact on our lives.*

I tried to describe to Dr. Munro how complex and detailed Stan's delusion was, how intricately thought out it was and often backed up by or tied to events in the news, and how it all existed alongside a life that appeared completely normal. He nodded. "It's a strange, partial psychosis that leaves part of the personality unaffected."

I'd read that some experts include misidentification syndromes in the domain of delusional disorder, including Capgras syndrome. Munro has written about this as well. That's the delusion that a close friend or relative has been replaced by an imposter. I felt a jolt when I first read the description of this, thinking of all the family and friends we'd been told had been grabbed and replaced by doubles.

Interestingly, some researchers link Capgras syndrome to physical damage to the brain. One review says:

> Recent studies have shown that between 25 and 40 percent of these cases are associated with organic disorders, which include dementia, head trauma, epilepsy, and cerebrovascular disease . . . neuroimaging evidence revealed a link between Capgras syndrome and right hemisphere abnormalities, particularly in the frontal and temporal regions.[4]

I don't know when Stan's delusion began, but I thought about the childhood tobogganing accident that had left his face scarred. Had that impact or some other injury caused damage to the frontal or temporal regions of his brain? I will

---

4   A review of the phenomenology and cognitive neuropsychological origins of the Capgras syndrome. Edelstyn, N.M, and Oyebode, F. *International Journal of Geriatric Psychiatry*, 1999 Jan; 14(1):48–59.

never know. And it will likely be years before anyone can reliably speculate, given how little research exists, and how hard it is to identify patients.

Over the years Dr. Munro contributed much that is known. He worked with and studied fifty patients with delusional disorder. They were men and women, from thirteen different ethnic groups, as young as teenagers but more usually from their late twenties into old age. He found the condition to be generally life-long and progressive. He decided there was less of a genetic component to the illness than seen in schizophrenia. His educated guess is that there's a biochemical cause and the brain chemical dopamine, a neurotransmitter, plays an important role. He pioneered the use of pimozide—a drug previously used to treat Tourette's syndrome—which blocks the chemical from bonding with dopamine receptors in the brain. He found that while it didn't necessarily make patients admit they were wrong or abandon their delusions, he could see it helped them relax and be less driven by those delusions. "And in some cases, people who were treated did eventually admit their ideas were crazy," he said.

As I sat across from the doctor taking notes, it was hard not to wonder how my life might have been different if Stan had somehow met and been treated by Dr. Munro. Where would I now live? I may never have left Vancouver. Would I be a reporter, producer, writer? Everything might have been so different. And yet, I concluded, I could not fathom or wish for a life without my children, my girls, who were an indirect product of the path determined by Stan's delusion.

"It's not really so rare as people say," Dr. Munro interrupted my thoughts. I had read various studies that put the prevalence in the general population at between 0.02 percent and 0.05

percent, compared to a 1-percent prevalence for schizophrenia. But Dr. Munro believes that, as more people learn about it, it will be shown to be much more common.

"You do hear about these things sometimes, we just don't hear them called delusional disorder." He cited a shocking event that was widely covered in the news in the late 1970s, the Jonestown "revolutionary suicides."

Jonestown was a commune established in Guyana, South America, by American Rev. Jim Jones, who led a quasi-religious group called the Peoples Temple. He believed the CIA and other intelligence agencies were conspiring to destroy the settlement, part of a complex conspiracy theory he fostered in his cult. He staged fake sniper attacks on himself to convince his followers of the threat and ultimately led more than nine hundred Americans to commit mass suicide by cyanide poisoning in November of 1978.[5]

Our situation could have been worse, I thought wryly. At least our mother didn't sign us up for a death cult. But I had to ask Dr. Munro about her, about the *folie à deux* phenomenon.

"She was a smart woman. How did she fall for this?"

Dr. Munro said he'd seen physicians and lawyers taken in by their patients' or clients' delusions, particularly with smart individuals. "When they're highly intelligent, they can develop very complex and smart delusions." He said even the smartest people around them can be susceptible because of the intensity of the belief, the tightly structured nature of the delusion, and the sometimes exquisite pseudo-logic used to bolster it.

I shook Dr. Munro's hand and thanked him for his time and

---

5   Reiterman, Tim; Jacobs, John (1982), *Raven: The Untold Story of the Rev. Jim Jones and His People*, E.P. Dutton, ISBN 0-525-24136-1, pp. 360–72.

willingness to share his knowledge. He was gracious. "Your writing about this could be important," he said, and then we parted.

In the days following our meeting, I reviewed my notes and my feelings. The diagnosis changed everything. The miasma of confusion and resentment, the darkness of my anger toward Stan began to dissipate. I felt lighter. I no longer had to hate him for what he'd done to our family; I could let go of that weight. It wasn't malevolence or guile. He had not deliberately set out to deceive us. We had become caught up in his delusion by chance.

I thought of my mother, looking for help to deal with the pain and dysfunction of living with an alcoholic husband, and the helpful person at Al-Anon who'd recommended a great counsellor, the minister at the local church, Stan Sears. That referral had put us—Mom, Ted, and me—on an unimaginable path.

TWENTY-SIX

SYBIL DIED LATE in 2014. We'd kept in touch with cards at Christmas and on birthdays, but never broached the topic of the Weird World. I visited her once after Mom and Stan had told me about the Mafia threats. It was about nine years after Stan died. By then she was in her eighties, losing her sight, and living alone in the mobile home where she and Stan had retired. I was in Vancouver for work and took the ferry to Gibson's. I hoped she could help me understand what had happened, and why. Had Stan been living with her during the time he'd told Mom and me that he was inside? Did she believe in the Weird World? If not, did she have any explanation for why Stan would make it up? I had many questions, but I hesitated. She seemed frail and I didn't want to upset her.

We went out for lunch and when we came back she made us tea. I took a breath and then began.

"When I was twenty-three I was told our families were in danger."

She nodded.

"You were aware of that danger?"

Again she nodded. "Yes."

"And do you think there's still a threat to you, to us?"

She looked steadily back at me. "I don't know right now, but there was and it's possible there still is."

"Do you worry? Are you afraid?"

She gave a slight shrug. "Oh, I just live my life."

I tried a few more questions but it was clear she didn't want to talk about it. I didn't want to push her. I decided I couldn't tell her Stan's delusional world was all a fantasy. It was too much and I sensed that, like Mom, after decades of being part of it, she would not believe me.

After Sybil died I thought about contacting their surviving son, John. I knew he'd been living in Vancouver and then retired somewhere in the Interior of B.C. I found a phone number for him in the eastern Fraser Valley. Ironically John lives not far from the fictional location of PH, Place of Hope. But I was afraid to call. He was the last link to Stan. If he knew about his father's delusional story, he might not welcome reminders and questions. If he didn't know about it, he might not believe me. He'd conclude I was crazy, trying to besmirch his father's memory.

But I needed to know when Stan's delusion began, how many others were caught up in it, and whether John had any information about what might have prompted it. Finally, I made the call. As he answered, I thought that there was no way he could imagine what was coming. I asked him if he remembered my family, and how we'd moved around the country with his parents, and he said yes.

"Some strange things happened back then," I told him. "I'd really like to talk to you about that."

"Oh-oh," he said, half-joking. *He knows*, I thought. But he didn't hang up. He agreed to see me and I booked my flight to Vancouver.

JOHN SEARS AND his wife, Pat, live in a new development of attractive West Coast–style homes in rural British Columbia, near a golf course. As I pulled my rental car into their driveway, I was nervous. I'd imagined this conversation for so long, but there was no way to predict how they would react. As I'd driven from Vancouver that morning, along the Fraser River, I'd gone over the things I wanted to ask them.

John opened the door to my knock. He looked younger than his almost seventy years, with short hair, and eyes like his dad's, although they were a more subdued blue. He and Pat welcomed me warmly. They'd made a lunch of salmon and salad, and we began by talking about where our lives had gone since we'd last met, some forty years earlier, when I was an elementary school-aged child and John was a young man. We were easing in to the conversation we were both eager to have, laying a foundation for a discussion about the events that had such a profound impact on all of us.

After we'd finished eating, I told John and Pat about the night I went to the motel in Sussex and what I'd learned there, and about the running, and the Weird World, and about Stan and my mother's decades-long love affair. And then I told them I believed Stan had suffered from delusional disorder; that it was the only thing that could explain what had happened to him, to all of us.

"Wow," John kept saying. And finally, "I've used up my quota of wows," he laughed apologetically. "It's hard to stop saying it." But it was a true response to what I was telling him.

"So what did you know?" I asked.

He said the first time anything strange happened with his father, John was in his early twenties. He and his brother, Michael, four years younger, were watching television with their dad one night when Stan decided to take the dog for a walk. He was gone a long time and the brothers began to worry.

"Mike and I went to the door and looked out, and the dog was there. So the dog's come back—where's Dad? Later he came kind of stumbling through the door and he looked dishevelled, and there was moisture in his eyes, like he'd been through something, and he was shaky in the breath."

When they asked what had happened, Stan said he'd been attacked. John and Mike wanted to go after the attackers, or at least call the police, but Stan said no.

"He said, 'It's been handled, everything's fine.' That's about all he said. Weird. But that was just one of several things."

There were times when Stan and Sybil said they had to go to the church retreat at Paradise Valley, saying there was danger. "And there were other nights when he'd say, 'Don't go out, don't take the dog out tonight. Stay inside. There's danger.'"

Stan didn't talk about the Mafia to them, but told his sons about bad guys with guns who posed a threat. And about the weird ones, "some RCMP special services who were involved and on his side, looking after things." John remembers his father saying my family was involved, that the danger had to do with my father. John thinks this would have been in the early 1970s, about the time my mother met him.

John was skeptical about it all but Michael, then in his late teens, was spooked, John said, "about all this talk about bad guys out there in the middle of the night, and guns. So one night in the basement, my dad had a hunting rifle, bolt action. I don't know where we ever got the bullets. But Mike was a little bit terrified, so he said, 'I'm going to see if I know how to shoot.' So we put a couple of boxes of books and comic books side by side and he fired that rifle into that box. It made a hell of a racket. I don't know what we thought we were doing, but I guess it was in case he needed the rifle to shoot somebody."

John said he'd wondered whether the stories about danger that sometimes required them to stay home at night were made up as a way of keeping the family together at a time when he and his brother were growing up and would soon be leaving home. The theory was an attempt to make sense of his father's disturbing behaviour.

Pat told me about camping with Stan and Sybil in 1975. "They camped about three sites from us and we went down to have a campfire with them one night and it was, 'There's danger here, you've got to be really careful, somebody just shot at us.' And we just went back to our campsite and went on as normal. And John and I talked several times about . . . this is strange, there's something wrong here. Because I didn't believe it and none of it made sense to me."

But it wasn't that simple for John—who loved and respected his dad—to dismiss.

"I didn't know what to say; it's my dad. He coached me in baseball, he coached me in hockey. He'd been a good dad. He always supported me. So it's hard to think, Oh, are you lying to me?"

John asked his mother if she believed the story about the bad guys. She told him she had faith in their father. And there was a talisman of her belief—a small, secret package she kept in her purse. She never went anywhere without it, keeping it close by her even in situations in which it was strange to take a purse. When I'd told John and Pat about the small transistor radio Stan had given me to call for help if I thought I was in danger, they looked at each other. "The mysterious package in the purse," John said, nodding.

When John was twenty-seven he told his father to stop talking about the bad guys and the Weird World. There was never any proof and he didn't want to hear it anymore. "I parked this weird stuff on one side and I just tried to ignore it," he told me. "Until this day I had no idea whether it was the truth or not."

He never talked to anyone about it, other than Pat. "It was embarrassing to me. Why is my dad, otherwise a normal guy, a respected guy in the community, doing this?" As evidence of how his father was respected, John recalled the words of the funeral director in Gibson's, the day of Stan's funeral. "He knew Dad because when he was a minister, they'd shared funerals together, and he said, 'You know, John, your dad was one of the straightest-shooting guys I ever met. You could always depend on Stan Sears; his word was gold. I really respected him.'"

But John, Pat, and I knew that for those closest to him, his word was suspect. At least about one thing.

John confirmed that Stan had lived with Sybil until the day he died, but would sometimes be away on his own.

"He used to take a week or two, he said he needed to get away and think and he'd go back east. I had no idea what he was doing, but he said he just rented a cabin and was alone for a while and that was good."

That explained, at least partly, the time he spent with Mom. But how, I asked, did he afford to fly back and forth across the country and pay for all the motel rooms and meals for the three of us?

John couldn't figure that out. He said Stan's pension was about $30,000 a year, and he'd never had an inheritance or come into money, as far as he knew. And Sybil had always been in charge of family finances.

Pat interjected, "Except she didn't keep any of the cash donations he got. Like when he married somebody, that money went to him." Still, we agreed the honorariums from weddings and funerals were unlikely to have funded his travels, the motel rooms, and the meals.

It's a part of the story that remains a mystery.

We spent several hours comparing notes and sharing stories. John and Pat said they were glad I'd come, glad to know the rest of the story. "We had suspicions anyway," Pat said. "And if I hadn't had them, I would have said, 'You're lying, can you prove this?' But, of course, I did have suspicions."

"I'm sorry," John told me. "That was a tough upbringing for you, bouncing all over the place and everything under pretense. My God, I'm so sorry."

I told him my theory that being well loved by a parent creates resilience, even in the midst of such chaos. And despite everything, I always knew my mother loved me. And Stan too. John recognized some value in this. But he asked, beyond the obvious, what effect it had had on me.

I'd thought about this after my mother died, as I worked to forgive her and come to a sense of peace about what happened to us. I realized the running and the secretiveness made it difficult for me to connect deeply with people. I think that, for a long time, I imposed varying degrees of distance in my relationships with most people, except my children, maybe because of the secret, or maybe because of what it did to my sense of confidence in determining who could be trusted and who might deceive me. I was shocked to realize this about myself, as I tried to understand the impact of the atmosphere I grew up in. And then I realized there was a part of me that had always felt alone; until I decided to tell the secrets, they kept me from being fully known.

Talking to John and Pat made me feel less isolated. It felt important to know that we've had a similar rare experience, and that we have all survived and even thrived in spite of it.

Our afternoon together also closed a circle for me. In the past year there have been many conversation and explanations. I visited my mother's sister, Penny, and my half-sister, Linda, and told them what happened and why we disappeared, and how we were warned they were dangerous doubles intent on our destruction. For them, these disclosures bring anger, relief, regret, and some understanding. For me, it's a great unburdening. As I tell the terrible secrets that lay like a great weight upon us, I feel lighter. I feel a freedom in this openness that is transcendent and hopeful.

TWENTY-SEVEN

SAINT JOHN. OF course, it's raining. I remember this as a grey place. Low cloud, lots of fog. I guess that's not fair. There were shiny days, warm with sunshine. But that's not what I recall about the place we ran to when I was thirteen. I am watching a thunderstorm light up the sky over the west side of the city and the ocean beyond, where a few hours ago I sent a scoopful of ashes flying into the wind at Saints Rest Beach. My mother's ashes. This is the final stop on a cross-country road trip.

My mother donated her body to science, inspired by a documentary I did about the silent teachers, the body donors, who play such a large role in the healing knowledge and skills of doctors and other health professionals. The department of anatomy at Dalhousie University in Halifax had the use of her remains for three years. Her body was used to teach the intricacies of anatomy to future doctors and researchers. When her ashes were returned to me, I could think of no one place they belonged, and kept them, waiting.

The trip had begun several weeks earlier with another scoopful of ashes released from Vancouver's Lions Gate Bridge. As that dust dispersed into the bay below, I pictured the old photograph of Mom near the entrance to that bridge span, on a trail in Stanley Park. In the photo she's leaning against her bicycle, with the girders and cables of the span soaring behind her, and the North Shore Mountains beyond that. She is smiling broadly—young, not yet married, and so unaware of all that was to come.

At Saints Rest fifty-odd years later, the waves rolled in, cold even in late July. The sky was low, threatening to soak us in rain later. I stood on a rock in the sand at the water's edge. The fragments and dust blew up from the cup as I tossed them, and then a gust blew them back at me. I turned my face away, but even now I can feel a few grains in my hair, against my scalp. I worry them against my skin with my fingertips. Her DNA is in me and now on me. Such a strange thing and yet I'm not repelled. I feel no squeamishness.

"This is to remember her love and selflessness as a mother," I said as Avery and I walked the few steps from the sandy parking lot to the beach. I'd told Avery and Laura the story of my orange-and-white tomcat Frisky. I got him when I was seven, and he came along both times we ran away. Each time, each new house, new school, for weeks or months he would feel like my only friend. After we moved here, to Saint John, the most difficult of all the new places we'd experienced, I relied on his company more than ever. And then, a few months after we arrived, he got sick. Feline leukemia, the vet said, shaking his head pessimistically. Over a few weeks Frisky wasted away and died, choking and flailing at the end, as I tried to squeeze a dropperful of desiccated liver into his mouth, a useless attempt to offer him nutrients and a few more days.

It was winter. The ground was frozen and we couldn't bury him in the yard. I angrily refused to let Mom take his body to the vet for disposal. So on a—yes—dark and grey early winter afternoon, Mom and I drove to Saints Rest Beach. The sand wasn't frozen. I stood in the mix of freezing rain and sleet as she hefted sand with her gardening shovel to make a grave just above the ocean's surf. The tide was coming in and soon the grave was filling with water. She shovelled faster. Frisky was in a cardboard box, carefully wrapped in with a baby blanket. I bawled, snotty body-shaking sobs.

"Go to the car, I'll finish," Mom said, pushing wet hair off her forehead. We were both shivering, our feet soaked, hands numb. And I did. I left her to finish the icy internment, and I huddled in the car, crying and feeling miserable, guilty that somehow my great love of Frisky didn't translate into the guts, the loyalty to brave the sleet and wind to bury him. It was Mom who did that, who persevered, planted the cat, trudged back to the car frozen and wet, and squeezed my hand, looking at me sympathetically with her warm brown eyes. "I'm so sorry, Pauline. So sorry."

From this motel that sits high on a hill in West Saint John, I can just see the beach at Saints Rest, illuminated every few minutes by flashes of sheet lightning. This is the same motel we lived in for the first weeks after we arrived, on the run from Winnipeg, while Mom looked for a house. Being here, taking care of Mom's ashes, feels as though I am closing another circle.

There was no one place to leave the remains of a restless soul who spent so much of her life on the run, on the move. My daughters and I have left portions of Mom's ashes across the country she loved, in all the places we could think of that were meaningful to her.

At the foot of the cedars she planted behind the house she loved on East 24th Street, the little stucco house with the over-grown roses climbing up the front porch and the massive old cherry tree in the backyard that towered over her hollyhocks and sunflowers. It was a fresh start, where we were all supposed to live happily ever after, where she'd planned to bring up her family and cultivate a fine garden, and one day welcome her grandchildren.

Near Hope, B.C., the imaginary location of PH, Place of Hope, where she believed she and Stan would one day escape to their log cabin in the safety of the Weird World, and finally be together. We leave ashes near the foot of a waterfall, hidden in the mountains, a place that stands in for another that never really existed.

In the wilds of the Rocky Mountains, on a trail near Banff, Ted and his partner, Jana, join us. We scatter ashes in a fast-flowing stream in memory of all the camping and hiking trips, and the way she filled our childhood with adventure even in the midst of fear and chaos.

In the little southern Saskatchewan town of Lampman, where she was born, in the garden of the church where she was baptized, where giant pink hollyhocks swayed in a hot late-afternoon breeze.

In the ghost town of Summerberry, where she grew up and sang and skated and played baseball, and learned her first lesson about loss when her mother died.

In the beautiful retreat of the garden that belonged to her lifelong friend Marlene. It was Marlene whom she turned to as a lost teenager and who always remained faithful and loving even when, as an adult, Mom would disappear and be out of touch for a while. Marlene didn't understand but she didn't judge. She continued to love Mom nonetheless and was always there when Mom would re-emerge.

In the back garden of the Dorchester house in Winnipeg, where she painted, scraped, and determinedly held the pieces together the year I fell apart.

In the front garden on Duchess Street in Saint John, the place we all lived together the longest, where she and Ted played baseball and built a utility trailer in the backyard, and she and I fought through my adolescence, and reconnected when that was over, and her children grew to young adults.

The ashes are dispersed and now we learn to carry on without her.

ANOTHER TWENTY CENTIMETRES of snow has fallen overnight. The snow continues to fall—a silent, steady whitening of the bare-branched poplars that surround Ted's cabin at Lac Sante, a couple hours east of Edmonton, Alberta.

We've both woken early. I lift the blind by the kitchen table and we look out the large window, across the snow-laden deck, and rails, and the swinging loveseat that recalls other seasons, other visits.

A magpie alights on a branch, triggering a shower of light snow. Nasty things, Ted told me yesterday, as we drove here. I was watching the striking black-and-white plumage of a single bird as it flew across a snow-skiffed field. "They'll peck out the eyes of cattle," he said.

The scene out the cabin window this morning is beautiful, we agree. I feel profoundly grateful to have this time here with my brother.

The moment passes. Ted is now bustling around, collecting tools for the next project. He doesn't stay still for long. He plans to insulate the walls of the latest addition to his ever-growing retreat. I have other plans for at least part of this day. I've told him I need to mine his memory, hoping he can help me find and place some of the missing or overturned pieces of the jigsaw puzzle that was our shared childhood.

I slip on a pair of boots and make my way to the outhouse ten metres away. I can't help laughing as I open the door to an already lighted and heated space. Last night he showed me the remote control he's rigged up; it's a small black fob, like one that would lock or unlock a car door. It hangs on a hook just inside the cabin door.

"Look." He showed me. "You press this button and it turns on the lights and the heater in the outhouse. Just start it up a bit before you want to go and it'll be warm for you. When you come back in, you can turn it off."

I enter the pre-warmed outhouse with two African masks decorating the back wall. *This is so Ted*, I think as I lift the insulated lid to the hole below. He applies his brilliant brain in such ingenious, practical ways, identifying a problem and losing himself in the creative solution of it. There's evidence of this around the lake house. He built every part of it himself—the sales and marketing executive without any construction training. He and his partner, Jana, cut the trees and planted the gardens that lies beneath the snow.

It's also like Ted to be so solicitous. He was up even before me to hit the remote so I can pee in luxurious warmth. Ted takes care of the people around him. For this trip he's brought a bottle of good red wine and clean sheets for me, shopped for the groceries we've brought with us, including steaks for dinner last night—my favourite. In these ways, he is so like our mother.

We talk about our memories, our mother, the madness that was our childhood, and the strength her belief in the Mafia story must have required of her: to keep going, to leave the familiar and known behind twice, and invite the condemnation and judgment of her family and friends for our disappearances. She did what she believed she had to do to protect her family. And we survived because of and in spite of that.

THE CRICKETS THRUM in the dusk. Charlie was by earlier to mow the grass in front of my trailer, and the air is redolent with the chlorophyll-green scent of late summer. A crescent moon is rising, perfectly outlined in the darkening sky and reminding me of how the moon looked the night I met my mother at the gas station in Sussex, the night of false revelations.

I am at my retreat, my place of reflection, where there is time and silence enough to reach a conclusion. I know now, he was sick. She was made uniquely vulnerable. Neither intended to hurt me; quite the opposite. Both wanted to protect me, and both loved me. Such irony here. My mother, making choices that resulted in such turmoil, loved me constantly and consistently in a way that gave me the resilience to survive the path she and Stan set us upon. Two smart people, likely above average intellectually, but damaged in ways that set the stage for such remarkable dysfunction.

His damage came from within, perhaps a result of a gene that didn't code properly, or some other malfunction of brain development, a seed planted early that blossomed into full-blown delusion at middle age. Maybe the day the young Stan survived the toboggan ride that left his cheek scarred by barbed wire there was some other, less visible damage—a bruise or slight tear somewhere in the folds of his prefrontal cortex. Perhaps those injuries could have become the roots of the delusion that came to control his life, and ours.

Her damage was inflicted from without, by heart-rending loss followed by neglect and abuse of many shades and colours, resulting in episodic depression. I think of her as a boxer in the ring, stunned by blows but pulling herself back to her feet again and again, only to face another punch, another loss, another betrayal. I am staggered by the strength and the weakness. In concert they created a life of deep joy at times, but mostly they created profound hardship. When she died, I stood at the reception following her memorial service as a line of people formed before Ted and me, one after another so anxious to tell us how she had helped them, supported them, changed their lives, lifted them up. My strong, sensitive, broken, loving, courageous mother had earned her rest.

For me, clarity has emerged from the chaos. My understanding of Stan's illness has freed me from the confused anger I'd felt toward him. It has allowed me to forgive my mother. Now, the sense of betrayal has evaporated, and, miraculously I am filled with gratitude for their love. It's a form of grace they would have appreciated, as though chains have fallen away. I realize that even within the tumult of our lives, it was their consistent support that upheld me. In a world where children are thought to thrive through stability and consistency, I have concluded that an unshakable sense of being loved is the paramount ingredient. Mom would quote Corinthians: "Love bears all things, believes all things, hopes all things, endures all things."

And despite her constant imprecations for secrecy—that drumbeat of "don't tell"—as I've been writing this and exposing the family secret, I've often felt as though she were peering over my shoulder, exuding her usual curiosity and enthusiasm for whatever I chose to do, her delight in my accomplishments. I am hopeful, and in some moments believe that wherever she is, she knows that I have let go of my resentment and can now freely miss and love her. My mother always told me I could be a writer, and she gave me a remarkable story. I imagine her now as I gaze across the water, the sun gone but still drawing dark purple designs against the sky, as I write these final words. "What a story, Polly!" she would exclaim. She would probably cry at the immensity of it laid out before her. And she would be proud, and happy for my liberation from it.

Yes, Mom. What a story.

This book is based largely on my memories and those recalled by my brother. Over the years I have occasionally made notes, begun and then abandoned journals, written essays about family meant for no one but myself. Other sources emerged with the deaths of my parents— treasures unearthed as I cleaned out first my father's and then my mother's homes. My father was a remarkably organized accumulator of information. He kept the letters his parents had written to him when he went to war, as well as my letters and even copies of some of his responses, neatly stashed in file folders in his big mahogany desk. It was an astonishing library of papers and court documents that summoned up times, places, and memories I had only dimly recalled.

My mother also kept files of correspondence, although over the years she burned most of the letters she received via Stan that purported to be from the Weird World. Still, when I was sorting through her belongings I found a grocery bag full of unburned letters. Perhaps she'd hidden them and then forgotten about them. I also discovered in her desk drawer the secretly recorded audiotapes I refer to in Chapter 12, as well as journals she'd written mostly in her later life.

In both parents' caches of belongings were photographs, which reminded me of places, people, and the flavour and meaning of certain times. They say that smell evokes the strongest memory response, but for me pictures have triggered strong memories and feelings.

The letters from all the people who were supposedly inside, which were remarkably researched and painstakingly written by Stan, offered important clues about when certain things happened, and what we were all thinking about or preoccupied by at particular times. Stan's personal letters to me also jogged memories and reminded me that whatever chaos he wrought in our lives, and despite his calamitous mental illness, he was a caring man who valued, loved, and helped to mould me, for good and ill.

Memories, particularly those of children, can be unreliable. Sometimes I have struggled to recall the order of events. Which campground were we at when Stan lost his memory? How old was I when a particular event occurred? I am confident that I have been true to a general chronology. Truly there are many details I have forgotten, but enough remains for some kind of reconciliation.

ACKNOWLEDGMENTS

An important purpose of this book was to reach an understanding from the perspective of adulthood. Since determining that Stan's story was not real, my overriding question has been: Why? My great thanks go to Dr. Theo Manschreck and Dr. Alistair Munro, who so generously took the time to hear my story, answer my questions, and confirm my belief that Stan suffered from delusional disorder. I hope this story can bring attention to this under-studied condition, and perhaps spur much-needed research.

My thanks also to my early readers—Louise Cameron, Jane Armstrong, Margot Brunelle, and Claudia Buckley—for their feedback. Cindy Bradette and Catherine Walker, my deep appreciation to each of you for being the backup for my kids when I had to travel, and for your friendship. There are many others whose support and love have been important. I name you in my heart.

I will always be grateful to Debbie Van Horne for the support that helped me stay afloat, and ultimately become buoyant, as I relived difficult situations and reinterpreted complex relationships.

I'm not sure I would ever have written this book without the support of my instructors, mentors, and classmates in the inaugural class of the master of fine arts in creative non-fiction program at the University of King's College in Halifax, where I now teach. Stephen Kimber and Don Sedgwick dreamed up a program that offered structure, attention to craft, and strong community as I revealed my story. Yay, Class of 2015, and our great mentors: Lori A. May, Lorri Neilsen Glenn, Ken McGoogan, and David Hayes!

Shaun Bradley, thanks for the "agenting," and so much more. Your encouragement kept me writing and your incisive critique made the manuscript better.

Diane Turbide, I have so appreciated your sure and wise, but never heavy, editorial hand, and especially your sensitivity as we worked on this book. Thanks also to Cheryl Cohen for her masterful copy-editing.

Most of all, my family—Avery, Laura, Ted, Jana, Tessa, and Jake—have loved and supported me in remarkable ways. "Thank you" seems inadequate. In particular, Ted, thanks for trusting me to tell what is also your story. Generous and loving as always, you somehow also retained your wicked sense of humour despite it all. Hugs, brudder!

Finally, as I wrote I tried, often unsuccessfully, not to think about the people who will be affected by my telling of this story. I understand that some who thought they knew me well will feel betrayed because I did not share this important part of my life. Others may be offended by my characterization of some people who appear in this book. I can only say this is my story, and while I regret any hurt or upset it may cause, the freedom of telling it is a gift I can finally give myself. I hope you will understand.